Billy Liddell

Other Robson Books by John Keith

Shanks For The Memory: Wit and Wisdom of Bill Shankly
The Essential Shankly
Bob Paisley: Manager of the Millennium
Dixie Dean: The Inside Story of a Football Icon

Billy Liddell

THE LEGEND WHO CARRIED THE KOP

JOHN KEITH

ROBSON BOOKS

This paperback edition first published in Great Britain in 2004 by Robson Books,
The Chrysalis Building, Bramley Road, London W10 6SP

An imprint of Chrysalis Books Group plc

British Library Cataloguing in Publication Data
A catalogue record for this title is available from the British Library.

ISBN 1 86105 804 7

Typeset by SX Composing DTP, Rayleigh, Essex
Printed by Creative Print and Design (Wales) Ltd, Ebbw Vale

Contents

Preface

The groundwork and research for this book embraced many sources and many people, to whom I am indebted for their enthusiastic assistance and support. I would like to thank Billy's widow Phyllis Liddell and sons Malcolm and David for their co-operation and permission to use many extracts from Billy's book *My Soccer Story*, published by Stanley Paul in 1960.

My sincere gratitude, too, to Roger Hunt for his enthusiastic and painstaking compilation of the foreword.

Thanks also go to the Reverend Malcolm Carter, Gerard Ormesher, Dave Ball, Ged Rea, Richard Whitehead, Malcolm Brodie, Jessie Paisley, Roger Hughes, Alf Mellor, Keith Stanton, Mark Platt, Brian Phillips, Alan Joshua, Rod Park, Ian Callaghan, New York Liverpool FC Supporters Club, Albert Stubbins (sadly to die during the writing of this book), Professor Andrew Lees and my colleagues at BBC Radio Merseyside.

Special acknowledgement goes to Dave Horridge, for enthusiastically supplying photographs, information and superb anecdotes, and to the dogged archival research of Eric Doig, who provided fastidiously checked statistics and other wonderful gems of information. Many thanks to them and to all the others who generously assisted in the production of this book.

John Keith

Foreword
by Roger Hunt

Imagine a player starring for Liverpool season after season, topping the club's scoring charts for eight years out of nine, representing both Scotland and Great Britain – and achieving all this despite training only two mornings a week while pursuing an accountancy career.

It is a script straight from a boy's comic strip, except that in Billy Liddell's case it happens to be amazing reality. No wonder he was a legend!

One day early in September 1959, shortly after I had signed professional for Liverpool after joining them as an amateur from the Army the previous year, I was called into manager Phil Taylor's office.

He said to me: 'You're going to be playing in the first team against Scunthorpe tomorrow because Billy Liddell's injured.' Any player making his debut is always a bit nervous and apprehensive and I was stepping up to play in the Second Division after only a few games in the reserves. But Billy was very helpful to me.

He was always there to offer little bits of advice, right throughout the short period in which his career, which was nearing its close, and mine overlapped. Billy was then 37 and I was 21 and he was full of encouragement.

For my debut I took over the No. 9 jersey that Billy had been wearing, even though I was, in 1950s terms, an inside forward and not a centre forward and it was the only time in my entire Liverpool career that I wore that number.

I was delighted that we not only beat Scunthorpe 2–0 but that I scored in the second half after Jimmy Melia had put us ahead earlier in the game. But Billy was declared fit for the next game, at home to Middlesbrough, and Phil Taylor told me: 'You did very well on your debut but the great man's coming back.' So I was left out.

Although Billy scored against a Middlesbrough side that included Brian Clough the team lost 2–1 and Billy's injury flared up again, ruling him out of the next three games. It meant that I was back in the team – and from then on I became a regular in the No. 8 jersey.

I first teamed up with Billy in the game at Swansea in October 1959. He played on the right wing and although I managed to get on the scoresheet we lost 5–4.

Billy then went out of the side until the second half of the season, by which time Bill Shankly had arrived to succeed Phil Taylor. But from February through to April, Billy and I played another eleven games together and our thirteenth and final appearance together in the first team was against Southampton in August 1960.

I also played in a few reserve matches with Billy and I am very pleased that I was able to line up with him in a Liverpool shirt, because there is no doubt that he is one of the all-time greats and was such a dedicated professional, even though his training was curtailed by his accountancy job.

It meant that I had the privilege of being in Billy's company on trips and I remember being at a London hotel when he introduced me to Jackie Milburn. I was so thrilled and excited because Jackie was another big star.

Billy was a religious man but would never try to preach to you. In fact, he was good company and liked a laugh and a joke. He'd come into the treatment room at Liverpool and take the mickey out of the lads who were on the table.

Born in Glazebury, I grew up a Bolton fan but I was well aware of just now big Billy Liddell was. He was such a key man for Liverpool that the club became known as Liddellpool. He was number one with the supporters for many years and players of his era invariably picked him in their best-ever team.

You could argue that he is Liverpool's best ever player, given that he was a loyal, one-club man. As well as winning a championship medal and playing in a Cup Final he stayed with them after relegation and starred through many years in the Second Division in teams that did not contain players of the quality that his skill deserved.

I think Billy would be tremendous in today's football. Look at the problems clubs and countries have filling the left-flank role. Then imagine Billy being available! The number of goals he scored coming in from the wing was amazing.

His shooting was explosive, he had fantastic heading ability, he was fearless and he could play anywhere. There were not a lot of frills with Billy. He was powerful and direct yet always fair and was never booked.

George Cohen, my colleague in the 1966 England World Cup team, was a hard, well-built full back and a defender to be reckoned with. George told me: 'I'd heard about this Liddell fellow. They were all talking about him and I wondered what all the fuss was about.

'I soon found out! When I was playing for Fulham against Liverpool I went into a tussle for the ball with Billy. I shoulder-charged him – and I just bounced off him!'

For as long as football is played and Liverpool FC exists the memory of Billy Liddell will be revered. He was exemplary as a man and a player. I am proud to say I knew him and lined up with him in a Liverpool jersey.

Chapter One

The Prince from Across the Border

William Beveridge Liddell swept on to the ball just inside the Liverpool half and accelerated in that majestic upright style that was as original as it was unmistakeable. On he sped down the left flank before cutting in across Anfield's snow-covered pitch, using his formidable strength to fend off Manchester City defenders.

Then, from an angle on the edge of the penalty box, he unleashed a ferocious shot that arrowed past City's celebrated German goalkeeper Bert Trautmann and soared into the Kop net. Ecstasy for the massed ranks of the Liverpoool faithful on the world-famous terracing behind the goal. They roared in relief and salute. Billy had come to Liverpool's rescue again. He'd kept them in the FA Cup. It was 2–2. Now extra time beckoned in the fifth-round replay.

But wait. The referee Mervyn Griffiths and both teams are walking off the field. What's happening?

For what seemed an age, but was merely a few minutes, hardly any of the baffled 57,000-plus crowd moved in the gathering gloom of that Wednesday afternoon in the pre-floodlight era of February 1956. Then came a Tannoy announcement: 'Ladies and gentlemen, the game is over. There will be no extra time. The referee blew the final whistle before Billy Liddell's shot went into the net. Would you kindly leave the ground.'

There was a collective gasp from home supporters, then a roar of disbelief at their club's Cup lifeline being snapped just when they thought it had been dramatically saved.

They trudged out of Anfield in shock and disbelief and, as they made their way home battling the wintry elements, it was not the continuing terrorist violence in Cyprus, nor Chancellor of the Exchequer Harold Macmillan's introduction of a 25-year-high Bank Rate of 5½ per cent, nor even the launch of regional Independent Television that dominated their thoughts and conversation.

Even that very day's landmark first League match to be played under floodlights, between Portsmouth and Newcastle, was off the agenda. The single, burning issue was Liddell's disallowed strike. The controversy over the referee's decision raged for weeks. Even now it prompts lively debate as one of the famous, enduring incidents of Merseyside football. Those still alive who witnessed it will take the memory to the grave.

Like a great beauty or precious stone enhanced by a slight flaw Billy Liddell will forever be associated with a goal he *didn't* score as well as the 228 that stand against his name in the records. It is an inherent weave in the fabric of a legendary player, a footballer and gentleman supreme, hailed by many as the greatest ever to don a Liverpool jersey and whose stature earned the club the soubriquet 'Liddellpool'.

Billy Liddell, the eldest of six children, was born at Townhill, two miles from Dunfermline, Fife, on 10 January 1922, less than a fortnight before a provisional Irish parliament approved a treaty with Britain to create the Irish Free State. Three months later another great British winger, Tom Finney, arrived in the world in Preston, Lancashire.

Like so many football luminaries of his generation, coal and the local pit played a major part in Liddell's environment and upbringing, and his family's Presbyterian influence would shape his entire life as a nonsmoking teetotaller.

Billy's father, James, was a miner and he and his wife, with the unusual name of Montgomery, had a further five children. Four were boys: Tom, Campbell, Alistair and George. The only girl, Rena, and George were twins and in later life Billy himself would marry and be blessed with twin sons. Like Billy, Tom was also destined to join Liverpool as a full back, although his appearances for the club were limited to the reserve side.

Life in Townhill in the 1920s was far from a bed of roses. Money was tight and the family diet included salt porridge, kail (a Scotch broth) and plenty of bread. Liddell recalled:

It was a struggle making ends meet but my parents were wonderful in the sacrifices they made, something I appreciated more and more as I grew up. When I was seven I asked for a pair of football boots for Christmas without realising how expensive they were, given the family income.

Nevertheless, my mother and father bought them for me and I remember being so excited seeing the boots in the pillow case at the foot of the bed when I woke up on Christmas morning.

Even though we couldn't afford a football that problem was solved because a boy down the road got one as a present. I put my new boots on that Christmas morning and didn't take them off until it was dark. I played in them morning and afternoon! I loved those boots. I would wear them when my parents sent me on messages and I'd practise with both feet, which stood me in good stead later.

On the way to the shop, or wherever I'd been sent, I'd kick the ball against the wall and control it with my natural right foot. And on the way back I'd use my left.

One day, Mr Wilson, my headmaster at Townhill school, saw me playing in a group of boys. He came over to me and told me to keep playing and keep practising, which was very encouraging. Shortly after I had a trial for the school junior team.

I was only eight and the average age of the team was over ten. I must have shown something because one Friday morning I learned I'd been picked at outside right in the school team to play the following day.

That meant a two-mile walk to get to the match. But I'd have walked 22 miles if I'd had to! It wasn't a story-book debut but I did well enough to win a regular place which delighted my proud parents.

My grandfather offered me threepence for every goal I scored, which was a lot of money for a boy of my age in those days. I went through a period when I didn't score many so my grandfather ensured I had even greater incentive.

He persuaded my grandmother and four aunts also to promise me threepence for each goal. I don't know whether it was coincidence or financial inducement but that same day I scored six!

My grandfather was there watching me but after handing over the promised money he told me that the women of the family would take a dim view of such an arrangement continuing! They also persuaded my grandfather that it was wrong to put such mercenary ideas in my head and the threepence-a-goal offer was withdrawn.

When I was eleven I passed the examination for Dunfermline High School. Pleasing though that was, I was disappointed to discover that they played rugby not soccer. But with the view that it was better to play some sport than none at all I took up rugby.

At his new school Liddell came under the aegis of an understanding games master in Ronnie Boon, a rugby union international who won twelve caps at wing three-quarter for Wales between 1930 and 1933. He assured the young Liddell that playing rugby need not be a barrier to his soccer aspirations, an approach that Liverpool and Scotland would later have reason to applaud.

'I was fortunate that Mr Boon was there,' said Liddell. 'He took me aside for a chat when he learned I was keener on soccer than rugby. He made me realise that if I applied myself thoroughly to the latter it need not handicap me with the former.'

Thus encouraged, Liddell continued to play soccer at every opportunity. He turned out for the Dunfermline and District Scout

League and at the age of twelve was chosen for the Dunfermline Schools team which played in the East of Scotland Schoolboy League and Scottish Schools Cup competition.

When there was no game for Liddell he would enhance his football education as an enthralled spectator at Dunfermline Athletic, who won promotion to the Scottish League First Division in 1934, only to be relegated back to the Second Division three seasons later. Liddell was a star-struck observer at East End Park as a parade of great names in Scottish football came to play. They included Celtic's iconic Jimmy McGrory, whose 410 goals in 408 matches gave him a scoring average unequalled in the history of League football in Britain.

'I longed to emulate Jimmy's scoring exploits and going to watch Dunfermline and seeing the big names in action fired my ambitions,' Liddell recalled.

Airdrie and Rangers inside forward Bob McPhail, Alan Morton – the gifted 5ft 4in 'Wee Blue Devil' of Rangers whose wing magic tormented England when Scotland thrashed the old enemy 5–1 at Wembley in 1928 – Jerry Dawson, Dougie Gray and Bertie Thomson were among a host of others who helped inspire Liddell on his football path.

In the spring of 1934 Liddell was selected for a schoolboy international trial match at Dunfermline but was omitted from the final trial game. However, he was named as a travelling reserve for the Scotland Schoolboys side that met Wales at Cowdenbeath, the home team including left half Alan Little, later to play for Rangers and Cowdenbeath and qualify as a doctor.

There was further disappointment for Liddell the following season when, despite playing in all three schoolboy trial games, he still missed out on a place in the Scotland side. But, finally, his dream came true when he was selected for the game against Ireland at Ayr, which Scotland won and from which Liddell took on board some valuable advice.

'A local reporter wrote that I would have done better if I'd shot for the far post instead of aiming for the near one every time,' Liddell recalled. 'It was something that stuck in my mind and I was grateful for the advice. If you shoot for the far post even if

your aim is faulty the ball may find a team-mate. But if you aim
for the near post and rocket the ball into the side netting nobody
can do anything about it.'

A fortnight after his schoolboy international debut against
Ireland in 1936, Liddell retained his place in the team to face
England at Villa Park but this time he was switched from outside
right to outside left. The game proved to be an important step in
his football development.

'It was the first time I'd been out of Scotland and it was a
thrilling experience to play in front of a 40,000 crowd,' he
recalled. 'That game stands out like a beacon in my memory. We
were beaten 5–0 and the man who did most damage to us was a
shrimp of a lad called Len Shackleton.

'That was my first meeting with the football genius who later
became one of the most brilliant and controversial players of his
generation.'

Liddell was a diligent, hard-working pupil at Dunfermline
High School, studying English, French, Latin, Maths, Chemistry
and Physics but still with no idea of what career he wanted to
pursue. He admitted:

Being a professional footballer had not entered my head and
while I thoroughly enjoyed my sporting outlets I kept my
nose to the grindstone at school.

When I became too old to play in schoolboy football I
signed for Kingseat Juniors, at a fee of 2s 6d per match. But
after playing for them for the best part of a season they got
into financial difficulties and the club was disbanded in the
spring of 1937.

The following season Blairhall Colliery gave me a trial
but nothing came of it. Then Hearts of Beath played me in
three trial games before they also lost interest. Fortunately,
there was another club on the horizon and that was Lochgelly
Violet.

Presumably, they saw something in me that the others had
missed because after two games they signed me for a 7s 6d
fee and 2s 6d expenses. During my first season with them I

was still playing rugby for the first fifteen at Dunfermline High, turning out for the school in the morning and for the Violet in the afternoon. On top of all that I was still swotting hard.

As the end of my schooldays approached I was still no nearer a decision as to my future and this uncertainty worried my parents. On one thing, however, they had made up their minds. I was definitely not going into the mines where my father spent all his working life.

The possibility of earning a living at football was still far from my mind and I had decided against a career in the Civil Service. I had also decided not to join the ministry, much to the disappointment of the Reverend Stewart, the minister of the church our family attended, who had suggested that I might follow in his footsteps.

He assured me that if I took that vocation I would never regret it. I'm sure he was right, too. But somehow, though attracted to the idea in many ways, there was a feeling at the back of my young mind that it was not the job for which I was best fitted.

Eventually, after many long talks with Rev Stewart and my parents, it was decided that I should go in for accountancy. I'd always been attracted to working with figures and Rev Stewart, when he saw that this was what I'd set my heart on, lost no time in contacting friends on my behalf.

He arranged for me to be articled to a leading firm in Dunfermline, depending on my passing the Scottish Higher Leaving exam. With that certificate the job was mine. But, unknown to me, events were unfolding that would determine that I would never join the company in Dunfermline and that when I entered the accountancy profession it would be on a part-time basis in Liverpool.

The reason for this act of fate was down to the shrewd judgment of a certain Matt Busby, who in years to come was to make one of the greatest contributions to British football by any individual in the history of the game in this country, as well as becoming close friends with Liddell and his future wife and family.

Scotland right half Busby was a product of the same Belshill Athletic club in Lanarkshire that turned out the golden talents of Alex James and Hughie Gallacher. After playing for Denny Hibs he and his widowed mother were about to emigrate to the United States when Manchester City stepped in to sign him in February 1928. It was a move that changed the story of football and the course of Liddell's life.

Busby arrived at Maine Road as an inside forward, but City manager Peter Hodge switched him to half back with great success. Busby's 226 appearances for City included successive FA Cup Finals, one lost to Dixie Dean's Everton in 1933, the second won against Portsmouth.

His midfield skills and constructive play had many admirers, not least Liverpool manager George Patterson, whose side were engulfed in relegation fears when he signed Busby for £8,500 in March 1936. It was one of Patterson's last acts in charge of the Anfield club before his resignation at the end of that season to be succeeded by George Kay.

Liverpool, though, secured their top flight status and Busby formed a memorable all-Scottish half-back line with centre half Tom Bradshaw and left half Jimmy McDougall. In the summer of 1938 circumstances conspired for Busby to ensure that Liddell would be Anfield bound.

'As a Liverpool player I still retained many connections with Manchester City and my playing colleagues there,' Busby recalled. 'Alex Herd and I, as City players, used to play a lot of golf together in Scotland during the close season. One particular day we were due to play but Alex didn't turn up for his usual round of the bunkers! So I went in search of him.

'I was told that he'd taken Hamilton Academicals manager Willie McAndrew in his car to watch a sixteen-year-old boy called Liddell playing for Lochgelly Violet.

'But when I saw Alex he told me that no business had been done with Hamilton because Billy Liddell's parents wanted some assurances about their son's future in the game and that the Hamilton club were not really in a prosperous enough state to make such lavish promises.

'So on hearing the story from Alex I immediately telephoned the Liverpool manager George Kay at Anfield and suggested he might succeed where Hamilton Academicals had failed. He did – and Billy Liddell became a Liverpool player.

'It was a very fortunate day for Liverpool and I have always been happy to recall the part I played in Billy's transfer, many years before I really started interesting myself in the buying and selling of footballers.'

Liverpool agreed to pay Lochgelly Violet £175 to sign Liddell, perhaps the best bargain in football history! But the player himself was unware of these career-determining developments. After the rejected approach from Hamilton he was invited by Partick Thistle for a trial for their second team, one eagerly accepted by the young forward but which produced nothing tangible beyond a promise that Partick would contact him.

'The turning point of my young life came after I'd been to a Saturday night youth-club dance in the summer of 1938,' Liddell recounted. 'When I got home shortly before midnight I was surprised to see a light in the living room. Usually my parents were in bed soon after ten o'clock and my first thought was that somebody was ill.' He continued:

I opened the door with a strange presentiment. Although my fears were happily without foundation I soon realised some-thing very much out of the ordinary had happened. Mother and father were still up and dressed and were obviously not there to tick me off for being out late. Clearly, there was something in the wind but what it was I couldn't imagine.

After answering questions from my parents about the dance I just wasn't prepared for their next words. My mother said: 'Willie, how would you like to live in Liverpool?' I could only stand and stare. I hadn't the slightest idea what the question meant. At that moment football was far from my thoughts and Liverpool had never been in them at all.

At last, when I found some words, all I could say was: 'What on earth do you mean?' Then the story came out, bit by bit, and as it did I realised that at the age of sixteen and a half I was at an important crossroads in my young life.

It seemed that while I had been out gallivanting around the youth-club dance floor, Johnny Dougary, one of Liverpool's Scottish scouts, had called on my parents and asked if I would sign amateur forms for the Merseyside club.

I quickly dispelled any notion that I was having my leg pulled. My parents would not sit up a couple of hours past their bedtime to do that. No, something important was happening which crucially affected my future.

Then my parents told me that two Liverpool officials – a director, Bill McConnell and manager George Kay – were coming up to talk the matter over the following Monday. They arrived as planned and had a long talk with my parents with me mainly a listener.

Mr McConnell and Mr Kay gave my parents the two assurances they really wanted – that I should be accommodated in homely lodgings and, because they considered football a precarious business, that I would be allowed to follow an accountancy career.

A week or so later a letter arrived addressed not to me but to my parents. I was at the front door when the postman called and as soon as I saw 'Liverpool Football Club' in the top left-hand corner of the envelope I knew I was holding my fate in my hands.

My father was at work so my mother opened the letter and we read it together. It told us that the club had fixed up a position for me with a firm of accountants and that I would get pocket money of £1 a week until I signed as a professional at the age of seventeen.

The letter also stated that good lodgings had been found for me and that the club would pay the cost of them. When my father came home we took the letter to the Reverend Gray, who had followed Reverend Stewart as our minister, and he suggested that before I signed anything we should ask about the professional standing of the firm I was to work for.

Maybe that was just his inherent Scottish caution but as it turned out we need not have bothered. The firm was one of the most highly respected in Liverpool.

The company, Simon, Jude and West, were also Liverpool FC's accountants and Liddell was to work for them throughout his playing days at Anfield prior to taking up a post as assistant bursar at Liverpool University's Guild of Undergraduates.

But before the teenage Liddell made his big move south, to leave behind the mainly cinder pitches of the Fife Junior League for the lusher turf of Anfield, he had another decision to make, as he explained:

One day the local Dunfermline newspaper carried a story about my impending departure to Liverpool. I was as proud as a peacock at the prospect of my move but that was dented somewhat by the reaction of the school rector when he saw the paragraph in the paper.

He told me he was disappointed that I should end my schooling to take what might become a blind-alley occupation. He said it would be far better for me to stay another year at school and sit for a university scholarship. He also held out the bait that by doing so I'd probably make a bigger name for myself at rugby than I ever would at soccer.

I went home that afternoon rather chastened. But the outcome of another family conference was that we would stick to our original decision and we advised Liverpool accordingly.

Two days later Mr Dougary brought along the necessary forms and the deed was done. For a time I walked around as if I was in a dream, eagerly anticipating what lay ahead while some of the village folk started to spin me yarns of the dangers of a big city.

They said that Liverpool was such a terrible and lawless place that the police went about in pairs. Other village people told me that if I didn't come up to expectations at Liverpool I'd find myself with no job and no prospects.

Fortunately, my mounting excitement enabled me to discount their tales of woe and when Willie Fagan, then one of the stars at Liverpool, visited my parents he soon set our fears at rest. His home was less than ten miles from mine and Willie had been asked by George Kay to make arrangements to travel to Liverpool with me.

It was a typical gesture by the Liverpool manager. With two boys of his own he knew what it meant to be a youngster who had never been away from home for more than a weekend to pull up his roots and live and work among strangers two hundred miles away.

I arranged to meet Willie Fagan at the station in Edinburgh and I was seen off from Dunfermline by the female members of the family. My father couldn't be there as he couldn't afford to miss even a few hours work. It was a tearful business for the women and almost for me, although I put a brave face on things for my mother's sake.

I felt very lonely until Willie arrived but before long we were on our way and on the journey he gave me a lot of valuable advice. Mr Kay met us at Liverpool and took me up to my lodgings. It turned out that my landlady was Mrs Doig, the widow of Ted Doig, the famous goalkeeper who played for Arbroath, Sunderland and Liverpool and won many Scotland caps before I was born.

The club could not have chosen a better place. Mrs Doig had several Liverpool players as lodgers. She was kindly and motherly and her house was a second home for all the youngsters who stayed with her.

My room mate was a fellow Scot from Alexandria named Eric Patterson. That was another good thing as we had plenty in common. Mrs Doig looked after the young players splendidly and that first night we all got well acquainted.

Matt Busby was captain of Liverpool but it wasn't until much later in my life that I discovered his key part in my move to Anfield before he'd even met me. In fact, I didn't know until

I read it in his book in the late 1950s! Although we got to know each other very closely over many years he never told me.

Perhaps the reason for that is that he didn't want me to feel under any obligation to him for what he did. I shall always be indebted to him. I am also very grateful for all his subsequent kindnesses and much helpful advice and guidance.

Busby's benign influence on his young fellow Scot was observed by Liddell's wife-to-be Phyllis, who reflected: 'Matt was a kindly father figure to Billy. He listened to everything Matt said and did everything Matt said. Billy thought a great deal of him and in later life we became family friends of Matt and his wife Jean.'

Liddell arrived in Liverpool on Wednesday 27 July 1938, two days after a terrorist bomb in the marketplace at Haifa, Palestine killed 43 people and wounded 42, while on the same day Australia won the fourth cricket Test in England to retain the Ashes. In Paris the previous month Italy's footballers successfully defended the World Cup, beating Hungary 4–2 in the final of a tournament in which the British countries did not participate.

And with the world about to be plunged into war it was to be more than eight years before Billy Liddell would make his League debut for Liverpool. By then his mentor Matt Busby had left Anfield for the challenge of rebuilding bomb-scarred Manchester United on his way to triumph, tragedy, further glory, a knighthood and iconic status in football. Liddell's path would also lead to the stars.

Chapter Two

Wings for Victory

The Liverpool that Billy Liddell joined in the summer of 1938 was a club struggling to recapture its former heady days. Mediocrity was almost their middle name from the second half of the 1920s and throughout the 1930s, an era decades before the domestic League Cup competition and European tournaments were on the fixture lists.

Since their back-to-back championship wins in 1922 and 1923, Liverpool's highest position in the First Division was fourth in 1925. They had also had to fend off several relegation scares, at least managing to preserve the top-flight status that had been theirs since 1905.

In the FA Cup a sixth-round appearance in 1932 was the furthest they had progressed since losing 1–0 to Burnley at Crystal Palace in 1914, the first Final watched by a reigning monarch – King George V witnessing the proceedings wearing a bowler hat.

Deepening the discomfort of the lean years for Liverpool was the success of arch rivals and close neighbours Everton, for whom the Dixie Dean-inspired 1930s had been a bountiful period. After the Goodison ignominy of relegation in 1930 Everton responded with a unique hat trick of Second Division title in 1931, League championship a year later and FA Cup triumph in 1933.

The pattern persisted in Liddell's first season at Anfield, with Liverpool finishing in mid-table limbo in 11th place while Everton lorded it as champions. Not that first-team matters as yet directly concerned the young Scottish recruit who was still starry-eyed at his new, very different surroundings. 'My eyes were here, there and everywhere,' Liddell admitted.

When I first arrived at Liverpool I recognised some of the famous players such as Matt Busby, Jim Harley, Phil Taylor, Berry Nieuwenhuys, Jack Balmer, Tom Cooper and several others, mainly because I'd seen their pictures in the papers from time to time. My friend Eric Patterson named those players I couldn't identify.

On my first morning at Anfield I didn't have much time to study the famous stars in the dressing room because in next to no time we were in training kit and jogging along the East Lancashire Road on a five-mile run to break us in.

The following days passed quickly enough but after a while I found I had time on my hands in the afternoons and suggested to Mr Kay that I would like to begin my accountancy job. Wisely, he advised me to wait until the season had got underway and I had my feet planted a little more firmly on the football ladder.

On the Thursday before the 1938–9 season began the team lists were posted on the dressing-room board and after eagerly scanning them I was pleased to see myself at outside right in the A team against Hindsford Colliery in the West Lancashire League.

I don't know quite what I'd expected to find at Hindsford but any hopeful ideas of luxurious dressing-room accommodation were soon shattered. After the match we all jostled around a large tin bath which was filled by buckets of water from a rather antiquated boiler.

The thought struck me that this was no better than I'd experienced in Scotland but I quickly realised that it was unfair to expect anything better at what was obviously a rather struggling minor club.

I also played in the Lancashire Midweek League and was in and out of the A team for some weeks. I began to wonder whether, after all, I'd done the right thing in joining

Liverpool. I didn't seem to be making much headway and I confided my fears to Albert Shelley, the former Southampton player who was then A team trainer and who became a firm friend and advisor throughout my career.

Albert pointed out there were other lads of my age at Liverpool and the club wanted to give them all equal opportunities. He told me it was quite usual for young players to be in and out of the junior teams. He advised me to be patient and although that was difficult at times it was the only course open to me.

My colleagues in the A team at that time included full back Eddie Spicer, whose career was to end so prematurely because of a broken leg, Ray Lambert, a future Wales international defender, and Bill Jones, a versatile player who would be capped by England.

There was also inside forward Abe Rosenthal, a charming fellow who later played for Tranmere Rovers and Bradford City and became a wartime glider pilot. He also built up a large ice cream and ice lolly business in Bradford and at one stage was reputed to employ more people than the city's football club had on their staff!

I became more or less an A team regular and I was eagerly looking forward to my seventeenth birthday in January 1939 when Liverpool had undertaken to sign me as a professional. When my birthday approached I went to the office to see Mr Kay. But as it was FA Cup week Mr Kay was engaged on more important matters and I was told to wait until the following Monday.

I thought a few days more were neither here nor there. In fact, it was another three months before I turned professional because of a nasty injury that could have ended my career before it had really started.

It happened on Blackburn Rovers A team ground when I was charged by a defender as I was going full tilt for the ball. I pitched over the touchline and caught my right knee with a terrific blow against a concrete post near the corner flag.

I had to be rushed to hospital where I had several stitches in the wound. Because of a shortage of beds the hospital wanted me out as quickly as possible and the following Monday I went by ambulance to the home of Harry Rawcliffe, a Liverpool player who lived in Blackburn and whose parents kindly invited me to stay with them until I could return to Liverpool.

It was a fortnight before I left Blackburn and I hobbled around on a stick for weeks. During that period all sorts of doubts went through my mind. The doctors told me that the damage to the tissue round the wound was extensive and I wondered whether I would ever be fit to play football again.

Liddell's deep anxieties over his future at that early stage were reflected in his future recollections to his colleagues every time the Liverpool team bus passed the Blackburn A team ground en route to Ewood Park. 'When our bus passed the spot Billy never failed to point out to us the pitch where he smashed his knee as a youngster,' revealed future team-mate Ronnie Moran. 'It clearly made a lasting impression on him.'

To make matters worse for Liddell he was still recovering from the knee damage when he received a worrying letter from home. 'It gave me the news that my folks had narrowly escaped with their lives when gas from a fractured main in the street had seeped into our family's house at night,' Liddell revealed.

My parents and three younger brothers had been saved only because a neighbour awoke, smelled the gas and raised the alarm. Seeing that I was a bit under the weather Mr Kay thoughtfully sent me home for a holiday and at the same time set my mind at rest by saying he'd write to me about signing me professional.

Finally, I put pen to paper on 17 April 1939 and I was to be paid £3 a week in the A team, £4 in the reserves in the Central League and £5 if I got into the first team. That seems little by present standards but to a seventeen-year-old lad in prewar days it represented wealth.

Three weeks after Liddell signed he was joined at Anfield by
another youngster from a similar background: a pit village where
coal was king and the value of money cherished. Left half Bob
Paisley, at twenty a little older than Liddell, hailed from Hetton-
le-Hole, County Durham.

Paisley's arrival from FA Amateur Cup winners Bishop
Auckland began half a century of service to Liverpool, as player,
coach, physiotherapist, assistant to Bill Shankly and, ultimately,
as the most successful English football manager of the twentieth
century.

It also forged a bond between Paisley, Liddell and Matt Busby
that would span the rest of their lives. 'Billy and I became pals
almost right away,' recalled Paisley. 'He was a good-living lad,
respectable and keen to get on in the football world. And what a
player he turned out to be! I always believed comparisons are
odious but Billy had everything. I don't care what era you talk
about, he'd be beyond price.

'It was also very beneficial to have someone like Matt Busby at
Liverpool when I arrived. As skipper, he was always ready to give
advice. He would give lads like Billy and I quite a few words of
encouragement. Matt was a man we could look up to and respect.

'He'd played the game and people like him weren't solely tied
down with tactics, which was a valuable lesson for me. I felt lucky
to have people like Billy and Matt around and the rest of the
players were a good bunch, too. I could have been pitched into a
gang of fly boys who couldn't care less about the game. So I was
very fortunate.'

By the time Liddell, Paisley and the rest of the Liverpool squad
reported for pre-season training in July war clouds were
gathering, the first-team party having made a summer tour of
Sweden that would be their last foreign football sojourn for
seven years.

In a move with echoes of Kitchener's finger-pointing First
World War 'Your Country Needs You' posters, players at all
clubs had been encouraged by the Football Association to join the
Territorial Army or other national service organisations. An FA
circular in April 1939 hoped that the game would display a

patriotic example to the youth of the country and Liverpool answered the call almost with a salute. As a club they became the first to join the Territorials, their intake including manager George Kay and assistant secretary Jack Rouse.

'Because of the world situation there was a feeling of apprehension in the minds of many people,' Liddell recalled.

We sensed we were on the brink of war. The senior Liverpool professionals responded to an appeal by the Football Association and Football League that players should set an example by joining the Territorial Army. I wasn't old enough.

Full back Jim Harley, from Fife like myself and a former Powderhall sprint winner, decided that the Navy was more in his line. 'I want to be sure I've got a bed to sleep in every night,' he cracked. He was an irrepressible character who ended up in destroyers and was mentioned in despatches.

The Territorials were called up before war was declared on Sunday, 3 September 1939 and though some of the older Liverpool players got leave to play in regional matches while doing their Army training it was obvious that before long the younger professionals were going to get chances to prove their football ability much sooner than expected.

More than thirty members of the Liverpool staff were prewar volunteer recruits. Among those who enlisted for the 9th King's Battalion of the Territorials were South African goalkeepers Arthur Riley and Dirk Kemp, both made sergeants, and Tom Cooper, Willie Fagan, Barney Ramsden and Tom Bush, who became lance corporals. Busby became a Sergeant Instructor in the Army Physical Training Corps while South African winger Berry Nieuwenhuys joined the RAF, a course later followed by Liddell.

Such were the manpower problems due to military duties that for their third and last game of the aborted 1939–40 season Liverpool struggled to field a team in the home First Division clash with Chelsea. They managed it thanks to friends of the enlisted Territorial players volunteering to take over sentry duties for Kemp, Ramsden, Busby, Bush, Fagan, Jack Balmer, Cyril Done and Jimmy McInnes, who were based in northern England and had only a few hours' sleep on the floor of a railway station waiting room.

The eight took their places in a team that lined up in old 2–3–5 formation: Kemp; Harley, Ramsden; Busby, Bush, McInnes; Nieuwenhuys, Done, Fagan, Balmer, Van Den Berg.

Liverpool still managed to beat Chelsea 1–0 with debutant Done scoring the club's last peacetime goal watched by a crowd of less than 20,000. Harley was sent off midway through the first half but the outbreak of hostilities meant that his case was never heard. The following day, 3 September, war was declared and the British liner *Athenia* was sunk by a German U-boat off the coast of Ireland with the loss of 112 lives.

In the early days of the war a first-team breakthrough beckoned Liddell and was then cruelly dashed. Highly respected local sportswriter Leslie Edwards had been impressed by the young Scot's displays and tried to use his influence on manager George Kay, whose selection role was restricted to advising the club directors who picked the team.

'I first came across Billy when he'd just come down from Scotland,' said Edwards. 'I met him at the entrance to the players' tunnel. He had his boots in a brown paper parcel. I had seen him in the junior team and I said to George Kay: "He's good enough to go in now."

'The outcome was that Billy was due to play for Tranmere against Liverpool in a wartime regional game in November 1939 with the aim of pulling in a bigger crowd. But at the last minute Tranmere decided to put one of their young local lads in instead, which was a pity.'

Liddell recalled: 'I jumped at the chance to play in the match for Tranmere. But when I reported to their dressing room I was politely but firmly told that there must have been a misunderstanding. Their director in charge told me: "I'm sorry but we'd rather play one of our own amateurs." It was a bitter disappointment to me.'

His Liverpool breakthrough came in two first-team friendlies against Preston and his display in the first, watched by a 3,000 crowd on 16 December 1939, was praised as one 'of great promise'. His debut finally came on New Year's Day 1940 when he was selected for the Wartime League Western Division home game against Crewe Alexandra.

'I was chosen at outside left, we won 7–3, and I scored one of the goals after just two minutes . . . there was no happier youngster in Liverpool that day,' he enthused. The team in which Liddell made his debut was: Mansley; Harley, Tennant; Busby, Halsall, S Eastham; Leadbetter, Nieuwenhuys, Done, Carney, Liddell.

Halsall and Tennant were guest players, a common feature of wartime matches. Star guests that illuminated Liverpool sides included Frank Swift, Peter Doherty, Sam Bartram, Stan Cullis and Charlton's Don Welsh – later to manage Liverpool – who scored six goals as an Anfield 'guest' in a 12–1 win over Southport in December 1944.

Five days later things got even better for Liddell, who retained his place in the side that went to Maine Road and beat Manchester City 7–3 in another Western Division match. He responded with the first of his eight Liverpool first-team hat tricks and what made the feeling even sweeter was that he claimed his treble against City's redoubtable Swift, the goalkeeper with dinner-plate hands who went on to win nineteen England caps:

As we left the field Frank ran over to me, patted me on the back and said: 'Well done, sonny boy.' Then he added jokingly, with a grin: 'Don't do that sort of thing too often. I don't like wingers scoring three goals when I'm under the bar!'

Frank was one of the most generous and kindly men I ever met. He never begrudged success to anyone. We became firm friends in later years, a friendship unshaken even when I ran into him at full tilt in an international and broke a couple of his ribs! It was a total accident and Frank used to joke I did it so I could score against him.

When his playing career was over, Swift turned to sports-writing and was one of eight journalists travelling with Manchester United who perished in the 1958 Munich air disaster, which killed a total of 23 people.

The tragedy also went perilously close to claiming the life of Matt Busby, but the United manager survived after a brave, protracted battle against his injuries. Restored to health, he built fine new teams and ten years later achieved immortality by leading United to the first European Cup triumph by an English club, a feat which earned him a knighthood.

In 1940, though, right half Busby was having a major effect on eighteen-year-old rising star Liddell who, in March that year, was hailed by manager George Kay as 'the best thing that has come out of Scotland in the past ten years'. Given the production line of tartan talent it was rich praise indeed.

'At that time Billy had the great influence of Matt Busby behind him,' recalled sportswriter Leslie Edwards. 'Busby made him tick. He fed him the passes along the floor and Billy would be off.'

Liddell concurred with that view, saying: 'Matt was a wonderful help on the field. You could hardly do other than play well with him behind you while off the field he was a constant source of good advice and valuable hints.

'I also learned a lot from Berry Nieuwenhuys, especially in centring the ball, and from the wartime guest players. They helped to keep football going and the government said that in their view football was doing a service to the country in maintaining morale.'

It was with that aim and to boost the coffers of the Lord Mayor of Liverpool's War Fund that a match was arranged at Anfield on 19 April 1941 between teams billed as The Football League and an All British XI. The game produced not only a sixteen-goal showpiece but through circumstance provided Liddell, now nineteen, with his first taste of representative football since his appearances for Scotland Schoolboys. Yet he went to the match as a spectator!

The teams lined up as follows:

Football League: Hobson (Chester); Lambert (Liverpool),

Gorman (Sunderland); Willingham (Huddersfield), Pryde (Blackburn Rovers), Galley (Wolves); Worrall (Portsmouth), Dorsett (Wolves), Lawton (Everton), Stephenson (Leeds), Hanson (Chelsea).

All British XI: Poland (Liverpool); Cook (Everton), Jones (Blackpool), Dearson (Birmingham), Cullis (Wolves), Busby (Liverpool); Nieuwenhuys (Liverpool), Mutch (Preston), Fagan (Liverpool), Stevenson (Everton), McShane (Blackburn Rovers).

Alf Hobson was drafted into goal for the League side as a late replacement for Frank Swift but he, in turn, had to go off after being injured in a collision with Liverpool's Willie Fagan. Tom Galley then took over in goal, which meant that someone had to fill an outfield vacancy. Opportunity knocked for the watching Liddell.

I'd gone along to the game because I wasn't going to miss the chance of seeing so many stars in action. Hobson played because Frank Swift couldn't get military leave but he got injured just before half time and during the interval I was asked by a League official if I'd go on as a substitute.

I didn't need a second invitation. I've never got ready for a game so quickly! I stripped like lightning and before the man in charge had a chance to find someone better qualified than me I was out on the field.

I went to outside left with Alf Hanson, the former Liverpool favourite who joined Chelsea just before I arrived at Anfield, switching to left half.Within two minutes of the resumption I'd scored!

The ball came to me with only the goalkeeper to beat and I made no mistake. The game finished in a 9–7 win for the League team and the spectators enjoyed a feast of goals as well as a brilliant display of football at its best, largely because there was nothing at stake and every player did his utmost to entertain the paying customers.

The breathtaking scoring sequence was: Stephenson (League) 1–0, Nieuwenhuys (British XI) 1–1, Dorsett (League) 2–1, Cullis

(British XI) 2–2, Lawton (League) 3–2, Busby (British XI) 3–3, Lawton (League) 4–3, Liddell (League) 5–3, Fagan (British XI) 5–4, Fagan (British XI) 5–5, Hanson (League) 6–5, Lawton (League) 7–5, Stephenson (League, o.g.) 7–6, Dorsett (League) 8–6, Stevenson (British XI) 8–7, Hanson (League) 9–7.

Liddell, having set his professional course in accountancy, was by now on deferred service with the RAF and awaiting call-up, having been accepted as an air crew candidate. But his blossoming football abilities brought his first Scotland call when he was chosen for the game against the RAF at Newcastle's St James's Park in February 1942, the same month that the tentacles of the war stretched to Australian soil with the Japanese bombing of Darwin.

While Liddell waited for action himself his Scotland selection came as a pleasant shock:

Although I knew that Matt Busby, who was then stationed in Scotland, had recommended me to Mr, later Sir, George Graham, the secretary of the Scottish FA, I was just twenty and felt it was expecting too much to be honoured at that early stage of my career.

On the Saturday before the international, Liverpool's game at Rochdale was called off because the ground was unfit and I was keen to have match practice before the Scotland match. I asked George Kay to let me play against Napiers, a works team, at Anfield. He said I shouldn't take any risks but I persisted and, finally, he let me play.

As it turned out my best intentions evaporated. After only a few minutes and before I'd even kicked the ball I got injured. I jumped to head the ball and collided with a defender. We clashed heads and I suffered concussion and a badly split lip.

I was carried off on a stretcher and taken to Walton Hospital, where I spent the next ten days. They treated me superbly but when I pleaded with the doctors to let me go to Newcastle, they told me there was no chance. You can imagine how I felt.

George Kay frequently came in to visit me and when I was well on the way to recovery he chided me about my determination to play against Napiers. In his gruff but kindly manner he told me: 'If you'd listened to me, Bill, you'd have been alright for Newcastle. Let that be a lesson to you.'

He was right. But, as it turned out, I didn't miss my first chance of playing for Scotland because the game at Newcastle was called off because of snow.

Liddell finally donned his country's dark blue jersey on 18 April 1942 in an unforgettable encounter with the old enemy England at Hampden Park. 'You can imagine how my mind was racing in the weeks leading up to the game,' said Liddell. 'I wondered if the selectors would include me again.

'There were plenty of players with strong claims, including former Everton player Jimmy Caskie who was playing with his Goodison team-mate Torry Gillick at Rangers. Others like Tommy Pearson, Johnny Deakin and Johnny Kelly were far better known names than mine.

'So when I learned I'd been selected at outside left I was overjoyed. To any Scot, the honour of appearing against England is the greatest of all and here it was happening to me at twenty years of age.'

It meant that Liddell would team up for the first time with a certain Bill Shankly of Preston, later to take charge of Liverpool and inspire an Anfield revolution. Shankly was at right half with Liddell's wartime mentor and clubmate Matt Busby at left half. 'Matt was instrumental in getting me into the team,' Liddell observed.

In those days arrangements for internationals were not so good as they are today. Some of the players didn't meet up until the morning of the match although the Anglo-Scots and many of the England team got together on the Friday evening.

I travelled north with Joe Mercer of Everton, who was stationed in Cheshire and, like Matt, was a Sergeant

Instructor in the Army Physical Training Corps. Joe did his best to calm my nerves by telling me what to expect on my first appearance at Hampden.

Joe had played there in the last prewar international when England won 2–1. 'It's a wonderful experience but it will put the wind up you at first when you go out and see the vast crowd and hear the tremendous cheering,' Joe told me, adding: 'Don't let it worry you, Bill. Once the match has started you forget it and if you play your natural game you'll be alright.'

Normally, competing international sides didn't stay at the same hotel. But it was different in war time. Everything was more informal and less highly organised and on this occasion the England and Scotland players were staying together.

The evening before the match I went to the pictures with Joe and his England team mates Jimmy Hagan, Alf Kirchen and Maurice Edelston. It was the first time I'd met the last three players, all of whom gave me a warm welcome and wished me luck. Jimmy Hagan, though, cracked: 'Not too much luck! Don't pinch all the limelight.'

Time usually seems to drag on the morning of a big game but that wasn't the case before this match. Apart from Matt Busby, I was meeting all the Scotland players for the first time and that, in itself, was an experience to remember.

I also met up with my mother and father for the first time in almost a year so there was plenty to talk about and it seemed no time before I got the signal to board the team coach for Hampden.

There were several other new boys as well as myself including Willie Waddell of Rangers, who shared with me the distinction of being the youngest on the field, as well as Gordon Bremner, Alex Herd and Jock Dodds, later to join Everton from Blackpool.

The older players did everything possible to put us at ease and help reduce the tension which can play havoc with the nerves of a youngster making his international debut.

This is how the teams lined up:

Scotland: Dawson (Rangers); Carabine (Third Lanark), A Beattie (Preston); Shankly (Preston), T Smith (Preston), Busby (Liverpool); Waddell (Rangers), Herd (Manchester City), Dodds (Blackpool), G. Bremner (Arsenal), Liddell (Liverpool).

England: Marks (Arsenal); Bacuzzi (Fulham), Hapgood (Arsenal); Willingham (Huddersfield), Mason (Coventry), Mercer (Everton); Matthews (Stoke), Edelston (Reading), Lawton (Everton), Hagan (Sheffield United), Kirchen (Arsenal).

'It was an enjoyable debut for me in what many people said was one of the best ever in the long history of games between England and Scotland,' Liddell recounted.

We won 5–4 and I got one of the goals. Jock Dodds got a hat trick and Bill Shankly scored the winner. Tommy Lawton scored a hat trick for England whose other goal came from Jimmy Hagan.

I'll never forget Bill Shankly's sheer delight when he put the ball into the England net for our winner. More than 17 years later he became Liverpool manager and he brought to the job that same enthusiasm, drive, courage and energy he had shown on the field in a Scotland jersey.

It didn't matter whether it was a Cup tie, a League game, a practice match or just a kick around. Bill Shankly lived for what he was doing.

I had a reasonably good game and, judging from the reports, I had done enough to warrant consideration again, which was encouraging. All things considered I was satisfied because the game had been something of an ordeal.

I didn't suffer from pre-match nerves but during the half-time interval I had to take some aspirins to settle my stomach and get rid of a splitting headache. It must have been delayed action.

Liddell's appraisal of his debut in front of an attendance variously recorded between 75,000 and 91,000 was cloaked in characteristic modesty. Others were not so inhibited.

The *Daily Herald* hailed Liddell's international baptism, enthusing: 'England's sequence of conquests was broken in a match which must live with the greatest in international memory. Pride of the crowd became Billy Liddell, the Liverpool boy. After equalising Lawton's opening goal he could do no wrong.'

Six weeks after his eye-catching Hampden performance, Liddell teamed up with Shankly again . . . this time in Liverpool colours. The club's final fixture of the 1941–2 season was the Liverpool Senior Cup Final against Everton at Anfield on 30 May, the day after Bing Crosby recorded the world's top-selling disc 'White Christmas' for the film soundtrack of *Holiday Inn*. 'Red Spring' was a more fitting title for the events at Anfield as Liverpool, with Preston guest player Shankly in the No. 4 shirt and Liddell this time operating on the right wing at No. 7, swamped their city rivals 4–1.

Shankly had an intriguing memory of the occasion, recalling: 'Before the game all the players, including Billy Liddell and myself, were in the passageway. But George Kay, the Liverpool manager, didn't speak. He just went round touching people on the shoulder. If he touched you, then you were playing!'

The following October, Liddell made his second Scotland appearance and his first at Wembley. Said Liddell:

Again, Willie Waddell was on the right wing and Bill and Matt at half back. Jock Dodds and Gordon Bremner were in attack along with a player I'd never met before, Tommy Walker of Hearts.

Tommy was one of the quietest men I'd ever played with. He rarely shouted for the ball, never complained if you did anything wrong but was always there to offer every possible help and encouragement.

He went on to play for Chelsea, then manage Hearts. Tommy was a gentleman on and off the field, an example to everyone by his sportsmanship. The Wembley game was nothing like the Hampden match. Instead of nine goals it finished in a goalless draw.

Liddell's RAF call-up arrived two months later and he was ordered to report to Lord's cricket ground on 7 December 1942.

I was billeted in St John's Wood and soon met several football folk, including the Chelsea trio of Len Goulden, Dick Spence and Joe Payne, the latter famous for scoring a record ten goals in a match for Luton against Bristol Rovers in 1936.

I also met the future England team manager Walter Winterbottom, then a Squadron Leader and later a Wing Commander, who arranged for me to play as a guest for Chelsea. I turned out for them a few times and scored a couple of goals but then I was posted to Cambridge.

The CO there refused to let me travel to London to continue playing at Stamford Bridge, even though, because he was a rugby fellow, he allowed chaps like Bleddyn Williams to go off to play rugby for Wales.

After much pleading on my part I was allowed to throw in my lot with Cambridge Town but only on the understanding that I signed a form to say that if I got injured, I wouldn't hold the RAF responsible.

I was still playing rugby occasionally and, in between, studied hard on a thirteen-week course. I wanted to qualify as a pilot but using my aptitude for maths I did so well in navigation that I was posted to the Air Navigation School at Bridgnorth in Shropshire.

Liddell made his third Scotland appearance in a 4–0 defeat by England at Hampden in April 1943. Raich Carter scored twice with Dennis Compton and Dennis Westcott the other marksmen. 'Carter and Jimmy Hagan were the men who put paid to our hopes that day,' said Liddell. 'They gave some of the best exhibitions of inside-forward play I'd seen.'

But in autumn 1943, while Liddell was stationed at Bridgnorth, he suffered an injury that haunts professional sportsmen. He recounted:

I was playing in a friendly scratch game with nothing at stake. We were winning with ease when, just before the end, I stumbled in a hole in the pitch and my ankle gave way.

I was taken to hospital and learned I'd broken my leg just above the ankle. That was on a Sunday. Three days later I was named in the Scotland team to play England at Maine Road. Naturally, there was little football news in the papers in those days and I realised the selectors hadn't heard about my injury.

I notified them immediately and Johnny Deakin of St Mirren took my place. When I read later what had happened at Maine Road I was rather relieved at having to miss the game. England won 8–0, with Tommy Lawton scoring four!

When I left hospital I went to the RAF Remedial Centre at Blackpool, which was a wonderful experience. Compared with some of the patients, there wasn't much wrong with me and I was soon alright again.

But what impressed me was the amazing devotion of the staff, from the top doctors and surgeons to the lowest orderly, to their task of getting men who had been maimed in the war fit and well again – or as well as they ever would be.

The medical people dedicated themselves to it and nothing was too much trouble. I must say I felt a bit of a fraud when people, seeing my air crew training badge, asked me how I'd been injured.

After a month at Blackpool I returned to Bridgnorth and was posted to Heaton Park, near Manchester, where we were not allowed out of camp until 4.30 p.m. on Saturdays.

One week, when Liverpool were playing at Manchester City, I applied to get away at midday so I could turn out in the game. My application was refused but I still got to Maine Road. I just hopped over the camp wall when nobody was looking!

I linked up with the Liverpool team at the station and went up to the ground in their coach. That was fortunate because there were scores of service police checking passes outside the ground. Luckily, they didn't check the passes of the servicemen on the team coach and I got away with it.

Liddell, with his powerful 5ft 11in, 12st 7lb frame and a hammer of a shot in either foot, also appeared for the RAF representative side. 'My best performance for the RAF was when that great Northern Ireland player Peter Doherty was in the team. I scored five goals that day and Peter, who was a fine inside forward, was laying them on for me.'

Another RAF match was unforgettable for rising star Tom Finney, who recalled: 'I was selected at outside right for an FA XI against the RAF at Stoke City's Victoria Ground. Among the other players on view were Billy, Eddie Hapgood, Raich Carter, Frank Soo, Len Goulden, Stan Cullis, Joe Mercer, Tommy Lawton, Jock Dodds, and Stanley Matthews.

'We won 4–3 but I was only a learner then. In fact, of the 22 players on view, only Jack Fairbrother and myself were not internationals. I'll never forget the impression the fabulous Matthews made on me. He was the opposing outside right and he had a wonderful game, the first of many I was destined to see from him.'

Finney would become a great England colleague of the Stoke and Blackpool inspiration, but Liddell would share with Matthews the glittering distinction of being the only two players selected for both postwar Great Britain teams, a massive honour still in the distance in 1943 as overseas duty as a Pathfinder navigator beckoned the Liverpool and Scotland star.

We were kitted out originally for a destination unknown. We speculated where it might be and it turned out to be Canada. We sailed from Gourock on the *Île de France*. It was a treat to tread Scottish soil again but depressing to see the magnificent view gradually fade as I left my native country once more.

We landed at New York which was a welcome sight after the British blackout. The city was ablaze with light despite the fact that there was supposed to be a sort of partial 'dim-out'. It was so partial you couldn't notice it!

After a few hours in New York we were on our way to Canada, first to Moncton for a couple of weeks' inactivity, then to the Central Navigation School in Rivers, a small town in Manitoba, working with Tiger Moths and Ansons.

I made many friends in Rivers and I don't mean to upset them by saying there are many more attractive places. The people were friendly and very hospitable but the township then consisted of barely half a dozen streets.

About every three weeks we got a 48-hour pass and that was the signal to hare off to the bright lights of Winnipeg. At the end of the course in Rivers I found myself with the rank of Pilot Officer Navigator and I returned to Moncton to await passage to England.

While I was there I played in several football matches along with players like Ken Chisholm, John Love, Les Medley and Peter Kippax, who would later become a colleague at Liverpool for a short time. The Scottish rugby international John Orr, who was quite a useful soccer player, also turned out.

When I was on leave in Toronto I played a few games with Toronto Scottish, helping them reach fourth place in their league. After returning to camp I had a week's special leave to take part in the semifinal play-off game in the League competition.

The Scottish won 3–2 and I scored twice but before the final I was recalled to Moncton and couldn't play in the game. Perhaps that was as well because I learned that the match was a real brawl, with fights among the players and demonstrations by spectators, to say nothing of a small fire in the stands!

The inside story of Liddell's appearances for Toronto Scottish was revealed by his widow Phyllis: 'He was just standing on the sidelines watching this team of Scottish ex-pats. Billy told them he was Scottish, although he didn't tell them he played for Liverpool. In fact, he went under the assumed name of Bill Tanner!

'They asked him if he'd like a game next day. He turned up and went on as a substitute. Within ten minutes he'd scored two goals

and the other team were asking him if he wanted a rest! He really
was football mad.'

Liddell wrote to George Kay to tell him he was heading back to
Britain after seven months in Canada – a fact celebrated by the
Anfield manager in his club programme notes – and Liddell duly
docked at Liverpool in September 1944. Kay met him and asked
if he could play for Liverpool the following day. But service
duties precluded such a swift return. Liddell was posted briefly to
Harrogate and his Liverpool comeback was delayed until late
October, in a goalless home draw against Everton in the Football
League North competition.

Whatever else was rationed during the war, derby meetings
between Merseyside's great combatants certainly were not.
Everton and Liverpool met a remarkable 36 times between
December 1939 and December 1946, with goals often in profusion
and attendances substantial. Liverpool won twenty of the wartime
duels and Everton ten, with six draws; Liddell collected twelve
goals in 22 appearances in the marathon Mersey series.

He scored in his last four wartime derby outings, two in home-
and-away League War Cup ties in March 1945 to give Liverpool
a 1–0 win on each occasion – the game at Goodison drawing a
wartime record crowd of 51,512 – and two further single strikes
in the Football League North in September and December 1945.

But the most breathtaking of the wartime Mersey meetings,
especially for Liverpool supporters, had an inspirational
contribution from Liddell who, according to a report, 'really
turned on the power to transform the match'.

In August 1943 Everton were leading 2–0 at Anfield with ten
minutes left in a fund-raising derby in aid of the Lord Mayor's
War Fund. But then Liddell took charge and Liverpool amazingly
scored five goals in eight minutes to capture an incredible
5–2 win.

A great Liddell cross was met by Jack Balmer to reduce the
deficit in the 80th minute before Liddell swiftly struck the
equaliser. The Scot's rampant raiding form then helped guest
player Don Welsh to hit a rapid-fire hat trick with two minutes
still left on the watch!

Liddell's sheer power earned rave notices at Hillsborough in November 1944 when he scored twice in Scotland's 7–1 rout of an RAF side that included Stanley Matthews, Raich Carter, Stan Mortensen and Ted Drake. 'Pilot Officer Liddell, recently returned from Canada, shot hard and often,' said one report. 'He scored after 27 minutes when he hit Delaney's cross as it fell. His second, and Scotland's sixth, was a glorious drive that gave goalkeeper Williams no chance.'

Following his brief RAF posting to Harrogate, Liddell was sent to Perth, which brought the oppportunity of a nostalgic four-match guest stint with his home-town club Dunfermline, where he had stood on the terraces as a wide-eyed schoolboy.

'After that I was off across the Irish Sea to Bishop's Court near Downpatrick, County Down,' said Liddell.

The idea was to acclimatise us to night flying in a blackout which there wasn't in Canada. One day, after an exercise, we were over the Isle of Man heading back to Bishop's Court when I had a scare.

I'd given the pilot the course back to base and was tidying things up when, all of a sudden, the nose went down and I thought we were going into the drink. The pilot levelled the plane out about twenty feet above the water.

I really got the breeze up. I was due to play for Scotland against England a couple of days later! I asked the pilot afterwards: 'What was all that about?' He replied: 'I'm going on leave at the weekend and I thought I'd have a bit of fun!'

While I was stationed in Northern Ireland I met Elisha Scott, the famous Irish international who kept goal for Liverpool for so many years and whose record number of appearances for the club stood as a record until I broke it in 1957.

Elisha had long been manager of Belfast Celtic and he came to Bishop's Court to ask me to sign for them as a guest player. I would have done so but for the fact that I'd half promised Linfield and didn't like to go back on my word.

Although Elisha promised me better terms I felt I'd be letting Linfield down if I accepted. I'd heard a lot about Elisha. Nobody connected with Liverpool could help doing that, especially when you spoke to former players and supporters who had vivid memories of him. So it was hard to refuse a request from a man who'd done so much for Liverpool. But, regretfully, I declined his offer.

I played only two games for Linfield but I was impressed by the quality of the Windsor Park pitch. It was well grassed. The stadium reminded me of Liverpool's in that the spectators on the terraces were below the level of the pitch and there was quite an atmosphere in the ground.

I became very friendly with the Linfield trainer, Gerry Morgan, who was also trainer of the Irish international team. In fact, I made quite a few friends there and kept in touch with them for years after.

Celebrated Northern Ireland-based journalist Malcolm Brodie, former *Belfast Telegraph* sports editor and veteran of covering thirteen World Cup Finals, vividly recalled Liddell's brief but cherished sojourn into Ulster football:

'Liddell was one of many leading English, Scottish and Welsh players who were wartime "guests" of Irish League clubs, a parade of stars who had a crucial role in ensuring the continuity of football in Northern Ireland.

'Their presence helped the regional league, established when the Irish League closed down during the war, prosper and survive. The crowd appeal of these visiting players like Liddell was immense.

'Linfield, Northern Ireland's best supported club, had created a remarkable "channel of communication", as they called it, with the Forces. They knew when a top player was about to be stationed at any of the Ulster bases and few escaped their network. Indeed, it was once said famously that they had a spy in the War Office!

'When Linfield secretary Joe Mackey and their legendary trainer Gerry Morgan learned that Liddell was to be posted to a base near Belfast they quickly tracked him and collected his signature on 13 January 1945. They were the envy of rival clubs who arrived too late on the scene.

'Because of commitments, however, Liddell was unavailable for a month and unfortunately played only two matches before being sent back to England. Both his games were against Ards, during February.

'He scored twice in the first match, an 8–0 victory at Windsor Park. He didn't find the target in the second game a week later but helped Linfield to a 2–0 win. I covered those matches and Liddell's class stood out. He was a powerhouse on the wing.

'Linfield's forward line was one of the most potent in the club's history: Dave Cochrane (Leeds United), Sammy McCrory (Southend), Davy Walsh (West Bromwich Albion), George Richardson and Liddell. They all dovetailed perfectly.

'Billy established many friendships during his short stay in Ulster, particularly with Billy Scott, a compositor with the *Belfast Telegraph*, whose son Jackie won Northern Ireland amateur caps with Linfield and went to live in South Africa.

'Billy Liddell was a frequent visitor to the Scott home. Indeed, this great player and a gentleman with sound principles was given a *cead mile a failte* (a hundred thousand welcomes) wherever he went. And Billy never forgot the hospitality extended to him.'

A decade later, Belfast's Windsor Park would be the venue for one of Liddell's greatest honours, his second selection for Great Britain. But his Scotland appearance against England in front of a 66,000 crowd at Villa Park in February 1945, shortly after his air 'scare' over the Irish Sea, had been eagerly anticipated by George Kay.

In the club programme two months earlier the Liverpool manager had written: 'Hearty congratulations to Busby, Harley, Fagan and Liddell for an excellent showing in the Scottish team which beat an RAF XI 7–1 at Sheffield last week, with Liddell (2), Fagan and Harley among the scorers.

'Should these players be selected en bloc to play versus England at Aston Villa in February it would write an interesting chapter in football, as perhaps the first time four players from one English club have played together for Scotland.'

The Liverpool quartet did play – Jim Harley at right back, Matt Busby at right half, Willie Fagan at inside right and Liddell at outside left – but Scotland lost 3–2, with Stan Mortensen scoring twice for England. Liddell recalled:

> The game was memorable for a wonderful display by Scotland's goalkeeper Bobby Brown of Queen's Park. He was like a human octopus, stopping shot after shot until the England forwards, brilliantly led by Tommy Lawton, must have been ready almost literally to tear their hair in frustration.
>
> I also remember the game for one of the most anxious periods I ever spent on a football field. It happened towards the end of the match when Matt Busby, who'd always been one of my soccer heroes, was carried to the touchline injured and ambulance men dashed up with a stretcher.
>
> They started tying Matt's ankles and legs together and I immediately thought that he'd broken his leg. Fortunately, it turned out to be only a severely bruised ankle.

After his spell in Northern Ireland, Liddell was sent back to England to join a Pathfinder navigational training unit at Worboys, Huntingdonshire. 'I was hoping to take some really active part in the war before it ended,' said Liddell.

> I'd been in the RAF more than two years, undergoing intensive training most of the time, and it seemed a pity so much effort should be wasted.
>
> Although I'd played plenty of football in off-duty time I'd worked hard to make myself an efficient officer and, on passing out of the Pathfinder navigational training school, I was ready to take my place in a bomber squadron.
>
> Again, I was doomed to disappointment. There was a glut of aircrews on the squadron to which I was attached, the 617 Lancaster Squadron, and though we had plenty of night exercises and other jobs to keep us up to scratch I couldn't get on a real operation over enemy territory.

Eventually, VE Day arrived and my hopes went! Later, I made several trips to Italy to bring back soldiers for leave as well as the usual routine jobs but nothing calculated to provide a big thrill.

When the transitional football season of 1945–6 started I was still in this country playing centre forward for Bomber Command together with well known players such as Bert Williams of Wolves and George Edwards of Birmingham.

Life for Liddell, as for millions of others, was to change in many ways after the global conflict officially ended with Japan's surrender in August 1945, following the US Air Force attacks on Hiroshima and Nagasaki with atomic bombs (whose origin stretched back to a Liverpool research laboratory).

Liddell's courtship with Phyllis had spanned the duration of the war and now a new beginning beckoned. 'We'd met when we were only seventeen in 1939, a few weeks before war was declared, when Billy was articled to the accountancy firm Simon, Jude and West,' said Phyllis.

'I'll never forget how it happened. Billy came to do an audit at the Liverpool company I was working for as a junior clerk. He was in the office on his own, checking over some books, and one of the girls said, "There's a young footballer in there . . . his name's Billy Liddell."

'I thought to myself, what a strange name. It was surprising, really, because my own maiden name of Farrance was very unusual in itself. I think it originated in France but Billy never commented on it. Little did I know then that I would carry the name of Liddell through my life.

'We got chatting in the office that day, we went out for a while and eventually, in December 1942, we became engaged. When I first knew Billy he lived in digs arranged by the club at Mrs Doig's house in Anfield.

'Then he went to live at a friend's house off West Derby Road where the mother and children in the family had been moved out to the country as war evacuees.

'That left the father, his son and Billy which wasn't a good thing in the respect of him being well looked after from a diet and physical point of view. As a footballer his fitness and condition was so very important.

'So my mum, Maria, stepped in and insisted that Billy came to stay with us. Unlike me, who didn't follow football until I met Billy, she was a great football fan, as was my dad, George.

'My mum was an avid Liverpool supporter and was overjoyed to look after Billy and cook for him. My mum and dad were great football followers and were regulars on the touchline at the Old Vics matches at the recreation ground in Garston, where our family lived.

'Once upon a time Garston was a village in its own right and it was a family joke that we were Garstonians not Liverpudlians! During the war Billy was away a lot, like me. I was in the WAAF, although the furthest I was posted was to Wilmslow, Cheshire where I spent about four years.

'Billy was very fortunate that at the end of the war he was posted to Warton near Blackpool where he was able to take a course to complete his accountancy studies and qualify. So the RAF was good for him in that respect.

'Because of the war we missed a lot of our youth, just like the players of that era lost a large chunk of their football careers. But at the time it wasn't something we really thought about. We just wanted to get the war over and return to some kind of normality.'

Nothing, though, would be quite the same again. Marriage, a championship medal and celebrity status were to welcome Liddell and his new bride Phyllis to a long-awaited, hard-earned peace.

Chapter Three

Peace and Glory

Wedding bells rang for Phyllis and Billy Liddell at Island Road Methodist Church, Garston, Liverpool on 20 July 1946, but two sets of close friends they would have liked to have been present unavoidably had to miss the couple's big day.

'We invited Bob Paisley and Jessie but they had to decline simply because they were away on honeymoon,' Phyllis recalled. 'Bob, like Billy, kept things to himself and we hadn't known that their wedding would be three days before ours!

'Jean and Matt Busby were also unable to come to our wedding because Matt had just taken over as manager of Manchester United and his club commitments prevented him attending.'

But when Billy and Phyllis moved into their club house at Bowring Park, Bob and Jessie were the first to wish them good luck. 'We lived opposite each other and the day my wife and I moved in, Bob was the first person across our doorstep to welcome us,' said Billy.

Jessie recalled: 'We paid 25 shillings a week rent for the club houses. As well as having Billy and Phyllis opposite us we also had Willie Fagan, Cyril Done, Phil Taylor, Albert Stubbins and others as neighbours.

'It really was fun and enjoyable in those days. The wives went to the games together and Phyllis and I used to sit on the wall outside the Anfield ground waiting for Billy and Bob to come out. There was no ladies' lounge or anything like that! Then we'd go to the sweet shop before getting the tram home.

'Phyllis and Billy were the first of the Liverpool football families to get a washing machine. It was quite an event and we all went to see it! Then Albert Stubbins got a new bedroom suite that wouldn't go up the stairs. So the upstairs window had to be taken out and we all spent a morning watching them get the suite into the house!'

It was an era unrecognisable today, when top footballers paid a team-mate to take them to work! 'When we were living near each other in Bowring Park we used to rely on Phil Taylor for our transport,' recalled Bob Paisley. 'He was the only one who had a car and Billy Liddell and I used to pay him tuppence a week to take us to the ground!'

The ravages and repercussions of the war still loomed large across the world, especially in Britain where rationing would persist in some form for almost another decade. The inquests, meanwhile, went on. On the very day that Billy – in his RAF uniform – and Phyllis walked down the aisle, a congressional committee in Washington exonerated President Roosevelt of any blame for the Japanese attack on Pearl Harbor in December 1941.

And after a brief honeymoon in the Isle of Man it was back to RAF duties for Billy for another three months, which meant he was still in uniform when League football resumed on its recognised basis in August 1946.

He had made a scoring FA Cup debut the previous season when the competition was run on a home-and-away basis. Liddell was on the mark in a 2–0 third round first-leg win at Chester. He missed the return but played in the first leg of the next round, an emphatic 5–0 defeat at Bolton, their record defeat in the competition, which signalled Liverpool's exit on a 2–5 aggregate, despite their 2–0 second-leg home win, for which Liddell was also absent.

Bolton's FA Cup progress, however, was to have tragic repercussions two months later. When the Lancashire club met Stoke City at home in the sixth round in March 1946, a wall and crowd barriers collapsed near a corner flag, killing 33 spectators and injuring 500.

The country was stunned by the disaster and, to swell the coffers of an appeal fund, England met Scotland at Maine Road,

Manchester the following August. Liddell was again on Scotland's left wing and the match was drawn 2–2, watched by a crowd of 70,000.

Liddell had now established himself as a high-calibre player of rich international quality, a flying winger armed with powerful scoring menace. His Maine Road outing for Scotland came only eleven days after he had helped his country beat England 1–0 at Hampden Park in front of a massive attendance of 139,468.

Earlier in the season he was in the team that beat Wales 2–0 at Hampden in November 1945, and two Liddell goals helped Scotland to a 3–2 victory over Northern Ireland in Belfast in February. An impressive international campaign for Liddell and Scotland was crowned when he bagged another brace of goals in a 3–1 win over Switzerland at Hampden in May 1946.

His extended RAF service, however, denied Liddell his League debut at the launch of the 1946–7 season when several of his Anfield colleagues were tasting First Division football for the first time. The debutants included centre half Laurie Hughes, a former Tranmere amateur who went on to play for England, two local boys in left half or left back Eddie Spicer and versatile Bill Jones, also capped by England, and winger Bob Priday, one of the club's South Africans. Wales goalkeeper Cyril Sidlow also made his First Division debut for Liverpool, following four prewar League outings for Wolves before his £4,000 move to Anfield in February 1946.

Others had played for Liverpool before the war, including Berry Nieuwenhuys, another South African winger who distinguished himself in the RAF. Just before joining up he had paid the well-known impresario Carroll Levis £50 for his Jaguar car . . . then left the vehicle in a journalist's garage for the duration of the war, in which he won the Czech Medal of Merit.

Full back Jim Harley, also a prewar player, joined the Royal Navy, his service illuminated by his mention in dispatches. Bill Jones, grandfather of a future Liverpool and England full back, Rob Jones, won the Military Medal for rescuing wounded comrades under fire during the Allied crossing of the Rhine.

Eddie Spicer became a lieutenant Royal Marine commando and captured a German NCO who was also a football international! Spicer was commissioned in 1942, later became a captain and was wounded at the Battle of Wesel in 1945.

Bob Paisley, a gunner in the Royal Artillery, had spent much of the war fighting Rommel's forces in the Western Desert and later rode through liberated Rome on a tank, a harbinger of a landmark football conquest in the Eternal City he would joyously experience as Liverpool manager 33 years later.

Only Crystal Palace with 98 and Wolves with 91 supplied more Football League players for wartime service than the 76 who went from Liverpool. One of the Anfield contingent, Tom Cooper, paid with his life as one of English football's 75 war victims, although in his case it was the result of a tragic accident rather than enemy action.

England full back Cooper, one of Anfield's first-team stars when Liddell arrived and a former Liverpool captain, became a sergeant in the Military Police and was killed on dispatch duty on 25 June 1940 when his motorcycle collided head-on with a bus at Aldeburgh, Suffolk.

In July 1945, less than three months after VE Day, Liverpool are believed to be the first English club to play on German soil when they took part in two games against Forces teams, with Liddell in his celebrated left-wing role. They beat 84 Squadron RAF 7–0, Liddell scoring twice, and then drew 3–3 with a British Liberation 21st Army XI.

The Liverpool line-up in their seven-goal romp, with service ranks and with Gulliver of Leeds United as a guest player, was: Capt. Dirk Kemp; Sgt Inst. Jack Westby, Cpl Joffre Gulliver; CSMI Matt Busby, Lieut. Tom Bush, Sgt Jimmy McInnes; Fl. Sgt Berry Nieuwenhuys, Sgt Phil Taylor, Sgt Inst. Willie Fagan, CSMI Don Welsh, Pilot Off. Billy Liddell.

Liverpool returned from Germany with a surprise prize. 'The club were presented with twelve shirts with neat white collars made from a material that was being used for Nazi flags,' reported columnist *Pilot* in the *Liverpool Evening Express*, adding: 'These will be very welcome to the club in these days of coupon rations.'

Busby's appearances in Germany were to be the last for Liverpool by the man who had been instrumental in bringing Liddell to Anfield, taking him under his captain's wing after he had been uprooted from Scotland as a teenager and later recommending him to the international selectors.

During the war Busby had been in charge of the British Army team as well as captaining Scotland. Liverpool, keen to keep him, offered him a coaching role. Busby was about to accept when Manchester United asked him to be their manager. It was to prove a defining moment for English football. 'Liverpool's coaching offer with a five-year contract and the probability of promotion seemed to provide my main requirement . . . security,' Busby recalled.

'I agreed verbally to accept but, while I was stressing to the directors that my football hopes centred on a managerial job despite being keen on coaching, I was informed quite unexpectedly that the Manchester United chairman Jimmy Gibson would like to see me.

'The sequel was that he offered me the manager's position at United, thus providing me with the opening I had been seeking. Liverpool directors did not take my decision very well.

'In fact, although I was as happy as a player could be with Liverpool, the one black spot on my career there concerned the unfortunate events surrounding my departure.

'Liverpool seemed to think I was going to United in the capacity of player-manager and there were suggestions about demanding a transfer fee from United.

'But I had no intention of trying to combine the two jobs. I knew it would be quite impossible to achieve all I wished as a manager if I were involved in the full-time playing duties and no transfer fee was paid.

'Having agreed terms with United and finally severed what had been a very happy association with Liverpool, I was asked by manager George Kay to play in a farewell exhibition match for them.

'But then I got a telephone call from George who told me: "There's been a change of mind here. The directors don't want you to play." I discovered later that the board were upset because I was joining Manchester United and they had taken the decision to cancel my sentimental journey.

'It hurt me to think that after nine of the happiest years of my life – yes, even the war years – the club directors should turn against me simply because I preferred to be manager of Manchester United instead of coach of Liverpool.'

Busby took over at United on 22 October 1945 at a time when Old Trafford was a blitzed wreck and the club staged their home fixtures at Manchester City's Maine Road ground.

It is hypothetical but intriguing to speculate on the impact on Liverpool and United if Busby's talents had remained at Anfield and ultimately grasped the managerial reins. Would those glorious eras of Shankly, Paisley, Dalglish and Fagan ever have happened? Would it have been the Kop rather than the Stretford End that would have warmed to those great domestic and early European exploits that Busby so thrillingly pioneered for United?

If so, what a superb stage it would have been for Liddell, whose redoubtable skills were confined for so many seasons to the old Second Division. Years later Busby responded to such conjecture when he observed:

'Billy is a really wonderful footballer but it's a fact that apart from the years between 1946 and 1950 he played with a club not enjoying a great amount of success.

'His main virtues are speed off the mark, strength on the ball and fantastic shooting ability, all of which would have been given considerably more scope if Billy had been in a really good team in the company of artists capable of serving the ball up to him.

'Instead, he has so often been compelled to go in search of the ball himself and that makes his triumphs all the more commendable. They have been hard earned.'

Long after Busby's departure from Liverpool supporters still cherished his Anfield contribution. In a 1966 poll of fans conducted by the supporters magazine *The Kop*, Busby was named as captain of a team of all-time Anfield greats, prompting the publication to comment:

'Why is it that this man Busby commands such widespread

respect and regard in all sections of soccer? A quick answer
would be the unparalleled success of United. But while that would
have merited a strictly professional admiration it would not have
inspired the warmth of feeling so generally extended to him.'

Busby's protégé Liddell scored seventeen goals in 28
appearances in the 42-match Football League North in the
transitional 1945–6 season, as well as two outings and a goal in
the FA Cup. But RAF duties prevented Liddell travelling on
Liverpool's tour of the USA and Canada in May and June 1946,
when they became the first English club to play on American soil
after the war.

It was the first of Liverpool's four North American summer
tours – their subsequent trips being in 1948, 1953 and 1964 – in
which they played 44 games and won 42 of them, a solitary draw
coming against Swiss club Young Boys Berne and their lone
defeat against Germany's Uwe Seeler-inspired Hamburg in 1964.

But their decision to escape austere, rationed, war-ravaged
Britain in 1946 and sail to the States to play ten matches was
visionary and paid a rich dividend in the following fierce winter,
which produced the longest season on record.

The climate and food were tonics to the Liverpool squad and
columnist Arthur Daley wrote in the *New York Times*: 'The
British booters have outscored their rivals on this side of the
Atlantic by a tidy count. They seem to be getting sharper, too, a
combination of continuous play and unrationed food.

'Don't snicker at the food item, either. Some experts figure that
their unlimited activities with knife and fork over here have added
25 per cent to Liverpool efficiency.'

When the curtain rose on the long-awaited resumption of
League football on 31 August 1946, Liddell was still absent.
'Unlike most of the other lads, who had been demobilised and
were ready and eager for the re-start of football, I was still
stationed in the RAF at Kirkham and missed pre-season training
and the first two matches,' he recalled.

Liverpool opened with a 1–0 win at Sheffield United thanks to
the only goal of amateur Len Carney's six-match first-team
career. It was a piece of club history for debutant Carney who had

been wounded in North Africa during the war and won the Military Cross. He became, at the age of 31 years and 94 days, the oldest postwar Liverpool player to score on his debut, and the value of his header that brought his solitary Liverpool goal would prove priceless in the winning of very different medals almost ten months later.

After a 1–0 home defeat by Middlesbrough in the second match of the new campaign, Liddell was available, at the age of 24, for his League debut at home to Chelsea, playing at outside left in front of wing half Paisley who was also having his First Division baptism.

'Bob Priday, one of the many South Africans at the club, had played in the first two games but was unfit for the third so I came in for my League debut,' said Liddell.

There were several changes, including our captain Willie Fagan's return after illness to take over from Len Carney.

Bob Paisley made his League debut, like me, and from then on I played in front of him for years. It was a great comfort to have him there, pushing the ball through for me. He was a left half in the old style: tremendously strong and rugged, never quitting, a wonderful tackler and great with long throw-ins. He could hurl the ball from the touchline to the near post.

Off the field he was a tremendous joker and kept us all laughing. We had a commissionaire at Anfield called Paddy Walsh who used to clean the manager's car. While he was doing this one day he went off to get another bucket of water and Bob nipped in, opened the car doors and wound down all the windows.

When unsuspecting Paddy came back he threw the water and it went right through the open windows and saturated the whole of the inside of the car!

Of course, we had no idea then of what Bob would go on to achieve for the club in so many different roles over half a century.

He became the most successful manager in Liverpool history and as well as being proud to regard him as a special friend I think he's the greatest servant the club has ever had. His record is matchless.

On the day we made our League debuts Chelsea were captained by John Harris, later manager of Sheffield United, with Tommy Lawton, signed from Everton the previous season, leading their attack.

They also included Len Goulden, who I'd first met when I was a wartime guest for the London club.

Liddell took only three minutes to register his first League goal and when he bagged his second of the game after 50 minutes it put Liverpool 6–0 in front . . . and Lawton had hardly touched the ball!

The England centre forward's team-mates, though, clawed back four goals through Alec Machin, who scored twice, Goulden and Jimmy Argue before Fagan notched a seventh for Liverpool three minutes from time.

Service duties precluded Liddell's appearance in the next game for which the directors, who picked the side, recalled Priday. It was an unhappy experience for everyone connected with the Anfield club. Liverpool crashed 5–0 to Matt Busby's new charges Manchester United in a midweek clash at Maine Road, spawning their nickname of 'The Crazy Gang' because of switchback results that would hallmark their season.

The painful defeat by United prompted a swift response at Anfield as chairman Bill McConnell and manager George Kay drove to Tyneside in pursuit of Newcastle United's free-scoring transfer-seeking centre forward Albert Stubbins.

They had a few hours start on Everton, whose boss Theo Kelly was one of a batch of managers also chasing flame-haired Stubbins, who was plying his trade in the Second Division after his glut of 231 wartime goals in 187 Newcastle matches, a total bettered during the hostilities only by Jock Dodds and Lawton.

However, his boss at Newcastle, Stan Seymour, believed that Stubbins compared favourably with the celebrated Lawton, saying: 'The only advantage Lawton might have over Albert is with his heading but Stubbins is cleverer on the ball.'

The wartime haul of Stubbins in his size eleven boots included 29 hat tricks, a sequence of fifteen goals in five matches during 1941 and five in a match on five occasions, against Middlesbrough twice, Gateshead, Stoke City and Blackburn Rovers.

Stubbins, born in Wallsend, spent two years in America as a boy when his father worked for a telephone company, a spell in which the sports-mad youngster threw himself into baseball, American football and sprinting. But the Wall Street crash signalled the family's return to England shortly before his eleventh birthday.

Eventually, he signed as an amateur inside forward for Sunderland, the town in which he worked at the dockyard in the reserved occupation of draughtsman during the war. But when his beloved Newcastle came knocking Stubbins jumped at the chance to join them at sixteen, and it was there that he made the big switch to centre forward.

His wartime scoring exploits earned him an England outing in the Victory international against Wales in October 1945, but when the Merseyside rivals arrived on Tyneside battling for his signature Stubbins could not be found! Eventually he was traced to Newcastle's Northumberland Street News Theatre where a message was flashed onto the screen saying: 'Would Albert Stubbins please report to St James's Park immediately.'

The £12,500 fee was agreed. It was just a question of whether Stubbins would opt for Anfield or Goodison. 'I tossed a coin to decide which of the two clubs I'd speak to first,' said Stubbins. 'It came down heads for Liverpool and I met George Kay and Billy McConnell.

'I was 27, Newcastle were in the Second Division, I wanted to play in the top flight and, suddenly, I had a choice of two big First Division clubs. But I was impressed by Liverpool and agreed to join them even before I met Everton.

'I explained to their manager Theo Kelly that I'd decided to go to Anfield and he was most courteous and gentlemanly about it and wished me all the best. The transfer fee seemed gigantic in those days. Years later it seemed laughably low. But I never felt under any pressure. In fact, it was an incentive to me.'

The fee, a Liverpool club record, was the second-highest ever paid in English football, surpassed at the time only by the £14,000 Arsenal had paid Wolves for Bryn Jones in August 1938.

'While I was at Newcastle I wrote for the local *Evening Chronicle* and I was looking to a career as a journalist when I finished,' added Stubbins.

'Liverpool said they would arrange for me to write a column for the *Liverpool Echo* and after meeting the sports editor Bob Prole I duly began doing articles for the Saturday night edition.'

Liverpool's acquisition of Stubbins provided its own headlines; he was an inspired signing who exploited the wonderful wing talents of Liddell and who, with Balmer, formed a potent strike force.

'The fee the club paid for Albert remained Liverpool's highest until they signed Kevin Lewis from Sheffield United in June 1960, but he quickly settled in and he was the type of centre forward a winger could aim for with crosses,' enthused Liddell.

'He soon struck up a good understanding with Jack Balmer and Willie Fagan, although later we lost Willie for three months with an Achilles tendon injury.'

The arrival of Stubbins coincided with Liddell's autumn demobilisation from the RAF and the Scot's return at Bolton on 14 September launched a remarkably consistent thirteen-year run in which he was never out of the team, except through international calls or a rare injury.

The game at Burnden Park, three days after the five-goal debacle in Manchester, also saw a stunning scoring debut for Stubbins in a 3–1 win. The new capture ran with the ball from the halfway line before unleashing an unstoppable shot eight minutes from the end.

It was the first of 83 goals he scored for the club in 178 senior appearances before his return to his native northeast in 1953. Fourteen years later Stubbins was included on the montage sleeve photograph on the celebrated Beatles album *Sergeant Pepper's Lonely Hearts Club Band* in 1967, apparently because his play was admired by relatives of John Lennon and Paul McCartney.

But the admiration Stubbins had for Liddell's talents was boundless. 'Billy was as strong as an ox and had the heart of a lion,' proclaimed Stubbins. 'He was a great player, fast and courageous. He'd run through a brick wall but he had abundant skill.

'Billy was a breed of player that later became virtually extinct – he moved head-on at defences. With his control, courage and two good feet he was superbly equipped for the job. His acceleration on the flank could easily turn a defence and his threat was even greater because he varied his crosses.

'He made more than a few goals for me and he was the most generous winger I ever played with. He never shirked a tackle but never once did I see him commit a foul. I can't think of a single weakness Billy had.

'I remember one game when Liverpool were playing at Newcastle and I was out of the team injured. When we got to St James's I went into the home dressing room to say hello to my old team-mates and got talking to Bobby Cowell, a very good, experienced full back.

'Bobby said to me: "Albert, could you do me a favour?" I said: "What is it?" Bobby replied: "How do I play against Billy Liddell because I never seem to have a good game against him?" It was quite a confession from a player like him.

'I told Bobby: "I'm in a difficult position. I can't tell you any Liverpool secrets. I can't really give you much satisfaction on that score. All I can say to you is that if Billy picks up the ball and you're not close to him when he does, then you're dead. He'll be past you so quickly." I think it was more a warning than advice!

'Billy Liddell was one of the all-time greats and in much later years my wife Anne and I stayed with Billy and Phyllis when we visited Merseyside.'

The win at Bolton, when Liddell and Stubbins played together for the first time, began an impressive unbeaten table-topping run for Liverpool stretching to the end of November. A fortnight after his memorable Burnden Park debut Stubbins was felled in the box in the home clash with Leeds and rose to take the penalty, an art he had peformed with blistering, 100 per cent efficiency at Newcastle.

As expected he struck the spot kick with venom, but goalkeeper Johnny Hodgson stopped it, fracturing his arm in the process. Stubbins had also broken a keeper's arm with a penalty in schoolboy football and another keeper's wrist with a shot on an American tour.

He had no wish to extend that hat trick and never took another Liverpool penalty, although two years later, when appearing for the Football League against the League of Ireland at Preston, he failed to score from two spot kicks – one missed and one saved – before scoring from a third.

'I wouldn't have worried if I'd missed three and had to take a fourth,' declared Stubbins, showing the self-belief that is a prerequisite of all great goalscorers.

The role of Liverpool penalty taker, which would later go with marvellous distinction to Liddell, was filled by Balmer who achieved the remarkable feat of scoring hat tricks in three successive League matches, in which he scored ten goals, in November 1946. He hit all three goals, including a penalty, in the 3–0 home win over Portsmouth, scored all four in a 4–1 victory at Derby and bagged another three, including another penalty, in the 4–2 home defeat of Arsenal. He continued his hot streak by scoring in seven successive First Division games that brought him a total of fifteen goals.

Balmer became the first player to score three consecutive hat tricks in one season, although Everton legend Dixie Dean collected a trio of hat tricks spanning the end of the 1927–8 season and the start of the following campaign.

'We went twelve games unbeaten in the League and another four in the Lancashire Cup before losing by the odd goal in five at Blackpool,' recalled Liddell. 'But then we had a lean patch and lost ground.'

The gloomy spell comprised only three wins in ten League games starting with the end of their unbeaten run at Bloomfield Road. It was followed a week later by what threatened to be a calamitous result – a 5–1 home hammering by title rivals Wolves.

A 52,512 crowd, Anfield's biggest of the season, saw Wallasey-born Everton reject Dennis Westcott, who had played for New Brighton and made wartime guest appearances for Liverpool, score four for Wolves and have another strike puzzlingly disallowed. Wolves were 4–0 up at half-time, during which one spectator, clearly not amused, threw four apples into the Liverpool goalmouth. The fruits of victory for Wolves was to go top and, apart from a weather-hit spell during a fierce winter when they were prevented from playing, they stayed in pole position until facing Liverpool at Molineux in their last game of the season.

Liverpool responded with successive 4–1 wins over Sunderland and Aston Villa. Then they lost at Stoke on Christmas Day, won the return a day later and then slumped to four straight defeats, to Sheffield United, Chelsea, Bolton and Everton, in which they scored only twice.

But if their championship hopes were faltering Liverpool had rising hopes of winning the FA Cup for the first time in their history. In round three they travelled to Walsall, the Third Division South club who caused a prewar sensation by toppling Herbert Chapman's mighty Arsenal. When they went ahead against Liverpool they nursed ambitions of a repeat.

Even after an own goal put Liverpool level, Walsall regained the lead and Fellows Park began to sense another huge upset. But Cyril Done, who had made his Liverpool debut in the last game before the Second World War, ran through to level the score despite looking well offside.

Liddell, whose pace and skill gave Walsall nightmare problems, put Liverpool ahead only a minute later when he cut in and drove in a superb shot. Two second-half goals from Balmer eased his side through with a 5–2 win.

'We realised it might be a struggle and that's what it was,' admitted Liddell. 'The Saddlers hit hard from the start and were soon a goal up but gradually we got on top to go through to a fourth-round home tie against Grimsby.'

A Stubbins header from a Liddell cross and another strike from Done gave Liverpool a 2–0 victory, but the star of the game was visiting goalkeeper George Tweedy, who showed the kind of custodial artistry that had brought him one prewar England cap.

Liverpool were handed another home tie in the fifth round, against Derby, in which a late header by the injured Balmer from a long Liddell cross brought the game's only goal to set up an unforgettable home sixth-round clash with Second Division Birmingham.

The massive demand to see the game prompted Liverpool to adopt the then revolutionary idea of making the tie all-ticket. Just under 52,000 packed into Anfield for what proved to be a Stubbins extravanganza on an ice-bound pitch, with the centre forward collecting the first of his three Liverpool senior hat tricks in a 4–1 triumph.

It was the spectacular second goal of the Stubbins treble, which put Liverpool 3–1 ahead, that will live forever in the memory of those who witnessed it. It was an incredible diving header from a Liddell free kick with Stubbins little more than knee-high above the rock-hard surface.

'The key to that goal against Birmingham is something that happened in the previous round against Derby when Billy took a free kick on the left which flashed across the goalmouth,' Stubbins revealed.

'Jack Balmer and I failed to connect with it by two or three feet. I wouldn't say we were to blame for missing it! Billy used to hit a terrific ball and with the speed of this particular one, which he hit low, we just failed to reach it. It beat the entire Derby defence, too!

'But we knew that if we'd reached it all it would have needed was a touch with foot or head to divert it into the net. Billy was brilliant with free kicks and used to alternate them.

'One day he would send over maybe a high, hanging ball to the far post, next time to the near post and every now and then he would shoot one across about two feet high. When he did that you knew it would need just a touch to fly into the net.

'So after Jack and I narrowly missed that low one of Billy's against Derby I vowed to myself that if the chance came I wasn't going to let that happen again. Next time I was determined to be ready.

'Lo and behold not long afterwards, in the Cup tie against Birmingham, Billy took a free kick in the second half. I knew

what I was going to do. I took up position on the edge of the box
and I knew the Birmingham defenders were thinking, "if Stubbins
is back there he's not going to cause us any problems".

'So they left me virtually unmarked on the edge of the box.
Now Billy had a shot like a cannonball and he hit this one low, just
as he had done a couple of weeks earlier. But this time I started
running at top speed as soon as he hit the ball.

'I hadn't known where Billy was going to put the ball and it
could have gone anywhere. But as soon as his foot moved to kick
it I was already running. After three or four steps I was at top
speed and I was just obsessed with reaching that ball as it came
flashing across.

'I knew, though, that I couldn't get to it on foot. I had to dive to
connect with it, which I did. I was only about two or three feet off
the ground. The goalkeeper, Gil Merrick of England, was
standing more or less in the centre of the goal and I was able to
direct it past his left hand.

'And what velocity it had! With the force and pace of
Billy's kick and the power of my header connecting with it the
ball just flew into the net. It was an icy ground and the game
wouldn't have been played today. My knees were lacerated,
both of them bleeding, after I'd slid across the surface. But it
was worth it!

'I got a lot of my goals thanks to Billy. The manager, George
Kay, used to look on Billy, Jack Balmer and myself as his heavy
artillery.

'Free kicks were a tremendous part of Billy's armoury. In a
game against Preston at Deepdale we got a free kick just outside
the box slightly towards the left flank. Billy came up to take it and
was going to hit it with his right foot when the wind rolled the ball
towards his left one.

'Most players would have stopped to re-place the ball as Billy
was entitled to do. But he just let it run, hit it with his left and it
went in like a rocket. He was great with either foot. It didn't
worrry Billy at all.

'He could operate on the left or right wing. Sometimes during
a match, if we were finding it difficult to penetrate a defence, he

would switch with Berry Nieuwenhuys, Jimmy Payne or whoever was on our right flank.'

Liddell counted the diving Stubbins goal as one of the most extraordinary he had ever seen although, with typical humility, played down his contribution to it. 'It was an amazing goal by Albert and nobody who saw it could ever forget it,' he said.

> When I put the ball over it was going a bit off course but Albert literally threw himself through the air to meet it with his head when parallel with the ground, about two feet above the pitch.
>
> It went in like a rocket, giving Gil Merrick absolutely no chance, and Albert slid on his stomach for several yards on the frozen surface before coming to a stop!
>
> Jack Balmer also scored in the match and there we were in the semifinal, the first time Liverpool had been in the last four for 33 years and with a chance of pulling off the League and Cup double.
>
> The championship, though, hardly entered our heads because not only had we lost our place at the top of the table but seven of our remaining thirteen League games after our Cup win over Birmingham were away. We had to finish the season with four successive away matches, the last two being at Arsenal and Wolves. So it looked impossible.

That daunting challenge was thrown down to Liddell and Liverpool because of the severity of the winter playing havoc with bleak, ration-book Britain and with League football.

The arctic conditions – in which the sea froze at Blackpool – and a government ban on midweek games forced the postponement or abandonment of 146 games. It meant that instead of Liverpool travelling to Wolves as scheduled on 12 April the game was rearranged as a towering climax to their First Division programme on 31 May.

Football, though, had been greeted on its peacetime return with massive crowds eager to resume watching their national sport amid the hardships of life in a war-ravaged nation. Potatoes, for example, were rationed to 3lb per person, per week.

'Reaction after years of war has sent Britain into a football boom,' Ivan Sharpe observed in the *Sunday Chronicle Football Annual.* 'Attendances have reached new heights with crowds flocking to games as never before and this is reflected in the balance sheets of the more successful clubs.'

Britain's average weekly wage was £6 and most players earned little, if anything, more than that. It prompted the Professional Footballers Association to press for better rewards for its members, given the box-office attractions they were proving to be.

The players threatened to strike in February 1947 but that action was averted by a new agreement on a maximum wage of £12 during the season and £10 in the summer and a minimum level for a full-time player over twenty of £7 and £5 respectively. An increase in what was termed 'talent money' for players helping clubs to success was also agreed, meaning that players winning the championship could share a payout ranging from £275 to £550.

Liverpool and their fans were confident of success against Burnley in the FA Cup semifinal. Their Lancashire foes were in the Second Division, albeit striving for ultimately achieved promotion, and Kop dreams took wing.

The omens, however, were not good. When Liverpool arrived in the team bus for the match at rain-lashed Ewood Park a gateman refused them entry, claiming they did not have the necesssary tickets! The 'jobsworth' stuck to his guns for some time before admitting the first team. But the reserve players and other members of the party had a further wait before they were allowed in with the club skips.

On the field, too, Liddell knew it would be a tough, patient battle: 'Burnley were not so good in attack but they had a wonderful defence, which had conceded fewer goals than any other team. They went into the semi having lost only one of their previous 32 games and had kept a clean sheet in 16 of their previous 22 League and Cup matches.

'Obviously, Burnley were going to be a stiff proposition and so it proved. The game finished goalless after half an hour's extra time.'

Liddell had appeared in both Scotland games earlier that season – a 3–1 defeat by Wales at Wrexham and a goalless Hampden Park draw with Northern Ireland – but his requirement for Liverpool duty in the semifinal replay at Maine Road a fortnight later meant he had to miss his country's duel with England at Wembley the same day, in which goals from Raich Carter and Andy McLaren ensured a 1–1 draw.

In Manchester, the semifinal stalemate continued. 'The longer the game went it looked more likely there would have to be a third meeting,' said Liddell.

We made no impression on Burnley's rock-like defence in which Alan Brown, later manager of Sunderland, played magnificently.

But late in the game Ray Harrison saw a half chance following a corner and rammed the ball into the net before our goalkeeper Cyril Sidlow could move. Although we threw everything into attack we just couldn't break through and our Wembley dreams disappeared.

In the League we had seven games left, only two of them at home, and the championship seemed out of reach. But we were not a team to give up on anything and everybody was determined to have a go at it.

For Liddell's team-mate Stubbins the outcome squashed his ambitions of his past and present clubs meeting at Wembley: 'Charlton and Newcastle met in the other semifinal and all the newspapers were tipping a Liverpool v Newcastle final,' he recalled.

'Unfortunately, they were completely wrong. Newcastle were "murdered" 4–0 by Charlton and we lost to Burnley. We didn't play at our best and full marks to Burnley for the way they defended.

'But I still believe that if we'd played them ten times, we'd have beaten them on about eight or nine occasions. But that's Cup football. It was a bitter disappointment to us because we were confident we were heading for Wembley.'

The pundits were wrong also in their championship predictions. Most believed the title was between Matt Busby's Manchester United, Wolves and Stoke. But Liverpool's resolve produced one of the most stirring closing runs in Anfield history.

From 1 February, when they beat Leeds at Elland Road, Liverpool won twelve, drew three and lost only one of their final sixteen League games. They even had to play three of those games without the inspiration of Liddell, who pulled a muscle playing for Great Britain against the Rest of Europe at Hampden Park.

But as Liddell emphasised: 'Our team spirit during those last few weeks was as good as anything I'd experienced. There could have been no happier atmosphere anywhere.'

The dressing-room camaraderie also struck Stubbins as he enjoyed his first season at Anfield. 'There was a tremendous feeling of togetherness. We never really got tactical talks from George Kay. He treated us like men and we used to discuss the games, and how we played, light-heartedly in the bath afterwards. Any serious inquests were done later.

'After a match in the dressing room, amidst the piles of cotton wool, laces, boots and jerseys littering the floor, Phil Taylor's first move was for his cigarettes. He'd take two out of his case and flip one to Jack Balmer.

'Cyril Sidlow, from his long experience of catching trains after a game, was first in the bath, closely followed by his close friend and Wales compatriot Ray Lambert.

'But Billy Liddell and I usually made straight for the vast tea urn to have a cuppa while our trainer Albert Shelley did about ten things at once!'

This togetherness helped Liverpool regroup after their FA cup disappointment. They had won their last League game preceding the semifinal and drove on to complete a sparkling closing sequence of fifteen points from the last sixteen at stake, the only one dropped being in a draw at Brentford. They beat Preston, Sunderland and Manchester United at Anfield and won at Aston Villa, Charlton and Arsenal prior to a dramatic finale in the Midlands.

The 2–1 win at Highbury was the last of the three games Liddell missed, leaving Liverpool with one remaining League match, at Wolves on the last day of May. The Molineux club, who had rammed five goals past Liverpool at Anfield earlier in the season, reminded their rivals of their potency by beating Derby 7–2 and Chelsea 6–4 in April. By the time Liverpool went to Molineux the country was gripped by the four-club championship battle between Liddell and his team-mates, Wolves, Manchester United and Stoke City.

Charlton had already beaten Burnley in the first FA Cup Final to be televised in its entirety. The relatively few viewers who had TV sets – licences for which had been introduced less than a year earlier costing £2 – got plenty for their money with the Wembley duel going to extra time before Chris Duffy's 114th-minute goal won it for the London club.

But the outcome of the title battle was to be an even more tense and extended affair in a drawn-out conclusion to the longest season in football history – one that was to bring Liddell a prized medal.

'I was fit for our vital last game at Wolves but we were without the injured trio of Phil Taylor, Willie Fagan and Bob Paisley,' he recalled. 'Bob Priday had played so well in my absence that he remained at outside left and I moved to inside left wearing the No. 7 jersey!

The position in the First Division before kick off was that Manchester United, having completed their programme, were top with 56 points from 42 games. Wolves had the same total, we were on 55 and Stoke also had 55, although their last game wasn't for another fortnight.

So both Wolves and ourselves needed to win to have a chance of the championship. They'd had a spell when they scored sixteen goals in three successive matches and we knew they were a good side. But three weeks before our game they'd lost 3–2 at home to Everton and Liverpool have always maintained that anything they could do we could do better!

For Wolves skipper Stan Cullis it was one game above all that he wanted to win. A few days earlier Wolves announced that Stan had been appointed assistant to their manager Ted Vizard and that this would be his last game.

Stan had been bitterly disappointed in 1939 when Portsmouth beat Wolves in the Cup Final and everybody at Wolverhampton was keen for him to get a championship medal as consolation.

The day, though, was more suitable for cricket than football. It was extremely hot, with the thermometer somewhere in the 80s. I remember remarking to Albert Stubbins about the vast number of spectators in shirt sleeves or summer frocks.

The heat was on – both on and off the field – and Phyllis Liddell recalled: 'All the wives went to that last match of the season at Wolves. We sat under a glass roof, we had chocolate and it became very messy!'

A 50,000-plus crowd crammed into sweltering Molineux and the teams lined up as follows:

Wolves: Williams; McLean, W Crook; Alderton, Cullis (captain), Wright; Hancocks, Dunn, Pye, Forbes, Mullen.

Liverpool: Sidlow; Harley, Lambert; Jones, Hughes, Spicer; Liddell, Balmer (captain), Stubbins, Watkinson, Priday.

Referee: J Biggs (Cheadle).

The contest was 22 minutes old when Liddell launched a move that put Liverpool ahead. The Scot moved menacingly down the left flank and delivered a cross to Balmer. The Liverpool skipper, dubbed the 'Alastair Sim' of football because of his balding pate, pencil moustache and slight frame, exchanged passes with Priday before firing past England goalkeeper Bert Williams for his 24th goal of the season.

Seven minutes before the break Balmer's attack partner Stubbins reached the same total to send Anfield's travelling fans into ecstasy. 'I said to Bob Priday before the game: "If you lie deep and pick up the ball just hit a long pass, not to my feet but past me and past Stan Cullis," revealed Stubbins.

'Sure enough, Bob was able to collect the ball in his own half and, without wasting any time, I was ready. Bob hit a beautifully accurate left-footed pass right down the centre of the field over the head of Stan Cullis and I went after it.

'Stan was caught out and had to turn and chase after me. As he did so Billy Wright and the two full backs closed in on me. But I got the ball, accelerated and took it past them.

'Bert Williams came running out as I approached him. It was a terrific race for the ball and as Bert came out, I just managed to get my toe end to the ball and roll it past him into the corner of the net.

'It was a great moment and all credit to Bob Priday for doing exactly what we'd talked about before kickoff.The odds against our plan working could have been 100–1. But it came off!'

The brilliant strike by Stubbins gave Liverpool a 2–0 half-time lead and put them firmly in the driving seat. 'We thought the game was safely in the bag,' said Liddell. 'But Wolves were never a team to give up without a struggle and Cullis was a wonderful inspiration to them.

'In the second half he urged his players on and made them fight as though their lives depended on it and they reduced our lead when Jimmy Dunn scored.'

Dunn, son of the former Everton and Scotland player of the same name, sent a twenty-yard lob over Cyril Sidlow and it was the signal for a concerted assault by Wolves, which saw the Liverpool goalkeeper distinguish himself against his old club and Liddell demonstrate his great versatility by dropping back as an extra defender.

Liverpool held out and Liddell enthused: 'We did so largely because our defence gave one of its finest exhibitions seen at Molineux for many a long day and it was ironic that the man who did most to keep Wolves out was their former goalkeeper. Cyril made save after save when it seemed certain he'd be beaten.'

The Anfield team's joy at the final whistle was boundless. They had won, gone top and now awaited the fate of Stoke, who had just sold Stanley Matthews to Blackpool for £11,500, in their much rearranged match at Sheffield United on 14 June. 'It was a great day and a great feeling and I remember being carried off the Molineux pitch at the end shoulder-high,' skipper Balmer recounted.

But the emotions of former England captain and centre half Cullis, born on Merseyside at Ellesmere Port, were in stark contrast. The future Wolves manager tearfully left the field, but not before congratulating Stubbins, for whom the occasion left an indelible memory.

'When Stan and I shook hands,' said Stubbins, 'there were tears rolling down his face. I commiserated with him, he congratulated me. We respected each other. We played hard but there was never any ill feeling. But the goal I scored that day haunted Stan.

'Wherever he went in years to come people wouldn't let him forget it. They talked about it and asked him why he hadn't tugged my shirt and pulled me back as we were chasing the ball. But Stan's sense of sportsmanship wouldn't allow him to.

'The Wolves' right back Gus McLean told me that if he'd got near me he'd have pulled the shirt off my back. If Stan had tugged me probably he'd have got away with it. It only needs the slightest touch when you're at top speed to knock you out of your stride. But Stan didn't do it and he deserved so much credit.

'But for us, winning at Wolves that day was a marvellous result. After they'd beaten us 5–1 at Anfield on a heavy pitch halfway through that season I used to wake up at night thinking of the humiliation. I'd never been in a side as a professional that had lost so heavily.

'Wolves could do no wrong that day at Anfield. They were exceptional. But we had our revenge and had the last laugh on them. We'd come from behind in the League with a magnificent finishing run and all we could do was wait on Stoke.'

The Stubbins goal thrilled Liverpool fans. One of them, Joe Nolan, who later went to live in Australia, recalled: 'Somewhere between Molineux and Wolverhampton station was a statue of Queen Victoria. It had an inscription referring to Prince Albert. One of the lads quipped, "Blimey, they didn't waste any time erecting that!"'

When Stoke's mid-June game at Sheffield United arrived, racegoers were preparing for the start of Royal Ascot three days

later and Liddell, Stubbins and company were engaged in the
delayed Liverpool Senior Cup Final against Everton at Anfield,
which kicked off fifteen minutes after the key Bramall Lane
match and attracted a remarkable 40,000 attendance. Liddell
recalled the scene:

> Stoke had to beat Sheffield United to deny us of the
> championship and, not surprisingly, our minds were more on
> what was happening there than in our game, although we
> managed to beat Everton 2–1.
>
> Loudspeaker announcements kept us informed about the
> score at Sheffield and the last ten minutes at Anfield were
> purely academic with the news that Stoke had lost 2–1. We
> were champions! The crowd didn't care what happened
> after that.
>
> All they wanted was the final whistle to be blown so they
> could come swarming over the pitch from the Kop and
> Kemlyn Road and carry us off the field. It was a scene of
> amazing enthusiasm.

It was a joy many of the large crowd had never experienced.
Liverpool's previous championship triumph had been in 1923.
There was, though, a certain symmetry about their feat in winning
the first postwar title as Everton had lifted the last prewar
championship in 1939 and their players were the first to
congratulate their Merseyside rivals.

Sheffield United's win, ending Stoke's eleven-match unbeaten
run and crushing their lofty ambitions, was secured with a goal
from 40-year-old Jack Pickering in his only League appearance of
the season. This on the Bramall Lane stage where debutant Len
Carney had scored his only Liverpool goal to launch their
marathon season with victory the previous August.

The final table in that summer of 1947, as sun-kissed as the
winter had been icebound, saw Liverpool as champions with 57
points and Manchester United runners-up with 56. Wolves, who
would have won the title if they had drawn with Liverpool, were
third, also on 56, and Stoke fourth on 55.

As well as the championship and the Liverpool Senior Cup, Liverpool also won the Lancashire Cup and Lancashire Combination title. The board had another reason to be happy, reporting a profit of £17,208. It was the third highest in English football, marginally behind Burnley but way behind Stoke's £32,207. The company who had prepared the club accounts, Simon, Jude and West, was the firm for whom Billy Liddell worked, successfully combining the professions of sport and business.

Under the heading 'The Goalkeeper's Peril', John E. Reynolds wrote in his book *Stars Of Soccer* published in 1948:

Liddell of Liverpool is one of the most forceful wingers in the game and his speed and enterprise had much to do with bringing the League championship to Merseyside.

He is not content to stay on the touchline; he is adept at cutting in and his shots on the run have the velocity of well aimed cannon balls. He is first choice for Scotland and his direct style has nonplussed many an English defence.

There is no chicanery about Liddell's play. Speed and ball control are all he needs. On the ball he is tremendously powerful and difficult to dispossess. But it is the vicious, curling danger of his corner kicks and centres that captures him best.

His corners come across swift and curving, then sweep suddenly inwards beneath the crossbar. Many a goalkeeper has sweated with desperate anxiety over these swerving, menacing kicks.

As a winger Liddell had created many of the team's 84 goals and chipped in with 7 himself in his first season of League football to ensure the champagne flowed at Anfield. Liddell never touched a drop. His play, though, had a wonderful effervescence of its own.

Chapter Four

A Great Briton

In the entire titanic history of football only twenty professional players have had the honour of donning a Great Britain jersey in a fully sanctioned, official first-class international. Only two have done it twice.

One was Sir Stanley Matthews, England's 'Wizard of the Dribble'. The other was Billy Liddell, the flying Scot who changed Liverpool into 'Liddellpool'.

The vast majority of the masses who crammed into bars, pubs, clubs, school halls and town squares the length and breadth of England, to watch the exploits of Sven Goran Eriksson's team in the 2002 World Cup Finals, would have responded with consternation to talk of a Great Britain team.

As they waved the flag of St George, thereby seizing the English emblem from the grasp of football hooligans and right-wing extremists, a subsuming of the Three Lions into a united side drawn from the entire United Kingdom was the last thought in their minds. And in this era of growing devolution even citizens of Scotland, Wales and Northern Ireland were at least relieved that the English had reclaimed their own flag after years of cheekily and quite wrongly flying the Union Flag in times of nationalistic fervour.

Yet at intermittent postwar intervals, usually when England have suffered an embarrassing flop, come calls for a Great Britain team to compete on the foreign stage. Surely, say its proponents, if we emulate rugby and some other sports by collecting the cream of British talent, we could conquer the football world.

This new millennium had hardly dawned when the subject was back on the media agenda. Foreign Secretary Jack Straw, then Home Secretary, declared in the aftermath of England's Euro 2000 failure: 'The one area of sport where we have been consistently successful is athletics and that is the one area of sport where we do not have an English, Scottish and Welsh team but a British one. I personally look forward to the day when we have a British football team. I think we might start winning some games.'

Straw's spokesman explained: 'He was talking in the wider context on a question about Britishness and Englishness and how he felt Britishness was a more inclusive word to use. It was a personal view.'

Former Sports Minister Tony Banks unleashed an even more provocative call for the British nations to unite as he reflected on past World Cup and European Championship performances.

'Scotland,' he proclaimed, 'is one of the great football nations and have a fabulous qualifying record. But they have never got past the first round and if you think about them in English terms, they are the West Ham of world football. They never quite perform to their full potential.

'Nobody can argue that Scottish football at its best is some of the finest in the world. But Scotland can never make it past the group stage and England consistently fail to find that extra push in the final stages. As Britain they would win it.'

Leaving aside the correcting fact that athletics competes both with separate teams, as in the 2002 Commonwealth Games in Manchester, and with a united British team as in the Olympics, such comments bring a predictable response.

Preston and former Scotland manager Craig Brown asserted: 'I suspect such proposals wouldn't meet with much favour in Scotland. I don't think any country wants to lose its autonomy.' His words were echoed by the FA in London. 'We have always competed as individual nations,' said a spokesman. 'I think the majority of the public is also very much in favour of this setup.'

As recently as December 2002 world ruling body FIFA quashed renewed speculation that the four home countries would be forced to play as one United Kingdom team in future.

Uncertainty over the autonomy of the British associations had arisen because of the FIFA statutes being rewritten for its 2004 centenary year, with membership of the world body possibly hinging on the country concerned being a member of the United Nations which, if applied to the UK, would mean a single combined membership.

FIFA president Sepp Blatter, who in July 2003 threw back onto the table the suggestion that the four home nations should combine to field a Great Britain team in the Olympic Games, has nevertheless assured them that at senior level their autonomy is safe. 'There is no threat to the four British teams who will continue to play as individual sides,' he insisted. 'Changes to that situation are absolutely taboo at FIFA.'

The prospect of a British team never passes first base, never even reaches the table, despite the fact that the massive total of foreign imports in British football reduces the scope for UK-born players to graduate in top-flight football.

It remains an intriguing subject for the bar, or perhaps a board game where participants would have the luxurious indulgence, for example, of speculating on what might have been if Bobby Charlton, George Best and Denis Law could have played together for Britain as well as Manchester United, or if that formidable Liverpool duo Ian Rush and Kenny Dalglish could have been in harness on the international stage.

Today, a Great Britain team would be able to pick Ryan Giggs of Wales to help supply ammunition for England's Michael Owen, a combination many would drool over.

Yet apart from the dubiousness of the assertion that the unity of England, Northern Ireland, Scotland and Wales would be an irresistible force in the global game, the politics of such a blend are an impenetrable minefield. In essence, turkeys won't vote for Christmas. Each of the four home associations vigorously defends its independence and autonomy. None will willingly surrender that for the creation of a British international team which would spell the end of their individual voting power within the European and globally influential halls of ruling bodies UEFA and FIFA, even if the home nations were to still play each other.

The excitement, though, was tangible when the first Great Britain team took the field in May1947, their clash with the Rest of Europe in Glasgow being billed as the 'Match of the Century'.

The game was staged to celebrate the return of the four British associations to FIFA and was inspired by FA secretary and former referee Stanley Rous, a visionary who was acutely aware of the dividends of Britain walking the corridors of world football power.

The four associations had haughtily spurned the invitation to be founder members when the *Fédération Internationale de Football Association* was formed in Paris on 21 May 1904. The nations that were represented comprised France, Belgium, Denmark, Netherlands, Spain, Sweden and Switzerland.

Remarkably, two years later the Brits did join and an Englishman, D B Woolfall, was elected FIFA president. But bitter, acrimonious disputes within the organisation after the First World War led to the British associations withdrawing.

Their return in 1924 lasted only four years before they quit again in 1928, one of Britain's grouses being the definition of and payments to amateurs. This severing of the ties meant that none of the four home countries competed in the inaugural World Cup of 1930 in Uruguay, the 1934 tournament in Italy or the 1938 finals in France.

'Britain in the 1930s was a self-sufficient, self-confident country with a sublime belief that British was best,' Rous wrote in his biography *Football Worlds* published in 1978. 'There was a sense of natural superiority, a smug feeling that all was right in our enclosed world and others had nothing to teach us.' He went on:

We could tell *them* how to organise parliamentary democracy, or an empire or a football team. And so we were largely unaware of our need to learn and develop and to be part of the mainstream of European life.

This attitude was certainly reflected in our football administration. In my early days at Lancaster Gate (then FA headquarters) England and the three other home countries took no part in FIFA.

We could have been the leading influence within it when it started. Instead, we preferred to stay aloof. Now in, now out, whenever we objected to their approach.

Our haverings about joining the European Economic Conmmunity, and having joined about whether to remain in, followed the pattern set by football.

That was the position which I inherited and I certainly had no thought that this was splendid isolation. To me it was a matter of regret so my endeavours were always for a new integration when the chance came.

Britain's part in the war perhaps made Europeans even keener to have us back in their football community and us much readier to rejoin. The sense of comradeship and interdependence was the one happy relic of the conflict.

So there was no problem in getting approval for Arthur Drewry, the chairman of the FA, and myself to go as delegates to a FIFA Executive meeting in Zurich in November 1945, with the brief to see if re-entry might be negotiable.

The interesting team of personalities with whom we held detailed discussions included Dr Ivo Schricker, a former German international who was FIFA secretary, and Jules Rimet, the French president of FIFA whose name will forever be associated with the World Cup.

For years Schricker had run FIFA's business from Switzerland and he had no problems of relationships from any residue of bitterness over Germany's wartime role. We all knew that he had regarded himself for years as more a man of Europe than of Germany and had been antagonistic to Nazi philosophy.

Indeed, he had been in trouble with Goebbels when he attended an international match in Germany. A photograph showed him with his right hand dangling limply, level with his waist, while around him every arm pointed rigidly at the sky in the Nazi salute.

His reprimand was countered with the spirited defence by Schricker that he was there representing the world not Germany and that he could do as he felt appropriate.

FIFA were badly in need of finance and we were able to help after a basis of re-entry had been agreed. Once Drewry and I had agreed the ground rules with Rimet and Schricker, a committee meeting soon followed at the FA offices in London and the British associations were re-elected at a congress in Luxembourg in 1946.

After this, I was holidaying in Basle when Ernst Thommen, president of the Swiss FA, invited me to lunch and talked of FIFA's desperate financial problems. It was then that I suggested a celebration match, Great Britain against Europe, with the proceeds going to FIFA as our goodwill gesture on re-entry.

I saw it also as a kind of victory salute heralding the return to normal sporting friendships for all, including Germany. On my return I had to sell the idea first to the FA.

It was readily agreed there but, unfortunately, had been prematurely leaked to the press from Switzerland. At once, I had George Graham, secretary of the Scottish FA, on the phone. He complained, rightly, that the announcement had been made without any consultation with Scotland.

He was mollified when I apologised for the embarrassing leak and added: 'Of course, we are thinking of playing the match at Hampden Park if that is agreeable to you.' George, rapidly converted to the project, replied: 'In that case I anticipate no difficulty with my executive.'

The plan by Rous, who was knighted two years later and elected FIFA president in 1961, was a huge success. The game, on Saturday, 10 May 1947, captured the imagination of a public still to return to normality after the war and came 24 hours after 150,000 people marched through Hamburg in protest at food shortages.

Almost as many, a crowd of 135,000, packed into Hampden Park to see Great Britain, including Billy Liddell, take on the Rest of Europe. The team line-ups were:

Great Britain (dark blue jerseys): Frank Swift (England and Manchester City); George Hardwick (England and Middlesbrough, captain), Bill Hughes (Wales and Birmingham City); Archie Macauley (Scotland and Brentford), Jackie Vernon (Northern Ireland and West Bromwich Albion), Ron Burgess (Wales and Tottenham Hotspur); Stanley Matthews (England and Blackpool), Wilf Mannion (England and Middlesbrough), Tommy Lawton (England and Chelsea), Billy Steel (Scotland and Morton), Billy Liddell (Scotland and Liverpool).

Rest of Europe (light blue jerseys): Da Rui (France); Petersen (Denmark), Steffen (Switzerland); Carey (Republic of Ireland, captain), Parola (Italy), Ludl (Czechoslovakia); Lambrechts (Belgium), Gren (Sweden), Nordahl (Sweden), Wilkes (Holland), Praest (Denmark).

Referee: G Reader (England).

Liddell's selection came near the end of his first season of League football and his call-up for Britain meant that he had to step out of Liverpool's ultimately successful championship quest by missing the First Division game at Charlton the same day, which the Anfield club won 3–1 thanks to an Albert Stubbins hat trick.

'I considered it a great honour to represent Scotland in the British team,' said Liddell who, with the rest of the squad and travelling reserves George Young of Scotland and England's Raich Carter, reported to the pre-match headquarters of the Aberfoyle Hotel at Loch Ard.

'It's a great occasion: the inventors against the pupils,' said the match programme, revealing the patronising attitude of British football, with Scotland and England yet to taste home defeat by a foreign nation at that time. Britain duly won 6–1 and one report read: 'A combined Great Britain side celebrated the return of the four home countries to FIFA by giving a Rest of Europe XI a lesson in football at Hampden Park.

'Despite a long, hard season, which is set to continue for another month in England because of the winter freeze-up, the British side outplayed the cream of Europe, which comprised players from nine countries and whose captain, Johnny Carey of Manchester United, was the only one with English as his native language.

'Wilf Mannion, aided and abetted by his England wing partner Stanley Matthews, was outstanding for Britain and scored two goals, one of them a penalty. Tommy Lawton also scored twice.

'Billy Steel, who had played only nine Scottish League games at the time of his selection, cracked in a raking drive from 35 yards. Steel had, of course, emerged during the war years so his limited League experience is somewhat deceptive.

'The 135,000 crowd were treated to an exhibition, hard fought but without a single intentional foul and which lived up to its billing as the "Match of the Century".'

The great Swedish centre forward Gunnar Nordahl, who broke scoring records in his native land and then in Italy after joining Milan and Roma, struck Europe's solitary goal. Liddell, though, felt the scoreline was somewhat kind to the British team, reflecting:

I think we were a trifle flattered by our 6–1 victory. It was only in finishing that we were so far ahead of the opposition. Despite the European team's heavy reverse, I thought Johnny Carey gave a wonderful exhibition at right half in their team. We led 4–1 at the interval through two goals from Wilf Mannion, Billy Steel and Tommy Lawton.

I pulled a muscle just before half-time and it became increasingly painful later. Finally, I could do little more than hobble about. But we got a fifth when Carlo Parola put through his own goal and Tommy Lawton got our last one.

The injury kept Liddell out of Liverpool's next two games but he recovered to play in his club's last match at Wolves when their 2–1 win brought Anfield's first League championship for 24 years.

Liddell was all set to be joined at Liverpool by his Scotland and Great Britain team-mate Steel after the Morton star had transfer talks with the Anfield board and manager George Kay. But the planned deal collapsed and Steel signed, instead, for Derby County in June 1947 for a then British record fee of £15,500.

It would be another eight years before the second and last Great Britain team took the field. The match was staged at Belfast's Windsor Park on 13 August 1955, in celebration of the Irish FA's 75th anniversary. Liddell and Matthews were the only two British players retained from the 1947 side, no mean feat in the face of competition from wonderful wingers such as Tom Finney, Cliff Jones and Peter McParland.

By then Liverpool's fortunes had turned on their head. They were preparing for their second campaign in the old Second Division, having finished eleventh in their first season after relegation in which Liddell, having been appointed captain and switched to centre forward, responded with 30 League goals to help prevent an even more alarming decline.

Yet, with typical humility, Liddell admitted: 'I was rather surprised to see my name in the Great Britain team again. I felt I was rather fortunate for there were several others with very strong claims. But far be it from me to quarrel with the selectors!

'I still count it my proudest achievement that I should share with Stan Matthews the honour of being the only two players in both British teams. To be so linked with the illustrious Stanley is an honour I will always cherish.'

The British squad in 1955 was placed in the charge of England team manager Walter Winterbottom. The trainer was Northern Ireland's Gerry Morgan, with whom Liddell had struck up a friendship during his brief wartime guest appearances for Irish League club Linfield.

Scotland duo Tommy Docherty of Preston and Willie Fraser of Sunderland, along with England pair Don Revie of Manchester City and Roger Byrne of Manchester United, were members of the British squad who went to Belfast as reserves.

A crowd of 58,000, generating receipts of £13,000, crammed into Windsor Park for the match, the programme for which advertised a new Philips television with pictures it claimed were 'clear without dazzling'. It was the visitors who dazzled. The teams were:

Great Britain (green shirts, white shorts): Jack Kelsey (Wales and Arsenal); Peter Sillett (England and Chelsea), Joe McDonald

(Scotland and Sunderland); Danny Blanchflower (Northern Ireland and Tottenham, captain), John Charles (Wales and Leeds), Bertie Peacock (Northern Ireland and Glasgow Celtic); Stanley Matthews (England and Blackpool), Bobby Johnstone (Manchester City and Scotland), Roy Bentley (England and Chelsea), Jimmy McIlroy (Northern Ireland and Burnley), Billy Liddell (Scotland and Liverpool).

Rest of Europe (red shirts, white shorts): Buffon (Italy); Gustafsson (Sweden), Van Brandt (Belgium); Ocwirk (Austria, captain), Jonquet (France), Boskov (Yugoslavia); Sorensen (Denmark), Vukas (Yugoslavia), Kopa (France), Travassos (Portugal), Vincent (France).

It proved to be an afternoon of Continental revenge as the European team swept to an emphatic 4–1 win, thanks to a hat trick from Yugoslavian star Bernard Vukas to follow his superb display for a European select side in a 4–4 draw with England two years earlier.

Many pundits and spectators, though, hailed French forward Raymond Kopa as the man of the match. The Rheims player, who a year later was snapped up by Real Madrid after starring against them in the 1956 European Cup Final, gave a masterclass in Belfast to plot Europe's triumph after Bobby Johnstone had put Britain ahead and France winger Jean Vincent equalised. Liddell said:

> The outcome was very different from that of eight years earlier. Not only had the Continentals now learned to shoot but their all-round play was of a higher standard.We were also at a disadvantage as the match took place before the start of the English season and we were not thoroughly match fit.
>
> We took the lead in the 25th minute through Bobby Johnstone and almost got a second shortly after when Jimmy McIlroy just failed to make contact with a peach of a pass by Stan Matthews.
>
> Almost straight away Europe dashed to the other end and after Kopa had hit the woodwork Vincent equalised from the rebound. Then the Continentals turned on the heat.

Twice they hit the post, twice the ball was kicked off the
line by John Charles, who was undoubtedly the man of the
match for Britain.

But we were struggling against a side playing magnificent
football. Vukas added two further goals in the closing stages
and then completed his hat trick from a penalty with almost
the last kick of the game. The European skipper Ernst Ocwirk
played brilliantly throughout. So did Kopa and Vukas.
Although we fought hard we just couldn't score again.

A week after taking on the best of Europe, Billy Liddell kicked off
for Liverpool in the Second Division fixture at Nottingham Forest
to embark on another season in which he finished as Anfield's top
scorer, with 32 League and Cup goals. 'Liddellpool' could indeed
be thankful for their loyal, great Briton.

Chapter Five

Tartan Travels

It is powerful testimony to Billy Liddell's talents that he had made more international appearances than any player in Liverpool history until the 1970s when the Anfield revolution, ignited by Bill Shankly and fuelled by Bob Paisley, began to rewrite the record books more than fifteen years after his last Scotland outing.

Liddell played 37 times for his country, scoring eleven goals, between February 1942 and October 1955, the first nine of them in wartime, victory and fundraising matches, the remaining 28 in official internationals of which there were far fewer than today.

In official internationals alone only celebrated Northern Ireland goalkeeper Elisha Scott's 31 caps had previously surpassed the total of the 'Flying Scotsman' in Liverpool's international roll call.

One of Liddell's biggest regrets is that he never played in a World Cup finals, denied a place in the 1950 tournament in Brazil by a bizarre Scottish FA decision, and remarkably omitted from the 1954 finals in Switzerland, despite playing for Scotland before and after.

But Liddell, a man of conviction, with a deep sense of community and involved in the accountancy profession outside football, grasped the mind-broadening experience of travel in a world scarred by war and which was still grappling with its legacies, including the Iron Curtain that had descended across Europe. He observed:

I've seen a large part of the world at somebody else's expense, the sort of thing guaranteed to thrill any Scot! I'll admit there are more ways of doing that than by becoming a professional footballer.

You could, for example, join one of the branches of the services but I don't think you'd see the world under the same conditions of ease and luxury as I have had visiting France, Belgium, Germany, Spain, Portugal, Italy, Austria, Yugoslavia, Hungary, Denmark, Sweden, America and Canada.

On all these trips I have had the opportunity to make friends with people, some of whom I still correspond with. I have learned much about other countries, knowledge which otherwise I would never have acquired.

And I have not had to pay for the privilege. On the contrary, I've been quite well rewarded, although I wouldn't have objected to getting a bit more!

Considering that Liddell played in an era of the maximum wage – which stood at £20 until it was lifted in his final months at Anfield in January 1961 – and that a player was paid £50 per international appearance for England, Northern Ireland, Scotland or Wales, the justification for the players union, the PFA, to demand a new deal was overwhelming.

Yet before that new era dawned, Liddell appreciated the horizons his football talents opened up in those years before package holidays and charter flights for the masses shrank the globe.

'Only well-to-do people could travel in the manner we did and all it cost the players was what we paid in duty on presents when passing through Customs on our return,' he reflected.

'In short, it became a holiday without worry, apart from that obviously attached to the effort of trying to win matches and play well which was the primary object. And you travelled with the knowledge that you found yourself better off when you returned than when you left.'

One of the most eye-opening trips Liddell made came when he was 33, at a time when he feared his international career may have ended in the aftermath of his massive disappointment at being excluded from the squad for the 1954 World Cup Finals.

The tournament proved catastrophic for Scotland, who lost to Austria 1–0 in Zurich and crashed 7–0 to Uruguay in Basle to finish bottom of their four-nation group, a shattering result preceded by team boss Andy Beattie of Huddersfield quitting after an internal row. It would be almost four years before Scotland appointed another manager.

In hindsight, perhaps the selectors were kind to Liddell to spare him any part in that humiliation. After playing for Scotland in the 3–3 draw with Wales at Hampden Park in November 1953, he was left out in the cold as a succession of other left wingers donned his country's No. 11 jersey.

I was followed at outside left by Willie Ormond of Hibs, Neil Mochan of Celtic and Tommy Ring of Clyde and I was passed over for ten matches, including the World Cup Finals.

Even though I was disappointed at missing the tournament after the not-so-distinguished show which Scotland put up I felt it was perhaps as well I wasn't there.

I was left out of another four Scotland games following the World Cup and I didn't feel I had the slightest chance of being in the party for the tour of Yugoslavia, Austria and Hungary in May 1955.

But Scotland lost 7–2 to England at Wembley in April when the 'man in possession' was Tommy Ring. It must have been when they were smarting under that indignity that the selectors thought of me again, as well as several others.

When the team to play Portugal at Hampden in the next match was announced I found myself restored to the left wing, which gave me no small amount of pleasure, particularly as the selectors had passed me over for the ten previous games. I was also included in the party for the following tour.

In addition to my return, the Scottish FA also recalled Gordon Smith and George Young, two old friends of mine who'd been in the wilderness for some time, and brought in four newcomers.

Tommy Younger of Hibs, later a team-mate of mine for three years at Liverpool, made his debut in goal to begin a sequence of 24 consecutive appearances for his country until he was omitted during the World Cup Finals in Sweden in 1958.

Tommy was a great companion at all times, full of fun and a brilliant goalkeeper, with the largest pair of hands I've ever seen apart from Frank Swift. Another debutant that day was Alex Parker of Falkirk.

He was then a stripling of 20 but subsequently joined Everton and became one of the most competent full backs in the English First Division. The others making their debut were the inside forwards, Archie Robertson of Clyde and Tommy Gemmell of St Mirren.

After four days of special training at Largs, in weather more like midwinter than spring, we found the Hampden pitch very heavy. Not that anybody worried about that. We knew it would suit us far better than the visitors.

Despite this, the Portuguese put up a very good show. Their two inside men, Matateu and Travasses, were really brilliant at times, so much so that I often wonder what damage they might have done on a dry pitch.

Our defence, though, played extremely well, our forwards took their chances and we won 3–0. Laurie Reilly and Gemmell got the first two goals and I bagged the third. The scoreline suggests a clear cut win but it was not quite so decisive as it appears.

Indeed, the sportswriters in general didn't seem to be greatly impressed by our display and were still expressing fears at what might happen when we went abroad.

We had a laugh when one of our players noticed a paragraph stating that eleven reporters were to accompany the Scotland party abroad. 'That's fine,' he said. 'We'll be alright now. If anything goes wrong the selectors can put out a full team of journalists. At least they'll know all the answers!'

Tommy Docherty of Preston and I – the only two Anglo Scots in the party – were instructed to report to Prestwick Airport for the flight to Belgrade which seemed rather a waste of time when the aircraft stopped at Manchester en route.

The first thing that struck everybody when we landed in Yugoslavia was the primitive nature of the airport. It had only one runway, the control buildings looked like log cabins in the backwoods of Canada and, so far as we could see, there were less than a dozen airport staff.

After being used to Prestwick, London, Ringway and elsewhere this airport was a bit of a shock. But at least we arrived safely, which was the main thing.

I've always liked flying – though, when time permits, a boat trip is more enjoyable – but I know that some players are on edge when they're flying and don't fully regain their composure until their feet are firmly on the ground.

When we left the airport we found the most old-fashioned and antiquated bus imaginable waiting for us on the dusty road outside. It was obviously on its last legs and we didn't relish the ride into Belgrade. Unlike some other places, our arrival in Yugoslavia created not the slightest interest.

The only folk who took any notice were two unkempt characters in ragged jerseys, old corduroy trousers and battered sandals who stood silently near the door as we got into the bus.

As we feared,the ride into Belgrade in that old contraption was a hair-raising business. I don't know what the brakes were like. The driver never used them! He just belted along, hell-for-leather, on the rutted and pot-holed road, which was worse than an English country lane.

Every time we went over a hole – which was frequently – we either got a teeth-shaking jar or bounced so that we nearly hit the roof. As we approached the outskirts of the city we passed several huge blocks of flats still under construction.

They had no windows or doors yet dotted all over the window sills we could see washing hanging out to dry. This puzzled me and I asked the interpreter the reason.

He said that housing accommodation was extremely scarce and that scores of students, who were apparently the favoured class, had taken up residence in the incompleted flats.

This was only one of many strange sights for, in many respects, Yugoslavia appeared very backward by British standards. Their ploughs were pulled by oxen, there were donkeys and mules everywhere in the streets, improvised wooden bridges over rivers and canals and barges and junks that appeared to date back almost to Roman times.

Fortunately, our hotel was quite good, even by British standards, apart from the service which left a lot to be desired, especially at meal times. Food may be incidental to some people but to footballers who have to keep in good physical trim it's extremely important.

A Continental breakfast is not very filling. But requests for a decent breakfast of ham and eggs met with blank and uncomprehending stares.

The state of the country left the players a little apprehensive as to what they would find at the football ground. While the stadium itself was impressive, the same could not be said of the pitch, which was very uneven with grass 'fully four inches high' according to Liddell.

As soon as the Scottish FA secretary, Sir George Graham, saw the pitch he told the Yugoslav officials that the grass must be cut and the ground well watered and rolled before the game the following Sunday.

He was assured this would be done but wasn't told how they meant to tackle it, which was perhaps as well! We found out when some of us went for a game of tennis, on courts adjoining the ground, on the Friday afternoon.

Being so close, we went into the stadium to see how the pitch looked only to be greeted by the most comical sight. Two of the smallest sprinklers I've seen were lazily spraying water on the surface and one groundsman was cutting the grass.

But instead of a modern petrol-driven mower he was using an ordinary common or garden hand lawn mower – and only an eight-inch one at that! At least he was doing his best to get on with the job by running backwards and forwards at top speed, with the mower bouncing up and down like a balloon on a string.

We roared with laughter as we watched. But it didn't seem quite so funny when we realised that the pitch was likely to be little or no better by Sunday than when we first saw it. Still, when in Rome – or Yugoslavia – you must do as the natives do and make the best of it.

In the dressing room before the match Gordon Smith was having attention on the massage table when the head support collapsed and trapped his fingers. He must have suffered considerable pain but gave no sign of it on the field, turning in a first-class display in a fast, exciting game.

The weather was oppressively hot. The perspiration ran off us and we all got very dry in the mouth. The reserve players, sitting on the bench, passed us pieces of lemon or orange every ten minutes or so, which helped.

Like most Continental goalkeepers Vladimir Beara in the Yugoslavia goal liked to have the freedom of the penalty area and resented being challenged. When I tried to connect with a couple of Gordon Smith crosses in the first half and collided each time with Beara, I could see he didn't like it.

We both landed in the dust with no harm done. But the outcome was different when I tried to score from a similar opportunity in the second half. Beara got to the ball a fraction of a second before me belting it away with one fist.

Unfortunately, he caught me in the eye with the other. While I don't think it was in the slightest degree deliberate, the result was the same – I had a lovely 'shiner' for a week.

A few minutes later Beara went over to the Italian referee, who couldn't speak the language of either team, and explained by his gestures that there was something wrong with his own eye, after which he was substituted.

George Young, too, was injured soon after and although he played on he had to have hospital treatment and missed the remaining two tour games.

When Yugoslavia attacked, the excitement among the spectators became intense, but once we got on top they either went quiet or started barracking their own men.

We were on the defensive for the last 20 minutes but got a 2–2 draw which, given all the circumstances, I think we deserved.

Gordon Smith had a wonderful game and formed a splendid right-wing partnership with Bobby Collins, then of Celtic, later of Everton and Leeds. Until then Bobby had been regarded mainly as a winger but his tour performances sealed his fame as an inside man.

After the match in Belgrade it was on to Vienna for the next game four days later. This time the team stayed in the impressive Park Hotel – although they had to sleep three or four to a room as the hotel was overbooked.

As Liddell recalled the match had added significance for the home side.

The week before we were due to play at Vienna's Prater Stadium, Austria had signed a Treaty of Independence and, naturally, they were hoping to celebrate this important landmark in their history with a solid victory over Scotland.

The weather on match day was beautiful and the pitch, unlike the one in Belgrade, was perfect. The stadium was full, with quite a number of troops present, including a contingent of Russians.

Right from the start we surprised the opposition by carrying the game to them. Within ten minutes we were a goal up when Gordon Smith, who had taken over as captain from injured George Young, rammed home one of my centres.

This boosted our confidence and we played some top class football. Midway through the first half an Austrian official came to the touchline and shouted to one of the home players. I've no idea what he said but I noticed one of the track-suited reserves start to limber up and I suspected that we were going to be victims of a put-up substitution.

Sure enough, a little later one of the home players fell to the ground when nobody was within yards of him. When the referee – another Italian – went to him, he dragged himself up and limped off.

Like a flash, the substitute shed his track suit and dashed on to fill the breach. Possibly, the player who went off might have pulled a muscle or something like that. But to me it looked strangely suspicious.

Still, we were in front and playing well so why worry? Things got even better because we got a second goal from Archie Robertson to give us a 2–0 half-time lead.

When the teams came out for the second half we noticed that the Austrians had done another swap and it wasn't long before the game started to liven up and get rough.

First, Bobby Collins was heavily sandwiched. Then Gordon Smith was tackled viciously several times. After that somebody took a kick at Alex Parker as he lay on the ground. Now it needed just a spark to set things alight. Yet when the explosion came it happened in the most unexpected way.

Gordon Smith had been bowled over twice and when it happened a third time the full back also went down. Gordon was first on his feet and put his hand out to help his opponent up. Just what the spectators thought he was trying to do I don't know.

Maybe they thought he was going to hit the Austrian defender, which is the last thing somebody like Gordon would ever attempt. But whatever they thought there was no doubt about their actions.

Pandemonium broke out. For a few seconds I felt very anxious about the outcome. Hundreds of people jumped over the railings and invaded the pitch. Laurie Reilly, Tommy Docherty and wee Bobby Collins dashed over to protect Gordon and during the ensuing scuffle blows were aimed.

Fortunately, the troopers patrolling the ground soon had the crowd under control and, before long, they went back peacefully, but by no means quietly, to their seats and the game resumed.

But it was not the last incident. Gordon Smith was again heavily tackled and fell. Although the tackle was nothing like so severe as some of the others and the Austrian offender was a different player the referee sent him off.

That made things easier for us and after I got our third goal and Austria had reduced the lead through Ernst Ocwirk, Laurie Reilly came up to head home one of my crosses to give us a 4–1 win.

In the dressing room afterwards Tommy Younger had us all in stitches as he recounted his feelings during the game when it looked as if things might deteriorate into a riot.

When the crowd jumped over the railings Tommy was at the far end of the pitch from the dressing rooms, which were behind the other goal, and he wasn't too happy about his isolated position. Tommy had us all laughing by exaggerating his fears but we told him: 'You're big and strong enough to look after yourself!'

Tommy pretended to be very upset at what he called 'our callous indifference' to the dangers he might have faced. So we saw a funny side of a regrettable incident and, with a victory to celebrate, we were all in high spirits and after the match we were royally entertained at a banquet attended by Austrian FA officials and players.

This win set up Scotland nicely for the final match of their tour against Hungary, the 'Magical Magyars' who, the previous season, had become the first foreign team to beat England at Wembley. The 6–3 defeat they inflicted in November 1953 was followed by a 7–1 thrashing of England in Budapest the following May.

The Scots had ten days to prepare for their examination by the Magyars, some of which they spent in the Austrian mountains at Semmering. Here they enjoyed some light relief in the form of a friendly, as Liddell explained:

As a variation from training we played a friendly game against a local side, a light-hearted affair with most of the fun provided by that inveterate humorist Tommy Younger.

Bill Brown, later to be Tottenham's goalkeeper, was reserve keeper on the tour and to give him a run he was brought into the team against the locals after the interval.

Tommy, though, didn't fancy sitting out the second half and persuaded the Scottish FA officials to let him have a go at centre forward. As we trotted onto the field Tommy told everyone within earshot that he intended to get a hat trick.

Gordon Smith, who was not playing in the second half, took Tommy up and bet him he couldn't do it. Well, thanks mainly to the local team's poor defence rather than Tommy's prowess as a budding centre forward he scored two and, with ten minutes left, was chasing here, there and everywhere desperately seeking a third!

He was shouting for the ball in tones as penetrating as a foghorn on the Mersey and his voice echoed round the mountain side.

At the same time, Gordon Smith stood behind the goal and yelled at the players not to give the ball to Tommy. Finally, though, Tommy did get a peach of a pass to complete his hat trick and win his bet.

Due to a Russian security alert, the Scots had to endure a coach journey from Austria to Hungary instead of the flight they had been expecting. Liddell recounted:

When we went to Vienna to catch the plane to Budapest we hit an unexpected snag. The Russian Prime Minister was visiting Yugoslavia's Marshall Tito and for security reasons the Russians refused to allow any plane to fly within 100 miles of their air corridor.

So we spent the night in Vienna, only to find that the possibility of air travel was not much brighter the following day. With the risk of further delays we decided to travel by bus but that turned out to be almost a case of jumping out of the frying pan into the fire.

We set off in a coach with a small trailer behind for the luggage, facing a 10-hour journey which would have taken an hour by air. The journey was not one I'd recommend, despite the wonderful scenery en route!

When we arrived at the frontier our passports were collected and stamped and we were through the barriers in less than half an hour. 'That's fine,' we said to ourselves 'you couldn't beat that anywhere.'

But we'd made a slight miscalculation. We were not in Hungary, as we thought we were. We'd only been passed out of Austria. The procedure for entering Hungary had to be done at a control post a quarter of a mile away. And what a performance it was!

We had to leave the coach and produce all our passports and other documents. Then there was a long discussion between Hungarian immigration and customs men and Scottish FA officials.

That seemed to be getting us nowhere, despite telephone calls to Budapest. The customs people insisted on unpacking the trailer containing our playing gear, personal luggage and so on. The talks and arguments seemed to go on interminably.

At one stage, Sir George Graham got so fed up he threatened to turn back and take the team home to Scotland right away. I don't suppose for a minute he had any such intention but felt that the threat might end the impasse and, apparently, it did have some effect.

Shortly afterwards a compromise was reached and we didn't have to open our baggage. Instead, two soldiers accompanied us in the coach and stayed with us until customs officials went through our things after we arrived in Budapest at about nine o'clock in the evening.

The hotel room where this took place was decorated in red and had busts and photographs all over the place of past and present Russian leaders.

Prior to the game we were allowed to train on the Nep Stadium pitch and had full use of all the facilities at that wonderful ground. It hadn't been completed at that time but was being built to hold 120,000 people, a capacity which was later reduced.

The dressing rooms and refreshment rooms were the best I'd seen. That goes for any in America or elsewhere, even the fabulous Estoril National Stadium in Portugal, which took a lot of beating.

We were invited, along with the Hungarians, to a pre-match reception at the British Embassy where we met and chatted – through interpreters – with such famous figures as Ferenc Puskas, Nandor Hidegkuti, Josef Bozsik, Sandor Kocsis and others.

What struck me most forcibly at first was the sartorial elegance of all the Hungarian footballers. They stood out all the more against the rather drably dressed ordinary folk of the city.

There was no doubt that the Hungarian players were extremely well provided for at that time and were looked on as national heroes, not in a silly, hysterical way but in a down-to-earth manner.

It indicated that whatever we may have thought about that in Britain, football success was regarded abroad as something eminently worthwhile, materially affecting the country's prestige and wellbeing.

I was told by an embassy official that there'd been a lot in the Budapest newspapers about the match as well as the British way of playing the game, which was described as the fairest and most sporting of any country.

So to the match itself on 29 May 1955. Following the controversy in Austria it was agreed that no outfield substitutes should be allowed unless a player was genuinely injured before half time, although an injured goalkeeper could be replaced at any time. (This was in an era when substitutes were not permitted in British football, for any reason.)

The teams lined up as follows:

Hungary: Danka; Buzinsky, Varhidi; Lantos, Bozsik, Szojka; Sandor, Hidegkuti, Kocsis, Puskas, Fenyvesi.

Scotland: Younger (Hibernian); Kerr (Partick Thistle), Haddock (Clyde); Docherty (Preston North End), Evans (Celtic),

Cowie (Dundee); Smith (Hibernian), Collins (Celtic), Reilly (Hibernian), Robertson (Clyde), Liddell (Liverpool).

Again, Liddell himself described the action:

The first half was one of the finest in which I've ever taken part, with play switching from end to end at such speed that the spectators in the middle of the stand must have been turning their heads one way then the other like those at Wimbledon's centre court.

Our team blended well and gave as good as they got. It was fast, thrilling rip-roaring stuff. The crowd, who hardly ever stopped cheering, were as generous in applauding our moves as they were their own team's.

At least they were until five minutes before the interval when Gordon Smith gave us the lead with a brilliant solo goal after a 40-yard burst. It was received in such silence by the 102,000 spectators you could have heard a pin drop. The crowd were probably stunned by the realisation that any team could take the lead against their famous side.

Eleven jubilant Scots trooped off at half-time, little knowing what lay ahead. When we lined up for the second half we twigged at once that something was afoot.

Hidegkuti was switched to outside right in place of Sandor but of the diminutive Sandor there was no sign, either at centre forward or anywhere else. In the middle was a six-footer we later discovered to be Palotas and a long time afterwards we learned that the Hungarians had changed their goalkeeper as well!

In the first half Harry Haddock had kept Sandor very quiet but he didn't have the same success against Hidegkuti, whose deep-lying tactics let Kocsis get in behind the back and do a lot of damage.

Within twenty minutes Hidegkuti, Kocsis and Fenyvesi had scored for the Hungarians and the crowd were once more in a good mood. But we didn't give up without a hard fight. We kept pegging away hopefully, though without much success.

Then fifteen minutes from the end I was cutting in for goal when I was fouled. The Austrian referee signalled a penalty and you should have heard the uproar it caused. It wasn't far short of terrifying.

One of the Hungarian players grabbed the ball and sat on it while the rest of them surrounded the referee shouting and arguing with his decision. At the same time the crowd were stamping, screaming and unleashing that shrill, ear-piercing whistle only the Continentals can.

In short, it was bedlam and it was several minutes before order was restored and I had to face the ordeal of taking the penalty. And what an ordeal it was!

I found taking penalties in British football that usually there's an almost deathly hush as you put the ball on the spot and walk back to take the kick. This was very different. The crowd kept up their shrill whistling incessantly until the moment I was taking the kick.

When I did take it the ball went the wrong side of the post and, much to my chagrin, the crowd started cheering wildly. Although my team-mates were not unduly upset I was bitterly disappointed over my miss. A goal then would have put us back in the game with a chance.

I took 44 penalties for Liverpool and scored from 36 of them. Yet I took only two for Scotland and missed them both! The other was in the game against France in Paris in 1950.

Even after my miss in Budapest we had most of the remaining play but, unfortunately, had nothing to show for it except marks on the crossbar and uprights and Hungary finished 3–1 winners. The crowd gave us a wonderful ovation at the end, a large number of them staying behind to cheer us as our coach left for the hotel.

The tour had been more successful than many critics had anticipated and if we did have to bow the knee to the Magical Magyars at least we'd come out of it much better than England who'd conceded seven goals on the same ground twelve months earlier.

So Liddell's European tour came to an end. But as well as travelling far and wide to represent Scotland, he had many memories of playing for his country at Hampden Park. Here he recounts a few, beginning with a 2–0 defeat by England in April 1948.

Tom Finney put England ahead just before the interval and Stan Mortensen got their second goal. But what made the match unforgettable to me was my attempted charge on England goalkeeper Frank Swift . . . a move that went wrong!

Frank had fielded a ball and had it securely in his grasp as I came dashing in with the idea of giving him a shoulder charge. Big Swifty, realising the danger, twisted to one side to avoid me. But I was going at such a rate that I couldn't help barging into him.

Unfortunately, instead of making contact with his shoulder I caught him smack in the ribs with all my twelve and a half stone. Swifty was such a big fellow that I was the one who ended up on the ground. But I was most upset to learn later that Frank had two broken ribs.

I was pleased that the referee did not give a free kick against me and much happier about the whole business because of Frank's response. The next time I met him he assured me, in that friendly manner of his, that he bore not the slightest grudge against me and said: 'I know you didn't do it on purpose, Billy. If I thought you had, I'd have soon settled your hash!'

It was in that game that Scotland introduced a new goalkeeper, Ian Black, who followed Willie Miller of Celtic. Ian was almost unknown at that time north of the border. He'd not long been back from Forces service overseas and had thrown in his lot with Southampton.

He'd been playing for them only a matter of four months when he was chosen to face England, the match above all others in which every Scotsman wants to play. Ian later played for Fulham and Bath City but he got just that single Scotland cap before Jimmy Cowan of Morton became automatic choice for the next five years.

Another Hampden game that stands out for a very different reason is our 6–1 victory over Northern Ireland in November 1950 when inside forward Billy Steel, my left wing partner on many occasions, had a real blinder.

Billy was not the easiest man to play with because in so many ways he was a law unto himself. But there can be no disputing his great ability as a player. Ireland had a splendid tactician that day in Peter Doherty.

Peter was then getting to the end of his long and brilliant career and he was not the Doherty of old. Even his agile brain and clever scheming could make no impression on a game which went all one way from start to finish.

Steel scored four goals in a 25-minute spell during the second half . . . and did so from only five shots. I had one of my best games up to then for Scotland. At least, that's what the sportswriters said and they see more than the player.

One of the critics went so far as to say that the Liddell–Steel combination was the finest wing partnership in British football at that time.

Another match in which Scotland registered an even bigger victory was when we played the USA at Hampden in April 1952.

Two years earlier the Americans had caused a sensation by beating England 1–0 in the World Cup in South America and more than 107,000 fervent soccer enthusiasts flocked to Hampden to have a look at the side that had done this to the old enemy.

It wasn't quite the same American team but six of the players who'd taken part in England's amazing defeat were in the side, including goalkeeper Frank Borghi. This time the Americans were never in the hunt and we won 6–0 without having to pull out all the stops.

Yet, if I'd had to name one man as the outstanding player that day I think I'd have voted for Souza, the visiting inside left, who tried so desperately to overcome insuperable odds.

Laurie Reilly got three goals and Ian McMillan a couple, the other being an own goal by the American right back

O'Connell. It was unusual to see the visiting centre half Colombo don a pair of leather gloves at kickoff and wear them right through the game.

Had it been in the middle of winter you might have understood it. But this was the end of April, in spring-like weather!

One of Scotland's most disappointing international results from my point of view was England's 1–0 win against us at Hampden in April 1950. Both teams were unbeaten up to then in the home international championship and it had been decided that the countries finishing in the top two would qualify for the World Cup Finals in Brazil that year.

Unfortunately, the Scottish powers-that-be decided they would accept the invitation only if Scotland finished as British champions. So everything depended on the Hampden game, which drew a crowd of more than 133,000 and featured a Scotland forward line in which all five players were called William – Waddell, Moir, Bauld, Steel and myself.

The match was cut and thrust throughout with the teams evenly matched. Bert Williams of Wolves was in magnificent form in England's goal and he made some great stops from Hearts centre forward Willie Bauld.

Another save of Bert's was truly miraculous. As the ball was chipped over to me from the inside right position I was facing across the field. The ball bounced at my side, as it was running in front of me, I swivelled and hit it first time for goal. It sped like a bullet towards the left-hand corner, just below the bar. As soon as I struck it I had the feeling it was a winner, but not against a man of Bert's calibre.

With a marvellous leap he turned the ball over the bar with his fingertips. And he had sprung so well that he landed a good couple of yards past the post.

England won through the game's only goal, scored in a breakaway by Roy Bentley in the 63rd minute. That, and Bert's brilliance, denied us.

So instead of a World Cup trip to Rio we had to settle for one to Lisbon and Paris to play friendlies against Portugal and France which, though very enjoyable, was not the same.

Looking back over his long international career, Liddell explained some of the differences between playing for club and country.

Playing in an international is a much bigger strain than an ordinary club game. Everyone expects a brilliant display from every player. But it's not easy to play your normal game because you're among different players and you have to adapt to suit the style of the team.

There's not the same opportunity to be unorthodox, unless you have a perfect understanding with your team-mates. I think this is one of the reasons why so many brilliant club players fail to hit the same high standard in internationals.

Unless you have a regular partner for half a dozen internationals you have to keep to the accepted pattern. Playing for Liverpool I could wander around the field as I pleased and wasn't always to be found in the position I appeared in the programme.

I had the backing and understanding of the rest of the forwards so that the line was never lopsided and frequently I was able to catch the opposing defenders unaware by popping up at inside right to take a through ball from the wing half.

Invariably, I found it a bigger strain playing at Hampden than at Wembley or at grounds in Ireland, Wales or abroad. Maybe it was the fact that I was an Anglo-Scot made it so hard.

I don't know why it should be but I think the majority of Anglos have always felt they are more liable to be criticised than players with Scottish clubs.

It's something peculiar to Scotland. Most critics there seem to think that a team of home Scots is preferable to a mixed one and quite a lot of supporters appear to think that once a man goes to England he loses his birthright.

The Anglo-Scot is in the unfortunate position that he may be watched only once or twice by the selectors and doesn't get a real chance to show the spectators what he can do.

You have the feeling that your performance will be compared not with those of your team-mates but with the local idol whose place you may have taken.

I can assure all my fellow Scots that although we may have chosen to make our living in 'enemy territory' we are still intensely proud of the fact that we belong to Scotland.

We wish for nothing more than to justify ourselves in the eyes of our own folk and to prove that Scotland is still the greatest.

In his 1960 autobiography. Liddell outlined his thoughts on the future development of the game. Given the growing rift between demands on players by their clubs and their countries the plan he revealed was years ahead of its time. Today it seems even more revolutionary.

My idea is that England and Scotland first and, possibly, Wales and Ireland later, might have their own residential international players, instead of borrowing them from the leading clubs.

The schemes could be run jointly by the national associations and leagues, the players being registered as their country's 'property' instead of belonging to clubs.

They would work and train together and, when not engaged on international business, tour the country playing club sides or teams representing different areas or even counties.

This would raise revenue which could fund any scheme the football authorities so decided. Obviously, from time to time new players of international calibre would be discovered by clubs. They could be transferred to the international squad, probably at a much higher fee than they would otherwise command.

Clubs and players not wishing to take part in such a transfer need not be obliged to do so – though I can't imagine any player turning down such an opportunity.

It wouldn't please a club to be in danger of losing a star in this fashion but eventually there would emerge a changed attitude on the part of all clubs in relation to the needs of the country. At present it's mainly a selfish one.

Equally, there would be instances of players enrolled for the national team failing to make the grade. Though falling below the highest standard there would always be demand for them by clubs – and they could be transferred in the normal way.

Liddell's glimpse into the future from over forty years ago also embraced European competition, cut-price airlines and aviation technology, much of which has come to pass. 'Nothing,' he said, 'is more certain than that we'll see a European League established.' He continued:

Before long it will be possible to fly from the heart of any of the big British cities to the centre of football interest on the Continent in a matter of two or three hours, by machines combining the speed of a jet with the manoeuvrability of the helicopter.

Fog hazards will become a thing of the past, as planes will rise vertically from the ground into the clearer atmosphere above before starting up at speed. Long runways will be outdated.

Football barriers will then collapse far more quickly than they have in the past decade. Planes may even take off from the pitch of the travelling club and land on that of the team staging the match later the same day.

Even for League fixtures I reckon that in another decade or so rail and coach travel will be as outmoded as stage-coaches are today. You may feel some of these things are far-fetched.

But the same would have been said 30 years ago of anybody who predicted that it would be possible to send rockets to the Moon, to cross the Atlantic in a few hours, to split the atom, to send guided missiles 6,000 miles and land on target, or sit in the comfort of your own home and watch a football match played on the Continent.

The prospect is that many more matches will be televised in the future and football, therefore, must look after and give greater consideration to the paying customers, the supporters who are the backbone of the game.

Up to a few years ago the majority of football followers were ready to put up with almost any inconvenience. Now they are becoming more and more aware of what they have been doing without for so long.

They read of luxurious grounds elsewhere in the world and they demand a higher standard of comfort than they have been getting. Given more comfortable facilities many of the 'missing millions' of recent years would be tempted back into the game.

Liddell's foresight possessed the high accuracy ratio of his multitude of shots, headers and crosses that tormented opposing defences.

Chapter Six

In Limbo Before Wembley

Anfield ambitions took wing on Liverpool's gloriously dramatic capture of the first postwar League championship. The Kop faithful basked in their place in the sun and their hopes soared of new triumphs to come.

If Liverpool's form had been one of remarkable peaks and troughs, they had shown resilience, determination and an unquenchable team spirit among the 26 players used in the title quest. They had also proved entertainers, with Billy Liddell, Albert Stubbins and Jack Balmer filling the starring roles.

'The truth is that everyone knows them to be an attractive, compelling side with a strange mixture of the very good and the very bad ... and they so often produce the latter when least expected, hence their tag of "The Crazy Gang",' commented the *Sports Spectator.*

They set their supporters hearts on edge. Give them a trifling match and they make a race of it, just as some Derby horse makes a race with a donkey. At other times – and how contrary they can be – they will reveal form that one thought hardly possible.

Hence the Anfield brigade's fascination and allurement. You never know. The possibility of sensation is in their bones and in their make-up. Always mercurial and unpredictable the Reds are giving great pleasure to their hosts of loyal supporters.

This at a time when it is most needed, as a relief from nationwide troubles and inflictions. These are joyous times Anfield way.

Anfield's average attendance during the title campaign was 45,730 and amid this heady atmosphere nobody could have envisaged that Liverpool would not grasp another major trophy for seventeen years, by which time Liddell's compatriot Bill Shankly had ignited the Anfield revolution.

During the summer of 1947, as Liverpool bathed in the after-glow of their championship success, Britain paved the way for Indian independence and partition with Pakistan while the United States military faced questions over reports that a UFO carrying alien beings had crashed in the desert of New Mexico. Questions over the Roswell Incident continue to this day.

At home, Clement Attlee's Labour government tightened food rationing and its official slogans 'Export or Die' and 'Work or Want' were hammered into the public consciousness.

For Liverpool in general and Liddell in particular there was sadness with the death in August of club chairman Bill (W H) McConnell. He and manager George Kay were the men who had assured Liddell's parents that their son's future was in good hands at Anfield and McConnell's business acumen had secured the key signing of centre forward Albert Stubbins to dovetail menacingly with Liddell's wing play.

McConnell's illness had prevented him being at Anfield on the day Liverpool learned they were champions but, with a great sense of compassionate, sporting consideration, the match ball from Sheffield United's Bramall Lane win over Stoke City, which ensured the title went to Anfield, was presented to him in a London hospital.

The much respected chairman, whose passion for football was matched by his enthusiasm for poetry, died little more than a fortnight before his beloved club kicked off their defence of the championship. He was buried in Anfield cemetery, the funeral service being conducted by former Liverpool captain, the Rev. James Jackson. He was succeeded in the chair by Alderman S R

Williams but the McConnell name continued on Liverpool's board when Bill's brother Tom became a director a year later.

'I liked Bill McConnell from the first time I met him and I hope he valued my friendship as much as I valued his,' said Liddell.

I remember him telling me the story of his early struggles. Like myself he came from a humble family and as a boy had little pocket money.

He told me: 'I used to watch Liverpool as far back as I can remember. As a youngster, with the tail of my shirt sticking out of the holes in the seat of my pants, I usually wangled my way in without paying.

'One day in a fit of boastfulness I told my young, working class pals that one day I'd become a Liverpool FC director.' Not only did Bill achieve that ambition but he went one stage higher and became one of the most popular chairmen the club has ever had.

He worked his way up, after many years at sea, to become the proprietor of Liverpool restaurants and a chain of dockside canteens. His popularity was evident from the large number of people from all walks of life who attended his funeral.

They ranged from the highest legislators in football to humble dock workers, who had sacrificed half a day's wages to pay their respects to the man who had done so much for Liverpool FC.

Manager Kay, whose team was still selected by the directors, went into the new season with the same squad of players, apart from winger Berry Nieuwenhuys.

'Nivvy', as he was affectionately called by fans, had been appointed assistant professional at West Derby Golf Club prior to returning to his native South Africa as assistant to the famous Bobby Locke at Transvaal Country Club. His place on the opposite wing to Liddell was shared between Bob Priday, Billy Watkinson, Ken Brierley and Alex Muir but the great Scot's talents were hailed both inside and outside the club.

'Liddell's power of drive is one thing . . . his inward drift to inside left is another,' said the *Sports Spectator*. 'His unerring endeavour, his charm and his shots from any angle or distance keep the crowd on their toes.

'He has been known to hit a ground shot not rising six inches which rocked the goalposts and made the crossbar shake. A lovable character, a fine athlete and a studious and competent man.

'Liddell is Scotland's natural selection for outside left and his value is incalculable. Has the club ever possessed a better outside left? Skilful and fast, he covers ground very quickly and must have one of the most powerful shots ever.'

The superlatives for Liddell flowed, too, from his team-mate Laurie Hughes, who made his senior debut on the same day as the Scot in the FA Cup tie at Chester in January 1946 and went on to win a title medal at centre half. Hughes became the first Liverpool player to appear in a World Cup Finals, playing impresssively for England in the ill-fated 1950 tournament in Brazil – when they sensationally lost to the United States – only for subsequent cartilage damage to end his international career prematurely

'Billy was the finest player I ever played alongside,' enthused Hughes. 'He could win a match on his own. Finney and Matthews were great footballers but Billy was a match winner.

'He had a great shot on him and he'd run down that wing like a rocket. He was always quiet, a very religious man. You had the "Liddellpool" thing but we didn't mind. He earned that.

'If a Liverpool player got invited to a function Billy always got offered the tickets first. We were getting a £2 win bonus, though, so we'd a lot to thank him for.'

To prepare for Liverpool's title defence Liddell's routine was one that had been agreed between the club and his accountancy firm. For the first month he trained every day with the squad and, after that, on Tuesdays and Thursdays.

Liddell's accountancy job caused a regular *frisson* of excitement in Liverpool city centre when he finished his half-day's work on Saturdays before travelling to Anfield to play in the afternoon match.

Pat Boylan, then a young fan who later emigrated to Ohio in the United States, recalled: 'I served my apprenticeship in Tithebarn Street and Billy's office was in Victoria Street. We all idolised him and on Saturdays we'd go and stand outside his office until he came out.

'He'd jog along to get the number 26 tram, travel with the fans up to Anfield and then play in a big match. He was a wonderful person and a star in every sense. What an example he was to the young kids who watched him.'

These were the days before Liverpool had their Melwood training ground – which they bought in 1950 from St Francis Xavier School – and daily sessions were held on the Anfield pitch or on land that became the main stand car park. They also used Penny Lane playing fields.

Stubbins provided an insight into the pre-season fitness regime when he wrote in the club's handbook:

Many fans will be surprised to learn that while some players can gain weight during the summer, others can lose several pounds. When this happens, due to the spell of inactivity, it is important to build muscle and increase weight.

We report at 10 a.m on the first day of training in July and after the preliminary greetings are over we go on scales for a height and weight check-up, under the watchful eye of trainer Albert Shelley.

This completed, the players don sweaters and football knickers over which are worn flannel trousers and, complete with a heavy pair of shoes, we set out on a road walk of four to five miles.

I say 'walk' but actually it is a combination of walking and running. Should a hot July sun be blazing down the men who have gained surplus weight begin to lose it from this moment on!

The players are strung out along the road in small groups and a brisk pace is set and maintained throughout. This is perhaps the most gruelling part of the breaking-in routine, the first pipe opener under summer conditions.

Once this opening run is over, however, we have the sense of physical wellbeing common to all athletes. From now until the start of the season the players will be training with gusto, morning and afternoon, lapping, sprinting and exercising until a state of 100 per cent fitness is reached.

Before that peak is reached, though, there are always a few minor aches and pains, tired muscles and blistered feet. But every player thinks it's all worthwhile when they hear that welcoming roar that heralds the beginning of a new season.

When the curtain did go up on the 1947–8 campaign Liddell scored Liverpool's first goal, with Stubbins adding another two, in a 3–1 home win over Preston. After a 2–0 defeat at Manchester United, a brace of Liddell goals clinched a 2–0 win over Stoke before Liverpool hit a sequence of six games without a win.

They resumed winning ways in the sweetest way possible with a 3–0 Mersey derby victory over Everton at Goodison Park through goals from Balmer, Stubbins and Willie Fagan. It was, though, a brief interruption of joy in an autumn and winter of gloom for Liverpool.

The launch on 1 November of the world's longest-running radio programme, BBC's *Sports Report*, told the story of Liverpool's 2–0 defeat at Blackpool, an all too familiar fate for the reigning champions. By the end of February they had lost fifteen games, winning only eight, and their title was beyond rescue.

While the BBC were launching their new programme they had made an arrangement with Liddell which, in today's high-profile, frenetic, media-driven football age, seems unbelievable.

The BBC's Liverpool studio at the time consisted of a small unmanned city centre base over the Washington Hotel, which stood above Lime Street's Guinness Clock. They gave Liddell a key and, in the event of anything newsworthy occurring in Liverpool's matches at Anfield, he was asked to catch a tram to town, open up the studio, switch on the lights and broadcasting equipment, contact the main studio in Manchester or London, do his piece, close down the studio after him – and get the tram home!

Liverpool certainly missed the bus in the FA Cup of 1948 after building Kop hopes of a run by emphatically clearing the first hurdle. They disposed of Nottingham Forest 4–1 at Anfield in the third round, Liddell scoring between two goals from Stubbins following an opening strike from Priday.

Liddell's shooting power again earned press comment. 'From well outside the penalty area he struck a free-kick which was so truly hit and at such pace that the ball, hitting the concrete surround of the Kop on its rounded portion, rebounded almost to the roof,' one reporter observed.

Liverpool's reward for that victory was to be drawn away to Matt Busby's Manchester United. But with Old Trafford still out of action as a legacy of Luftwaffe raids and United's temporary Maine Road home required for Manchester City's home clash with Chelsea, the tie was staged at Goodison Park, vacated by Everton's away tie at Wolves.

A crowd of 74,721, generating receipts of £8,810, crammed into Goodison on a biting January day, some three weeks after Britain's railways had been nationalised and only six days before India suffered more torment with the assassination of Mahatma Gandhi.

The Goodison gates were closed half an hour before kickoff, with an estimated 12,000 locked out, while inside people who had fainted were passed over the heads of spectators for treatment by the St John Ambulance Brigade. The massive crowd set a new attendance peak for the Everton ground, although it was surpassed the following September when more than 78,000 watched the Mersey derby.

A week before the Goodison tie, United's First Division clash with Arsenal had been watched by a Maine Road crowd of 83,260, a Football League record and a barely believable total in this post-Hillsborough and Bradford disasters era of safety-first, all-seat stadia.

The Cup rivals lined up at Goodison like this:

Liverpool: Minshull; Jones, Lambert; Taylor, Hughes, Paisley; Liddell, Balmer, Stubbins, Done, Priday.

Manchester United: Crompton; Carey, Aston; Anderson, Chilton, Cockburn; Delaney, Morris, Rowley, Pearson, Mitten.

With both teams having to wear change strips because of the colour clash, Liverpool played in white and United in blue. It was, however, Liverpool and their fans who were soon feeling blue. United's attack sparkled and Liverpool's defence was confused by their tactic of winger Charlie Mitten and half back Henry Cockburn fluently and frequently interchanging positions.

A blitz of three United goals in a six-minute spell late in the first half, from Jack Rowley, Johnny Morris and Mitten, decided the tie. Only a second-half goal-line clearance by Bill Jones saved Liverpool from further embarrassment as, according to the *Liverpool Echo*, 'United simply toyed with their opponents'.

United won 3–0, a sweet moment for Busby against his old club and former boss Kay. His side went on to lift the Cup, beating Blackpool 4–2 at Wembley, and finished runners-up to Arsenal who succeeded Liverpool as First Division champions.

Liverpool's Cup knockout came in an alarming sequence for Liddell and his colleagues of seven defeats, a draw and only one win in nine games in the first two months of 1948. During that spell they failed to score in five consecutive First Division matches.

The run was ended in dramatic style, thanks to a bizarre, brave personal incentive for Stubbins: 'We had a home game against Huddersfield who were in relegation trouble and, like us, needed points,' said the Liverpool centre forward.

'Just before the match I received a telegram. When I opened it, it warned me that if I tried to go near the Huddersfield goal, I'd get my leg broken. I didn't say a word about it to anyone. But I was so angry that I was determined to be the boss. We won 4–0 . . . and I scored all four goals.'

That victory signalled a change in Anfield fortunes. Stubbins maintained the scoring habit with eleven goals in the last eleven games of which Liverpool won eight and drew two to pull themselves up to finish in limbo in eleventh place.

Then it was time for the squad to pack their bags for the club's second tour of the United States and Canada (although RAF duties had prevented Liddell making the first tour two years earlier).

Liverpool sailed to America on the *Queen Elizabeth* and Liddell's arrival was eagerly anticipated across the Atlantic. 'When the crack Liverpool Reds trot out on the field to meet the American League Metropolitan All Stars at New York's Triborough Stadium on May 16 all eyes will be focused on two internationalists who were not in the 1946 party,' wrote soccer columnist Erwin Single.

'One is the sensational Albert Stubbins, once a Detroit schoolboy, who leads a million-dollar forward line. The other is the mighty Willie Liddell, winger par excellence, a braw Scot and reputedly the man who possesses the most powerful kick in soccer today. He fires a cannonball.'

The transatlantic voyage by luxury liner was enjoyable for former RAF flier Liddell, who reflected: 'Unless you are an extremely bad sailor the five days aboard provide relaxation, plenty of entertainment and amusement and food which the finest hotels in the world cannot better.

'Flying certainly saves considerable time and possibly has other advantages but when you fly, you rob yourself of one of the finest experiences you could wish for, a sea crossing to New York or Montreal.'

Liddell's previous visit to the States and Canada had been on wartime RAF service, but his return with Liverpool wowed the football press and public and he was welcomed back in Montreal and Toronto by a lone piper donned in kilt, sporran and glengarry.

And at half-time in Liverpool's 5–1 win over Ulster United in Toronto a Scottish FA representative presented their celebrated forward with a brown leather holdall, an item of luggage that would have a long-running role in the Liddell family.

For years Billy used it to carry luggage on trips and also to carry memorabilia of his career when he toured schools to give talks to children. These exhibits included a US soccer jersey, collected when he swapped shirts with an opponent during the tour.

Later, one of his twin sons David used the bag to carry school books and other documents before it was given to the Liverpool FC Museum half a century after Billy received it in June 1948.

The Americans, too, pushed the boat out during the tour. Rear Admiral Gordon McLintock, superintendent of the US Merchant Marine Academy, invited the Liverpool squad to attend a regimental review and then to dinner at his residence, where he announced that soccer should be introduced as a regular sport for his trainee sailors.

Starting at outside right in all eleven matches Liddell finished third top scorer with thirteen goals behind Stubbins (17) and Jack Balmer (16) as Liverpool swept through the tour with a 100 per cent record.

The plaudits rained down on Liddell. After his two-goal show in a 4–2 win over St Louis All Stars the *St Louis Star Times*, under the headline 'Liddell's Style Thrills 7,326 Onlookers', declared: 'Bill Liddell, who had Eddie Linehan chasing him most of the night, amazed the onlookers with his clever brand of soccer and was the outstanding Liverpudlian.'

The *Newark Sunday News* enthused: 'Liddell possesses the most powerful drive of any forward we have ever seen. He's known as "Cannonball Willie" and justifies this tag every time he shoots the ball.

'At Ebbets Field against the All Stars he beat Gene Olaff twice from twenty yards. Any forward who can do that must pack dynamite in both feet as Olaff is one of the best goalies this country has produced.'

The *Toronto Daily Star* reported that 'the play of Liddell was like watching one of the Barrymores on stage', while *Montreal Herald* columnist Elmer Ferguson quoted tour arranger Erno Schwartz proclaiming of Liddell: 'America has never before seen such a player. He has both finesse and power to a degree we have never before found in the many great players who have visited this continent.'

Liverpool were visited in Montreal by former Everton favourite Sammy Chedgzoy, who had been a father figure to the young Dixie Dean in much the same way as Matt Busby had been a guiding influence on Liddell. Sammy, who had emigrated from Britain, dropped in to the Anfield squad's hotel eager to catch up on football news and gossip from home.

The tour, for which Liverpool were guaranteed $30,000, saw the first match between foreign clubs on American soil when the Merseyside visitors met Swedish side Djurgarden at Ebbets Field, Brooklyn.

The Stockholm team built a 2–1 half-time lead through two goals from Hans Jeppson, his brace split by a goal from Liddell, who went on to inspire a 3–2 victory through second-half strikes from Ken Brierley and Balmer.

'Sparked by the brilliant play of Bill Liddell, Liverpool FC trimmed the Djurgarden team,' reported the *Brooklyn Eagle*, which was even more effusive about his two-goal display in Liverpool's final tour match, an 8–0 win over Kearney Scots Celtics in New Jersey.

'Liddell put on a one-man show all by himself,' said the paper. 'He headed in Priday's pass ten minutes from half-time and also booted in Balmer's assist for Liverpool's eighth.

'Actually, the great internationalist had a hand (foot or head) in earning no less than five of the other goals gathered by his fast-moving comrades. He was here, there and everywhere.'

Another player who was on the move as a result of Liverpool's visit was American-based centre half Joe Cadden. His potential led Liverpool to sign him, although in four years at Anfield he made only five first-team appearances before joining Grimsby Town and then Accrington Stanley.

'A Scot by birth, Joe had gone to America some years before and played for Brooklyn Wanderers,' said Liddell. 'He played against us on the 1948 tour and gave such a solid display that Liverpool invited him to sign on. Joe came back with us and duly put pen to paper.'

The tour, on which Liddell and his team-mates met a host of celebrities including world light-heavyweight boxing champion Gus Lesnevich, Jackie Robinson of the Brooklyn Dodgers, the world's first black professional baseball player, and film and TV star Lucille Ball, was a huge success. Liverpool extended their record on American soil to 21 wins out of 21, scoring 133 goals and conceding only 26, although Jim Harley's tour injury forced his retirement and he was succeeded at right back by Bill Shepherd.

During the summer of 1948 Attlee's Labour Government introduced the National Health Service, but the compelling question at
Anfield was whether Liverpool could find a prescription to cure
the homesickness of Albert Stubbins and his wife Ann.

The 29-year-old had won a place in Kop hearts by scoring more
than fifty goals in his first two seasons at Anfield, but he and his
wife both deeply missed Tyneside and a rift developed between
the former Newcastle player and the Liverpool board. Stubbins
failed to report for pre-season training, refused to re-sign and
asked for a transfer when Liverpool rejected his plan to move
house back to Newcastle and train there while he built up a
business for his retirement.

'The dispute between Albert and the club was the main topic in
the dressing room and, for that matter, all over Merseyside,' said
Liddell. 'It deprived us of his services for the opening thirteen
games of the season.' He went on:

Albert was as mild mannered and inoffensive a man as you
could ever meet. Never within my hearing did he say an
unkind word about anybody. But he hadn't really settled
down on Merseyside.

Although he had a nice, modern club house in the 'colony'
where eight or so of the Liverpool players lived, he and his wife,
both Geordies, hankered to get back among their own folk.

Albert wanted to train with Newcastle at St James's Park
and travel to Liverpool's matches each Friday. But the club
had a rule that all players should live on or near Merseyside
and train together.

Nobody could quarrel with that. It was a sensible idea.
Obviously the highest level of team work can be reached
only through players being together and trying out various
moves, experiments and tactical schemes.

Despite his quiet manner and apparent gentleness Albert
had a streak of determination in his make-up. When the club
refused to allow him to live in Newcastle he was adamant
and refused to re-sign. For a time it was stalemate and when
the new season started there was no Stubbins.

So Les Shannon took over at centre forward. It was not a position for which he was physically suited, as he lacked both height and weight. But he tried manfully enough and was unlucky on many occasions.

Eventually, after ten games, he gave way to the more powerfully built Cyril Done but Les later went to Burnley and developed into a splendid inside forward and an even more brilliant wing half. He later coached Everton's youngsters before becoming Arsenal assistant manager and then manager of Bury and Blackpool.

The impasse between Albert and Liverpool was resolved, finally, when the club agreed to his original proposal, with certain modifications.

He re-signed in the lounge of a Southport hotel in October 1948 and although he was hardly match fit after being out so long, he had kept in trim by training regularly at Gateshead back in his native North East. He made his comeback for us in our fourteenth match of the season, at home to Middlesbrough on 23 October and he celebrated by scoring in our 4–0 home win.

During my years at Liverpool I'd say Albert was one of the most popular players with the crowd. He was a brilliant centre forward, with delicate and accomplished ball control and a terrific shot.

He was also one of the most gentlemanly of players. In all the games we played together I never once saw him guilty of anything approaching a deliberate foul.

The sports headlines had been made that summer by Don Bradman's winning retirement from Test cricket and at the Olympics in London when Dutch woman Fanny Blankers-Koen won four track events – the 100 metres, 200 metres, 80 metres hurdles and the 4 × 100 metres relay – and Emil Zatopek of Czechoslovakia set a new 10,000 metres record.

London was also the venue when world light-heavyweight king Gus Lesnevich, who had met the Liverpool squad less than two months earlier, lost his crown to Britain's Freddie Mills, who won on points in front of 46,000 at White City.

Liverpool, though, made a losing start to the campaign with a 2–1 defeat at Aston Villa and could only draw 3–3 at home with Sheffield United the following Wednesday, with a Liddell goal and two from Balmer ensuring a point. Liddell was also on the mark in the next two games, a 4–0 home win over Sunderland and a 2–1 win at Sheffield United, and his goal early in the second half at Highbury secured a 1–1 draw against Arsenal.

Middlesbrough's Anfield visit in October, the game in which Stubbins made his long-awaited first-team return, saw Liddell involved in penalty drama.

After Balmer and Stubbins had put Liverpool 2–0 ahead they were awarded a 77th-minute penalty, which Liddell took and duly beat Boro's Italian-born goalkeeper Rolando Ugolini for his first spot-kick goal in official, peacetime football. Shortly after, Liverpool earned another penalty, but this time Ugolini bravely got in the way of Liddell's blast to pull off a creditable save, although he had to receive treatment before he could resume between the posts.

Still in pain from his heroics the keeper suffered more anguish when his centre-half colleague Bill Whitaker conceded an own goal in the last minute to condemn Boro to a 4–0 defeat in front of a then record post-war Anfield crowd of 57,561. That clinched successive wins for Liverpool but they never bettered two consecutive victories throughout the League season in which they finished a mediocre twelfth.

Without the injured Hughes for most of the campaign, versatile Bill Jones took over at centre half and Liverpool conceded only 43 goals, the best defensive record in the top flight apart from title winners Portsmouth, who let in one fewer.

When the champions-to-be visited Anfield in November they fell victim after just nine minutes to a Liddell goal Dixie Dean would have been proud of, the Scot powering a header into the Portsmouth net from outside the penalty area!

Liverpool won that duel 3–1 but it was one of only five home League victories. They lacked a cutting edge, scoring a meagre 53 goals and failing to find the net in fifteen games, nine of them at home.

One of the reasons was that having been without Stubbins for the opening quarter of the campaign through his dispute with the club, fate conspired to keep him out of much of the rest, restricting him to a total of fifteen appearances and six goals, two fewer than Liddell who was second top scorer behind fourteen-goal Jack Balmer.

'Soon after re-signing, Albert ran into a succession of injuries and was in and out of the side for the rest of the season,' Liddell reflected. 'Although he played for us for another four seasons he never fully recaptured the wonderful form which had made his light shine like a beacon during his first two years on Merseyside.'

That winter brought a special memory for Wirral man John Martin, for whom Liddell has been his lifetime hero. 'My uncle was quite well connected and as my tenth birthday present he took me to the home game against Burnley on December 4, 1948,' John recalled.

'The prospect of seeing my hero Billy in the flesh was almost too much for me to bear during the run-up to the game, which I watched from the splendour of the directors' box.

'When we took our seats I found myself next to Ted Ray, who was a huge radio star at the time and it would be difficult to overemphasise my sense of excitement!

'At half-time everyone retired to the boardroom, except for me. Because of my tender years I wasn't allowed in and I had to stand outside with the commissionaire.

'But just before the second half started a buzzer sounded and the commissionaire opened the boardroom door and announced: "Teams coming out, gentlemen."

'Imagine my excitement as I heard the clatter of studs on concrete. Then the players walked past me, within touching distance. I, of course, had eyes only for Billy and he must have recognised my idolatry because he winked at me as he passed.

'It's a moment I still relish all these years later! I also remember it finished 1–1. Burnley scored first and I'd given up all hope before Cyril Done scored our equaliser about ten minutes from the end.'

It was the season when local boy Jimmy Payne burst onto the First Division scene, making his debut in a 1–0 home defeat by

Bolton when his display on the right wing somewhat offset the disappointment of the result.

Liverpool suffered a similar defeat next time out, at home to Arsenal, but again Payne's performance stirred the Kop faithful. His dribbling talent even prompted premature comparisons with Matthews and Finney and when Payne won an England B cap, it seemed certain that full England recognition was only a matter of time.

He never achieved that peak or fulfilled those over-hyped and unfair early expectations. Yet Payne, an enigmatic figure, went on to make 243 Liverpool first-team appearances, scoring 43 goals, before joining Everton for £5,000 in April 1956. It was a move that was short in both distance and duration. Payne made only six Everton appearances, scoring twice, before retiring from the game at the age of 30 later that year to open newsagent and confectionery shops.

He did so with due deference to Liddell, saying: 'Billy was a great player . . . a match winner. He could win you a game on his own after you'd been pulverised. That's why they called us Liddellpool.'

The 1948–9 season was one that bore testimony to Liddell's brilliant, ubiquitous talents. He filled four different forward positions for Liverpool, including one game at centre forward as a sign of things to come.

He also found himself operating at left half in the 1–0 defeat at Newcastle in October after switching positions with the redoubtable Bob Paisley, who had been concussed. Paisley was eventually carried off but returned in the second half only to connect with a Liddell cross that knocked him out again and saw him carried off a second time!

It was Paisley's last-minute goal at Nottingham Forest in the FA Cup that snatched Liverpool a third-round replay which they won 4–0, with the fans almost seeing more than they bargained for. 'The Liverpool trainer Albert Shelley was kept busy supplying everyone with tape for their shorts, the mud and the general sliding about having caused these to go to half mast,' noted one reporter.

The win earned Liverpool a home tie with Forest's rivals Notts County, captained by Tommy Lawton, which drew an attendance of 61,003, surpassing the Middlesbrough total and only 33 short of the turnout for the 1934 FA Cup win over Tranmere, which was then Anfield's all-time record. The big crowd, paying receipts of £5,419 to swell the healthy Anfield coffers, launched yet another salute to Liddell, who scored the game's only goal in spectacular style.

When Stubbins was obstructed in the 58th minute Liverpool were awarded an indirect free kick in the penalty area. 'The taking of this became quite a lengthy procedure,' reported the *Liverpool Echo*. 'Taylor paced out the distance between the ball and the opposition when the referee commanded him to desist.When all was set, Done merely tapped the ball two feet and Liddell smashed it straight through with a terrific shot.'

The timing of Liddell's thunderbolt could not have been better, as the *People* underlined: 'Liverpool had begun to wear a worried look and the victory goal came when it was least expected and with County looking the more likely scorers. But Liddell slammed the ball into the net over the heads of the packed County defenders.'

Liddell once again finished the match at left half after another injury to Paisley, who played a huge part in ensuring that his friend and team-mate would go through his majestic career without a booking.

'The referee spoke to me and said he was taking my name for swearing,' Liddell revealed. 'I hadn't sworn and the referee was clearly mistaken. At that point Bob stepped in on my behalf and told him: "If you put his name down you'll never referee again. He's never sworn in his life."

'The referee admitted he'd made a mistake and didn't book me. So I'm very thankful to Bob for what he did. He always had a great sense of fairness. He was a man of great principle.'

Liverpool's Cup exploits that season ended with a 3–1 fifth-round defeat at Wolves, a game in which late goals from Sammy Smyth, later to move to Anfield, and Jimmy Mullen took the Molineux side through after a Stubbins goal had cancelled out a Jimmy Dunn strike for the eventual Cup winners.

During the summer of 1949 Liddell was joined at Anfield by his brother Tom, a full back signed from Dunfermline junior club Lochore Welfare to become one of Liverpool's 37 professionals.

'A younger brother of Billy, he showed every promise in Scottish junior football and will be an acquisition to the staff at Anfield,' said the club handbook.

Tom played in the reserves but never received a call up to first-team action with Billy. Later he managed a family sweets and tobacconist shop in Oakfield Road near the Anfield ground.

By the time the 1949–50 season dawned sweets and chocolates had come off postwar ration and Liverpool and their fans were hoping for a mouthwatering campaign on the field. It certainly proved to be tasty, even though Kay and the board had bought no new blood.

Liverpool kicked off on a scorching August afternoon with a 4–2 home win over Sunderland – Paisley opening the scoring against his boyhood idols with Balmer, Kevin Baron and Stubbins also on the mark – and proceeded to rattle up a sizzling nineteen-game unbeaten First Division run. It was the club's best start to a season since their inaugural League campaign in the Second Division more than half a century earlier in 1893–4, when they were unbeaten in all 28 games and then won a Test match for promotion.

At the time it was also the longest unbeaten run from the start of a season by any side since the First Division was enlarged to 22 clubs. The record endured until Leeds United strung together 29 matches undefeated in 1973–4, later equalled by Liverpool in 1987–8 when the top flight contained 21 teams. But Liverpool had 22 wins to nineteen by Leeds.

'Our unbeaten run in 1949 is one of my greatest Liverpool memories,' said Liddell. 'It was down to wonderful team spirit which ran throughout the playing, coaching and training staff.'

After beating Sunderland we drew 0–0 at Stoke before going to Everton in our third game of the season on a hot Saturday afternoon, watched by a crowd of more than 70,000.

Although they didn't have a goal to cheer it was a match packed with thrills and excitement and without an intentional foul from start to finish. It could almost have been played without a referee!

In contrast our return with Stoke, in which I scored our only goal in a 1–1 draw, was rough. Our right back Bill Shepherd and skipper and inside left Jack Balmer received injuries which kept them out for several games.

Fortunately we had a capable man to step into the breach in Eddie Spicer with experienced Willie Fagan taking over Balmer's position. We won 2–1 at Arsenal in our next match, thanks to two Albert Stubbins goals, and earned high praise from the London press.

We followed that successful trip to the capital with 1–1 home draws against Manchester United and Bolton. In fact, we'd have beaten Bolton handsomely but for the wonderful goalkeeping of Bootle-born Stan Hanson, brother of the former Liverpool winger Alf.

Stan always seemed to save his most amazing performances for games against us. This one was another right out of the top drawer and Stan got a tremendous ovation from the Kop at the end.

Our eighth game took us to St Andrews to meet Birmingham where we won 3–2. I scored twice late on after Cyril Done put us ahead in the opening two minutes.'

Liverpool made it four straight wins with victories over Derby County at home (3–1), West Brom away (1–0) and Middlesbrough at home (2–0) before a goalless draw at Blackpool when Liddell's shooting was too powerful even for the match officials.

He unleashed a shot almost from the halfway line that flew around fifty yards past home goalkeeper George Farm, who was standing on the penalty spot. The ball crashed off the bar and bounced down over the line. Travelling Kopites rapturously celebrated their hero's spectacular strike but neither the referee nor the linesmen were anywhere near the incident to confirm the 'goal' and after Farm ran back and grabbed the ball, play continued, with Liddell robbed of a wonderful winner.

His skills, though, were not lost on opposing centre half Harry

Johnston. 'Billy was the type of winger every manager seeks,' declared the England international. 'Defenders feared him because he was always there when scoring situations arose.

'He never chickened out. He was big, strong, speedy and played it hard but fair. He put his heart and soul into a game. A great competitor.'

Liddell scored one that did count early in the next match, a 2–2 home deadlock with Newcastle, who forged a 2–1 half-time lead. But Preston-born inside right Kevin Baron, who had established himself in the first team after a patient wait in the reserves, struck a second-half equaliser which was followed by a bizarre incident.

Ten minutes from the end Newcastle left winger Bobby Mitchell volleyed past Liverpool goalkeeper Cyril Sidlow for what seemed the winner, only for Geordie celebrations to be doused by referee J J Russell's whistle. The official had blown to signal a free kick to Liverpool, explaining that as the ball was crossed, Mitchell had shouted 'leave it to me', which had distracted Liverpool right half and captain Phil Taylor. Mr Russell declared it 'ungentlemanly conduct'.

The Newcastle match launched a Liddell run of scoring in five successive matches, the last four of them wins, which brought him seven goals.

He was the lone scorer in Liverpool's defeat of Fulham at Craven Cottage, followed by a brace in the 4–0 home demolition of Manchester City, an explosive display on Guy Fawkes Day.

Liddell lit the touchpaper against City with a memorable angled low left-foot drive to put Liverpool ahead after eleven minutes after Bill Jones had flicked the ball over his head and the second of two Stubbins shots had rebounded to the Scot, who was doing one of his occasional stints at No. 7. Ken Brierley, playing at outside left, headed a second goal and Baron scored the fourth. But sandwiched between was an incident that was to confirm Liddell as the club's penalty taker. City goalkeeper Ron Powell's push on Baron prompted Sheffield referee B J Flanagan to award a spot kick.

It was taken by Lambert but saved by Powell who pushed the ball onto the bar and caught it as the Liverpool full back attempted a follow-up. However, another penalty later in the game brought Liverpool's third goal, described by the *Liverpool Echo* as 'an extraordinary affair'.

The paper reported: 'The referee stopped play for what appeared to be a City free kick and raced to the other end of the field to see if Ron Turnbull needed attention to an injury. When he returned he signalled his decision was a penalty to Liverpool – and Liddell made no mistake.'

Liddell scored from another penalty when he gave another two-goal show in Liverpool's next game, a 3–1 win at Charlton, and he reflected: 'Scoring from the penalties meant I was given the job as our regular taker.

'Curiously, of the total of 44 that I took in postwar football, five of the eight from which I failed to score were at Anfield – and each time at the Kop end. Four of the eight I failed to convert were saved, two hit the post, one was inches wide and the other just over the bar.'

Being in range of a Liddell thunderbolt could be a high-risk business for players and public! But even if you were in the flight path there was pride to accompany the pain, as long-time Liverpool supporter Sam Leach revealed.

'I was standing behind the Kop goal at one match when I was hit by a Liddell special,' he recalled. 'It was like being struck by a hammer and I was concussed for a few days. But I proudly refused to wipe the ball mark off my face!'

A Liddell goal after just two minutes set Liverpool on their way to a 2–1 home win over Aston Villa, achieved despite playing most of the second half with ten men after Baron had been carried off.

'The next match was at Wolves, who'd done even better than us as far as points were concerned in the early weeks of the season,' said Liddell.

They won nine and drew three of their first twelve games before the thirteenth proved their downfall.

Our 1–1 draw at Molineux, thanks to a goal from Willie Fagan, was followed by a 2–2 home draw against Portsmouth.

Cyril Done, deputising for the injured Albert Stubbins, scored twice against Pompey to stretch our undefeated sequence to nineteen games, from which we'd taken 29 points.

But our run ended on 10 December at Huddersfield Town, who had won only four of their twenty games. So we felt we stood a great chance of coming away from Leeds Road still unbeaten.

We should have done. We scored through Willie Fagan after only four minutes and another goal from Ken Brierley put us 2–1 ahead at half-time. Huddersfield got back into it after the interval but we failed to take several chances.

To make things worse, we felt we were robbed. All our players were convinced we should have been awarded a free kick in our penalty area. But the referee gave it to Huddersfield and their Northern Ireland outside right Johnny McKenna scored to give them a last-minute 3–2 win.

To some extent it was a relief because the longer we remained unbeaten the greater became the strain. Every game was as intense as a Cup tie and each team we met wanted the glory of being the first to beat us.'

Nevertheless, Liverpool ended the 1940s in pole position at a time when football was massive box office. The aggregate attendance for the League programme on 27 December 1949 was a record 1,269,934, around three per cent of the population of England and Wales. The average gate for the four divisions was 28,862.

An Anfield crowd of 55,000 saw Liverpool beat Arsenal 2–0 on New Year's Eve to send them into a new decade on top of the League. Liddell opened the scoring after 32 minutes. He is also credited in some record books with the second goal, eight minutes from the end, but contemporary reports indicate that it was an own goal, the ball crossing the line off visiting goalkeeper George Swindin's knee after he failed to gather a Liddell corner under pressure from Willie Fagan.

Nevertheless, Liddell's goal in his last game of the 1940s edged him towards a top-scoring League haul of 17 goals from 41 appearances in a season when he also had his only right wing outing for Scotland, in a 2–0 Hampden Park win over Wales.

Kop hopes of a second championship in four seasons, however, evaporated with four defeats and a draw in their last five games. Liverpool collected only five League wins from January and slid to finish eighth on 48 points, yet only five behind Portsmouth who retained the title.

Liddell, though, experienced confirmation of the old adage that many a true word is spoken in jest. 'On the way home after our unbeaten run had ended at Huddersfield I said to Willie Fagan and Cyril Done: "Now that's over we can relax a bit before the Cup ties come along. If we can keep playing as we have been we might get to Wembley."

'While there was a certain amount of seriousness in my remark, it was not meant to be taken too literally.' But Liddell's off-the-cuff comment was to have a long-awaited sequel.

Chapter Seven

Cup Final Agony

Liverpool and the FA Cup had been uneasy bedfellows. In almost sixty years since they first entered the competition they had never won it. They had never even trod the Wembley stage, their only appearance in the Final coming in 1914, shortly before the start of the First World War, when they lost 1–0 to Burnley at Crystal Palace.

So when Billy Liddell and his colleagues embarked on the Cup trail in January 1950 the hopes of the Kop were tempered by a suspicion that perhaps Liverpool just were not destined to reach the Twin Towers and ascend the 39 steps to lift the prized trophy. Liddell knew exactly how they felt, admitting: 'Like every player my ambition was to play in the Cup Final but Liverpool had been trying to win it for so long without success that everybody had rather a fatalistic attitude about our chances, and that applied even when our prospects seemed bright.'

Liverpool were drawn away to Second Division Blackburn Rovers in the third round of the 1949–50 season, a game that was played on a mud-bath Ewood Park pitch and which ended goalless.

In the Anfield replay, Liverpool were rocked when Blackburn took the lead against the run of play with a 21st-minute goal from Ernie Edds. Jimmy Payne fired his side level before the interval with a spectacular shot.

Liverpool attacked the Kop end in the second half and shortly after the restart they took the lead in controversial circumstances. When Baron's shot rebounded off the underside of the bar Fagan was there to hit the ball into the Blackburn net with a batch of Liverpool players apparently offside. Referee R A Mortimer of Huddersfield thought otherwise, however, and despite Blackburn protests he allowed Fagan's effort to stand.

The visitors, stung by what they felt was an injustice, surged forward and gave Liverpool's defence a host of problems. A minute from the end they went desperately close to equalising when Edds smashed a curling free kick against a post with goalkeeper Cyril Sidlow beaten, although there was still time for Liddell to demand a scrambling save from Sidlow's oppposite number John Patterson.

'We got through that rather luckily and we also had a bit of a struggle in round four when we were drawn against Exeter of the Third Division South,' said Liddell.

On a treacherous, icebound pitch the lowly Anfield visitors held out until seconds before half-time when Baron side-footed in a Stubbins pass. Exeter gave their top flight foes a few anxious moments before Fagan scored with an 82nd-minute shot that trickled over the line, with Liverpool again the beneficiaries of the referee rejecting offside claims.

Within a minute aggrieved Exeter reduced the deficit through a Dick Smart header and it needed an 88th-minute header from Payne, which made it 3–1, to book Liverpool's ticket into round five.

'We were drawn to play Stockport County at Edgeley Park and it almost proved our undoing,' said Liddell. 'The Third Division side included Alex Herd, the former Manchester City inside forward and a Scotland colleague of mine, and they put up a magnificent fight.'

The tie set a Stockport attendance record officially logged as 27,833, although many more fans got into the ground by scaling a wall and there were echoes of disasters past and portents of those to come when a section of fencing collapsed. Fifty fans were thrown to the ground, although none were seriously hurt, and after police and ambulance men attended the scene the spectators continued watching the game by standing close to the touchline.

The first half was goalless and home supporters were incensed soon after the interval when Sunderland referee R Wood dismissed penalty appeals when Liverpool captain Phil Taylor appeared to bring down Herd from behind. Liddell was involved in the move that put Liverpool in front after 57 minutes, his pass into the goalmouth seized on by Paisley who set up Fagan to score from close range.

The pitch began to churn up, the legacy of heavy pre-match rain, and Stockport kept Sidlow as busy as home keeper Jack Bowles at the other end, a remarkable tribute to their spirit against opponents who were leading the Football League. Stubbins, though, doused some of the Stockport fire with a second Liverpool goal in the 70th minute, steering in the rebound after his first shot rebounded off Bowles.

The home side gained some deserved reward in the last minute thanks to the impressive Herd, who won respective losers and winners medals with Manchester City in the 1933 and 1934 Finals and whose son David was in the victorious Manchester United side in 1963. The 40-year-old met Terry Swinscoe's corner and sent a header beyond Sidlow to reduce Liverpool's winning margin to 2–1. Nevertheless, their passage into the last eight began to stoke thoughts of a League and Cup double, although the home sixth-round pairing with Blackpool was a testing one.

The Seasiders, boasting the First Division's best defensive record, stepped out at Anfield without injured Stanley Matthews but still with plenty of class players and also a live duck, complete with its own bucket of water, as a pre-match mascot.

It seemed that Blackpool's goose might have been cooked when Fagan, extending his record of scoring in every round, struck Liverpool ahead with a right-foot shot before the tie was twenty minutes old.

But within four minutes the visitors were level when Laurie Hughes handled to concede a blatant penalty. England's Stan Mortensen sent the spot kick to Sidlow's left and, although the Wales international got a hand to the ball, he could not keep it out. Blackpool showed their quality and composure to protect the 1–1 scoreline and edged ever closer to a Bloomfield Road replay. With nine minutes left the game was still deadlocked.

Liverpool were frustrated and increasingly desperate for a second goal, and in a bid to unlock the door Liddell and Payne switched wings. It was a change that paid a spectacular dividend and had the Kop rapturously acclaiming their hero Liddell.

'Payne jigged up the left wing, attended by a retinue of three Blackpool defenders,' reported the *Liverpool Echo*. 'Just when it seemed that he would shoot, he passed the ball a few yards to his right where Liddell slewed it with his right foot beyond the dismayed Farm.'

It was a wonderful goal which, after Mortensen's brave flying header just failed to snatch an equaliser, took Liverpool into the sixth semifinal in their history. Their opponents would be none other than neighbours and arch rivals Everton, who had gone to the Baseball Ground and beaten Cup favourites Derby County 2–1 after previously knocking out London trio Queens Park Rangers, West Ham and Tottenham.

Manchester City's Maine Road stadium was named as the venue for only the second all-Mersey semifinal – Everton winning 2–0 at Villa Park in the previous meeting in 1906 – and the first in any round since 1932.

The other semi was also a derby, with Arsenal taking on Chelsea at White Hart Lane. It meant that if the Gunners prevailed, they would set a record by reaching Wembley without travelling outside London after being drawn at home in every round, to Sheffield Wednesday, Swansea, Burnley and Leeds.

The FA broke with tradition by staging the semifinals on different dates. Arsenal and Chelsea played first and drew 2–2, the Highbury club coming back from two goals down to earn a replay, also at White Hart Lane, which they won 1–0 through an extra-time goal from Freddie Cox.

The all-Mersey meeting on Grand National day, 25 March, generated massive public interest and also prompted Tophams, then Aintree's owners, to protest to the FA about the clash of these great sporting events. Their complaint was sympathetically rejected, leaving police and transport operators to draw up plans to avoid traffic congestion.

Residents also had their grouses. A meeting at Anfield Methodist Church, Oakfield Road, close to the Liverpool stadium, complained about the disturbing noise from fans when semifinal tickets went on sale. And somewhere in the queue for semifinal train tickets at the city's Central Station was a certain Jessie Paisley, wife of Liddell's friend and team-mate Bob.

'I remember my dad and I sharing a place in a day-long queue at the station to get his train ticket to go to Manchester for the game,' recalled Jessie. 'You didn't think anything of it. There were no privileges then and nobody in the queue knew who we were.'

Four days after Liverpool secured their semifinal place Blackpool extracted revenge by returning to Anfield for a League match and winning 1–0. It was one of a run of results that ultimately cost Liverpool their chance of the championship, which went to Portsmouth who finished level on points but 0.4 of a goal ahead of Wolves, the first time the title had been decided on goal average for a quarter of a century.

'Had we been meeting Everton three months earlier, doubtless we'd have been strong favourites but after our opening nineteen League games without defeat we'd been slipping,' recalled Liddell.

Of our seven League games immediately before the semifinal we lost four, drew two and won only one. Everton had not been doing much of note, either, but their record over the same period was a bit better.

We lost 2–0 at home to Wolves the week before the semi and a few days prior to the big game Laurie Hughes, who had been in brilliant form but had missed our previous two games, was pronounced unfit by the club's specialist.

Bill Jones, who had played in only one of the previous Cup games, took his place. It was the only change from the team that had played in the previous four Cup games, including the replay with Blackburn. In the first Blackburn match Bill had been at left half in place of Bob Paisley.

Everton's passage to Maine Road had been rather more difficult than ours, having been drawn away in three of their four ties. Their only home game had been in the fifth round, against Tottenham, who were carrying everything before them in the Second Division and were promoted as champions.

We were told that Everton had been fortunate to beat Spurs by a rather dubious penalty award in the opening minutes. Eddie Wainwright scored from the spot and although Tottenham did most of the pressing after that they couldn't break down Everton's defence.

Everton went to Buxton three days before the semifinal but we stayed at home until Friday afternoon, when we left for Alderley Edge in Cheshire. Although there was no chance of Laurie Hughes playing, he came along for the ride.

It was the second time in three years that he'd missed out on playing in a semifinal. A broken fibula kept him out of both games against Burnley in 1947. We spent the evening before the semifinal watching a film at a Wilmslow cinema and the weather for the big game next day was perfect – beautifully mild and sunny.

We got up for breakfast, had a walk round the village, read the papers and played cards. Then it was time for the pre-match meal. Before a home match I usually had poached eggs on toast and before an away game I had steamed fish. That's what I had before the semi, with semolina pudding to follow.

We left the hotel at about 1.15 p.m. so that we could get to the ground an hour before kickoff. We didn't see any fans on the way but they were out in force once we got close to Maine Road. When we arrived, I chatted to a few of them and signed some autographs.

I used to leave myself up to 25 minutes to get changed and I followed my usual routine. The last thing I did was to put on my No. 11 shirt. I was always the last to get ready and the last man out.

If for any reason I didn't come out last supporters would write to me and say it was the reason the team hadn't done so well in that particular match!

The team line-ups were:

Everton: George Burnett; Eric Moore, Jack Hedley; Jackie Grant, Ted Falder, Peter Farrell; Ted Buckle, Eddie Wainwright, Harry Catterick, Wally Fielding, Tommy Eglington.

Liverpool: Cyril Sidlow; Ray Lambert, Eddie Spicer; Phil Taylor, Bill Jones, Bob Paisley; Jimmy Payne, Kevin Baron, Albert Stubbins, Willie Fagan, Billy Liddell.

Maine Road was packed with 72,000 fans, paying receipts of £13,497 and, after Wainwright had sent a shot narrowly wide of an upright, Liverpool believed they had scored in the 24th minute. They claimed that a Stubbins header from a Fagan centre had crossed the line before Moore kicked it clear, but Northwich referee Colin Fletcher rejected their appeals.

Five minutes later, however, Liverpool did break through with an unlikely Bob Paisley goal that caused widespread confusion. Dave Horridge, later to become a well-known *Daily Mirror* sportswriter, was at the game as a *Liverpool Echo* messenger and described the sequence of events thus:

'I was behind the goal Liverpool were attacking in the first half. Paisley lobbed the ball back in after Everton goalkeeper George Burnett had punched away a Jimmy Payne cross.

'It was a high ball from Paisley and as Burnett and a defender went up for it, challenged by Liddell, the ball ended up in the net, despite Everton having men on the line.

'Nobody else touched the ball after Paisley had kicked it but the reporters in the press box assumed that Liddell had beaten Burnett to it and headed it in. Later, they had to send corrections to their papers saying it was Paisley's goal and not Liddell's.

'I'll never forget one report which read: "Paisley's lob was headed in by Paisley who outjumped Burnett!" Perhaps it inspired the old football gag about strikers getting on the end of their own crosses!'

On the day that 10–1 shot Freebooter was racing to victory forty miles away at Aintree, Paisley's own freebooter had brought him a rare and memorable goal, one of only thirteen he scored during his Anfield first-team career.

There was no confusion, though, about Liddell being the scorer of Liverpool's second goal after 62 minutes that clinched their long-awaited ticket to Wembley, although he admitted:

It was an absolute gift. The words 'good fortune' describe it precisely. Kevin Baron wormed his way through and centred just beyond the far post.

The ball struck an Everton man and was going for a corner when Eddie Wainwright tried to save the flag kick. But all he could do was put the ball right at my feet.

I had to shoot from the most acute angle but I hit the ball first time with all my strength. It sped into the net like a rocket, giving George Burnett no chance.

Rather than sit back, Liverpool tried to build on their 2–0 advantage and nobody was more determined than Liddell. One reporter wrote: 'Liddell showed notable speed and persistence and when he went head over heels over a group of photographers crowded near the dead-ball line the referee moved them further back.

'From Liverpool's twelfth corner, nine of which had come from Liddell's flank, he tried a 75th minute in-swinger which curved appreciably and struck the near post .'

Although Everton were as disappointed at their 2–0 defeat as Liverpool were jubilant, they had contributed to one of the most Corinthian of Mersey derbies.

'If there had been a gentleman's agreement to decide the issue purely on football, it could not have been kept more strictly,' Leslie Edwards wrote in the *Liverpool Daily Post*.

'Because so much was at stake I rate the game the finest of all city inter-club matches. There have been others full of fire and of drama and good football but none so to inspire our admiration by the good conduct and good sense of all who played.

'Liverpool won because they had greater punch and because their defence had one of its particularly brilliant days.'

As the final whistle sounded, securing a Cup Final collision with Arsenal on 29 April, Liddell remembered his off-the-cuff aside three months earlier. 'We trooped off the Maine Road pitch happy in the knowledge that my half-joking remark to Cyril Done and Willie Fagan after the Huddersfield defeat had, indeed, become a fact,' he said.

For Liddell and his wife Phyllis it was a joyous time. Two months before Wembley they celebrated the birth of twin sons Malcolm and David and just a few days before the Cup Final, there were pictures in the newspapers of the Liddells at the christening of their new arrivals.

For Liddell the player there was fulsome praise from some of his greatest contemporaries. Johnny Carey, the brilliantly versatile Manchester United and Ireland star, who had captained the rest of Europe side against Great Britain three years earlier and would later manage Blackburn, Everton, Leyton Orient and Nottingham Forest, declared:

'Every football team wants to play against a Real Madrid. As players we always want to test ourselves against Billy Liddell. As with Tom Finney and Stanley Matthews I know that meeting the Lion of Liverpool calls for something special.'

And Matthews, a Great Britain team-mate of Liddell's, proclaimed: 'What a fine player Billy is. He's brilliant on the field, wonderful as a gentleman, great as a friend and a credit to the game of football.' Even as they spoke, Arsenal were making uncompromising plans to curb Liddell's menace.

Liverpool's first visit to Wembley saw Anfield swamped with ticket demands from a host of fans who had not been born when the club had last reached an FA Cup Final 36 years earlier.

The ticket allocation for each club was a meagre 8,000. Liverpool received 100,000 applications, sufficient to fill the stadium on its own. Liverpool's response was to conduct a ballot, open only to people living within 25 miles of the city.

It was not only supporters who faced ticket headaches. Arsenal left half and captain Joe Mercer had problems, too. The former Everton star, who still lived on Merseyside and had a grocery business in Wallasey, trained at Anfield on a regular basis. When both clubs reached Wembley a potentially embarrassing 'spy-in-the-camp' situation was resolved by Mercer training on his own in the afternoons after the Liverpool sessions had finished. But the ticket situation was one he could not resolve and Mercer had to abandon plans to take employees to the Final because he could not get sufficient tickets for them.

'After the semifinal we had five weeks to wait for the Final and they were the longest five weeks of my career,' Liddell admitted.

During that time we all discovered we had more friends than we'd realised! They all wanted a Cup Final ticket.

The FA later introduced a rule allowing players in the Final up to twelve tickets but in 1950 there was no such regulation. Although Liverpool allowed us a reasonable allocation, it wasn't enough to allow every player to satisfy his family, relations and friends.

Yet the most casual of acquaintances would buttonhole us with requests for tickets until we were almost afraid to show our faces in public. It got worse in the last fortnight, with the excitement mounting, and it seemed that half the male population of Liverpool wanted to be at Wembley to cheer us on.

Prior to the semifinal I made an arrangement with Jackie Grant of Everton that whoever was on the winning side would see that the other one had tickets for the Final.

Both teams had League fixtures scheduled for Cup Final day so the losers knew they wouldn't be able to go to Wembley personally but wanted tickets for relatives. That was fair enough, and when I eventually got my allocation Jackie was among the first to be fixed up.

In the build-up to Wembley, Joe Mercer gave us plenty of warnings about our Cup Final fate! Joe, who lived at nearby Hoylake on the Wirral, trained with us and there was a suggestion that Liverpool would ban him from Anfield until after the Final.

Liverpool, though, were too generous to do that. They were not that kind of club. But, for obvious reasons, while still offering the Arsenal skipper every facility, they asked Joe to train on his own in the afternoons.

But we were all very pleased when it was announced shortly before Wembley that Joe had been elected Footballer of the Year by the Football Writers Association. It was an honour richly deserved.

Joe had been a tower of strength to Arsenal all that season and, in fact, during his entire Highbury career and it was a sad day for football when a broken leg, sustained against Liverpool some years later, ended his career.

Following our semifinal win over Everton, we won our next three League games, 2–1 at Manchester City, 1–0 at home to Charlton and 2–0 at Burnley, and I was pleased that I scored in each one of them, including a penalty against Charlton.

Those results started people talking of the possibility of either us or Arsenal doing the League and Cup double because both Cup Finalists were still in contention for the title.

After our run of three successive wins we had five League games left. But the outcome of the first two of them, over Easter, squashed our hopes. In the first of them we had one of those days at St James's Park and were hammered 5–1 by Newcastle, our heaviest defeat since November 1947.

Willie Fagan scored in the first half and we were only 2–1 down at half-time but conceded three second-half goals. Two days later, on Easter Monday, Burnley reversed our win against them on Good Friday by coming to Anfield and beating us 1–0.

With Portsmouth, Wolves, Sunderland and Manchester United all running strongly for the title we realised that any faint hopes we had of the Double had evaporated.

There was further massive disappointment for Liddell five days later when he lined up for Scotland against England at Hampden Park to do battle for a place in the World Cup Finals in Brazil that summer.

Football's world ruling body FIFA had decreed that the top two in the home international tournament would qualify for the World Cup. But Scotland decided they would go to Brazil only as British champions.

The contest drew a Glasgow attendance of 133,300. Scotland needed only a draw to book their ticket to South America, England needed to win. Roy Bentley put the visitors ahead in the second half but when Liddell connected with a headed pass from Arsenal's Alex Forbes – with whom he would come into close and painful contact at Wembley a fortnight later – it seemed certain to bring an equaliser.

Yet as Liddell's right-foot volley arrowed towards the top corner of England's net, goalkeeper Bert Williams flew through the air to claw the ball away with the save of a lifetime. Even when Williams was beaten shortly after by a stinging shot from Willie Bauld, the ball struck the underside of the bar and England survived to win 1–0.

England captain Billy Wright succeeded after the match in persuading his opposite number George Young to plead with the Scottish FA to relent and go to Brazil as British runners-up. The Scottish hierarchy, however, were adamant and the team stayed at home, denying Liddell and his colleagues a place at football's biggest global event, a decision that seems incredible today.

A week later Liddell returned to club duty at champions-to-be Portsmouth where Liverpool lost 2–1 with Ray Minshull, later to become Everton's youth development officer, making his second consecutive appearance in goal deputising for injured Cyril Sidlow.

Arsenal also had a forgettable last pre-Wembley match by losing 3–0 at Wolves, their third defeat in seven League outings since the semifinal, and Liddell revealed:

We read all we could about their performances and noted that, generally, they'd been scoring freely, particularly through Doug Lishman, Peter Goring, in his first season in the Arsenal side, and to a lesser extent, Reg Lewis.

It seemed that these three would be the main danger to our hopes and we discussed endless plans to outwit them. As it happened, Lishman didn't play against us.

Two days before the Final we left for what was supposed to be a secret hide-out at Weybridge but it's surprising how these so-called secrets leak out. This one did, just like the rest. A crowd of autograph hunters met us at Euston station and an equally keen but smaller batch of them was outside our hotel when we arrived!

On the way down from Liverpool, the manager George Kay was far from well and when we got to Weybridge he had to go to bed, where he stayed for most of the time until the morning of the game.

He insisted that he wouldn't miss Wembley but he was far from being fit and well. George devoted himself heart and soul to Liverpool; unfortunately he took everything far too much to heart.

I'm firmly convinced that it was the worry of the weeks before the Final, culminating in the last few days of intense nervous strain, that started the illness which eventually led to George's resignation the following year and his death a few years after that.

We all had the highest regard for George and while he was confined to his room at our pre-Wembley hotel, trainer Albert Shelley took charge of the team preparations until George picked up the reins again on the morning of the match.

Kay's health cannot have been helped by the controversy over Liverpool's Cup Final team selection, which then was still done by the board with the manager involved only in an advisory capacity.

By a split decision the directors, under the chairmanship of Alderman Ronnie Williams, decided to omit Bob Paisley, whose semifinal goal at Maine Road had helped secure Liverpool's Wembley ticket and whose tigerish, ball-winning style was seen by many as essential to Liverpool's cause. He had impressed in Liverpool's win at Arsenal earlier that season – they went on to complete a First Division double over the Highbury club – and Paisley was widely regarded as being ideally suited to negating the skills of Jimmy Logie or dousing the fire of Alex Forbes.

With England centre half Laurie Hughes back in action after missing the semifinal with a broken toe it came down to a choice between Paisley and versatile Bill Jones, also an England international, for the No. 6 shirt. Although Paisley had missed the previous four League games he was fit and available for Wembley and won the vote of four directors. But five opted for Jones and that snub shattered Paisley and almost changed the course of English football.

He confided in Albert Stubbins that he was thinking of asking for a transfer. 'He was at a really low ebb, very despondent,' said Stubbins. 'I told him that I understood how bitterly disappointed he was but advised him not to do anything on a whim.'

To Liverpool's massive good fortune, Paisley swallowed his anguish and stayed at Anfield to become, decades later, the most successful manager English football has known.

But the wisdom or otherwise of his omission from the 1950 Cup Final has been questioned down the years and Liddell reflected:

> It must have been an extremely difficult choice for the directors and manager to make.
>
> It was doubly disappointing for Bob because he'd been a member of the Bishop Auckland team which won the FA Amateur Cup in 1939 and it would have been a notable distinction for him to play in an FA Cup Final, too.
>
> Whether we would have fared any better had Bob played is purely a matter of opinion. His terrier-like tackling might have helped to sway the course of the game and offset the regular upfield excursions of Alex Forbes, who brought the ball into our half so frequently.

Liddell described how the Liverpool squad visited a sun-kissed Wembley the day before the match.

> We weren't allowed to train or have a kick-about but the idea was to see what the pitch was like and get the feel of the place, particularly for those who had never played there.
>
> The turf was its usual lush quality and as we strolled around we saw where our wives, parents and friends would

be sitting – in the open about ten rows from the front. In the brilliant sunshine of the Friday morning that seemed great but not in the weather we got next day!

When I woke up on the Saturday morning I looked out of the hotel window and saw the rain falling in torrents and there were pools of water on the lawns. Those dismal conditions were to be the story of the day.

Snow had fallen earlier in the week as an unseasonal precursor to the Final, although the drabness was somewhat brightened by the Wembley outfit chosen by Liverpool trainer Shelley – comprising red trousers, cream linen jacket and red shirt.

Liverpool, who recalled inside right Kevin Baron after injury-hit Jack Balmer's outing against Portsmouth the previous week, had won the toss for choice of colours necessitated through the red clash. They chose white shirts and black shorts while Arsenal wore gold with white shorts.

Arsenal were the oldest team to appear at Wembley in an FA Cup Final. Their average age was 31, seven of their players had been involved in prewar League football and the Final was the swan song for Denis Compton, whose knee damage spelled the end of the cricketing hero's football career a few weeks from his 32nd birthday. Ellesmere Port-born Arsenal skipper Joe Mercer was approaching 36 while the youngest member of their side, 21-year-old Peter Goring, had made his debut only nine months earlier.

Although Liverpool fancied their chances after beating them twice in the League, there was a warning of Arsenal's attacking potency in that only Sunderland surpassed their total of 79 First Division goals that season.

The teams lined up as follows:

Liverpool: Sidlow; Lambert, Spicer; Taylor, Hughes, Jones; Payne, Baron, Stubbins, Fagan, Liddell.

Arsenal: Swindin; Scott, Barnes; Forbes, L Compton, Mercer; Cox, Logie, Goring, Lewis, D Compton.

After the teams were presented to King George VI, Liverpool captain Phil Taylor won the toss. The action had hardly begun before there was evidence of the impact on the pitch of the incessant downpour, with players sliding yards on the treacherous surface.

But an eleventh-minute challenge by Forbes on his Scotland team-mate Liddell set the controversial tone of the contest. 'Arsenal were ruthless and aimed at confining Liddell,' wrote Percy M Young in his book *Football on Merseyside*. 'He [Liddell], Herculean in endeavour, was surrounded wherever in possession and on one occasion it took four men to prevent his escapes.'

Ronnie Moran, later to captain, coach and twice caretaker-manager Liverpool, was among the Wembley spectators at the end of his first season at Anfield as a teenage amateur. He was emphatic in his view that Forbes went beyond the bounds of fair play in his mission to stop Liddell.

'Arsenal knew that Billy was the big danger to them and they felt that if they stopped him playing, they'd stop Liverpool,' said Moran. 'Forbes, Billy's fellow Scot and a big, red-headed physical player, was given the job of marking him and he didn't half dish it out!

'Forbes caught Billy several times and obstructed him whenever he could. Billy, in typical fashion, kept on getting up and walking away. Forbes, I must stress, was a good right half.

'But he wouldn't have got away today with what he did at Wembley in 1950. He'd have been sent off. And with Forbes gone and Billy in full flow I'm sure we'd have won the game and lifted the Cup for the first time.'

Respected football journalist and author Brian Glanville also questioned the Forbes strategy. 'Would Arsenal have won the Final if Forbes hadn't painfully fouled Liddell, that peerless left winger, early in the game?' he asked. 'Liddell once told me that he couldn't get his jacket on the next day.'

However, referee A Pearce of Bedfordshire chose not to impose any sanction on Forbes and Arsenal full back and Wales captain Wally Barnes leaped to the defence of his team-mate by saying: 'I was sorry to see Alex accused in some press reports of fouling Billy Liddell maliciously.

'On one particular occasion referred to, Alex's knee barely came into contact with Liddell and at no time was it above thigh height. If Alex had really been guilty of a malicious foul the outside left would have been flat out on a stretcher and not flying down the wing again seconds later.'

Liddell, in characteristic, Corinthian manner, refused to point the finger at his compatriot or stoke the controversy.

Far be it from me to impute any malicious motives to Alex. I'm absolutely sure he had none. We'd played together for Scotland and always got on extremely well.

Actually, I thought nothing about the incident at the time, except that it struck me as a rather severe tackle. It was only later that I realised how it had appeared to many onlookers.

Several people told me that it seemed to them that Arsenal had gone out to stop me by hook or by crook, as part of their tactics. I'd hesitate to subscribe to that view. Though the game was a hard one I thought at the time, and later, that it was perfectly fair.

Liverpool's defence was undone in the seventeenth minute, thanks to the creativity of Logie, who had been missing when Arsenal made their pre-match entrance from the tunnel. Logie had sneaked out of the dressing room to telephone for the result of a dog race and joined his team-mates only during the presentation to the king, making his belated arrival by shouting to Forbes, 'It got beat, Alex.'

But for Liverpool it certainly was not a case of better late than never and Liddell applauded Logie's role in Arsenal taking the lead. 'Wee Jimmy set up the opening goal with some neat play,' he said.

'He put Reg Lewis in possession and Reg slid the ball past Cyril Sidlow with an assumption of impudent nonchalance that would have been very amusing had it not been such a blow to us.

'A few minutes later I crossed the ball and it eluded Albert Stubbins by the merest fraction as he tried to head it with only goalkeeper George Swindin to beat. Had we scored then, the game might have taken a dramatic turn. Instead, we went in at half-time a goal down.'

The interval was welcome in the heavy, stamina-sapping conditions – Denis Compton quaffing a large brandy during the break – but Liverpool resumed by penning back Arsenal and went close to equalising.

Liddell, whose legs had been cynically swept from under him by Arsenal right back Laurie Scott as he raced through late in the first half, kept striking fear into the opposition ranks.

'Early in the second half Liddell got the better of Forbes after a long tussle and sent in a beautiful high centre which Swindin misjudged and it went over his head,' said one match report.

'The ball went straight to Jimmy Payne who threw himself forward and connected with a header. The word "goal" was framing on the lips of the crowd but if ever a man made up for a mistake it was Swindin, who flung himself at the ball and just managed to grab it on the line.'

Just as the seventeenth minute of the first half had seen Arsenal take the lead, they virtually assured themselves of lifting the Cup by scoring again in the seventeenth minute of the second period.

Mercer launched the move by finding Denis Compton. He passed to Freddie Cox who beat Eddie Spicer and slipped the ball through to Lewis. The inside left turned and beat Sidlow with a brilliant shot for his second goal of the game.

'We were really up against it after that but we fought tooth and nail in the last twenty minutes and it took the Arsenal defenders all their time to keep us out,' said Liddell. He continued:

They lived up, though, to their 'stonewall' reputation in great style and though Jimmy Payne, Bill Jones and Willie Fagan all went close, the ball just wouldn't go into the net. My view was that over the course of the game we gave almost as good as we got and we didn't disgrace the thousands of Liverpool folk who were there supporting us.

But Arsenal were worthy winners. It would be easy for me to say that if such and such a player had done this or that and we hadn't missed reasonable chances, we might have won. But anyone can be wise after the event and nothing can alter the fact that Arsenal deserved their victory.

Before the game my wife Phyllis and I had hoped that the arrival of our twins Malcolm and David would be a good omen for us at Wembley. But by a strange coincidence, Reg Lewis, whose two goals beat us, was also the father of twins, in his case girls.

As we couldn't both be on the winning side the Goddess of Fortune apparently decided to bestow her smiles on the Arsenal player, as he was the senior parent with Reg's girls aged about eight at that time.

When Joe Mercer climbed the steps to receive the glittering prize from the king, he became the oldest FA Cup Final captain to lift the trophy while Paisley, the man who missed out, had a losers' medal specially struck for him as scant consolation for his twelfth-man watching brief. Liddell added:

On the Saturday night our directors, officials, players and our wives and friends attended a post-match banquet at a London hotel but there was something missing with the absence of the Cup from the top table.

The following day we went on a coach trip to Brighton before returning to Liverpool by train on the Monday afternoon. The reception we received on Merseyside could not have been warmer or more moving if we'd have been coming home as conquering heroes.

Mounted and motor cycle police were out in force marshalling the crowds who, we learned, had gathered hours before we were due. In the city centre thousands of wildly cheering people lined the streets ten deep on either side.

More people lined the two-mile route from the city to our ground, all of them bursting into frantic cheering as the coach came into view. Even the most hardened members of our party were really touched by this amazing expression of loyalty.

When we got to Anfield, where a junior match was in progress, a crowd of around 30,000 gave us a tremendous ovation as the players and officials walked around the pitch.

We then travelled to Liverpool town hall where another 10,000 people were packed in the nearby streets. We were welcomed by the Lord Mayor and Lady Mayoress, Alderman and Mrs Cleary.

The Lord Mayor, a keen football fan, was an Evertonian at heart but his wife's loyalties were with Liverpool! They both attended Anfield and Goodison regularly. All in all it was an unforgettable and moving homecoming after the disappointment of losing at Wembley.

Ironically, the Cup itself did come to Merseyside, brought by Arsenal skipper Mercer to be displayed for a week in the window of his family's grocery business in Wallasey!

But the estimated 100,000 people who turned out across the city to salute the valiant losers had no inkling that they were experiencing a watershed in the history of Liverpool FC. The club and its supporters were destined to suffer the agony of mediocrity and would not get as close to a major prize for another generation.

The 1950s would come and go and the calendar move into the swinging sixties before the Anfield faithful could stage another celebration. Liddell, though, remained steadfastly loyal to the club for whom his talents shone like a beacon in the mist.

Chapter Eight

Loyalty Beyond Price

The phrase 'loyalty bonus' is tossed around in a careless and carefree manner in modern football. Players at one club today and seemingly gone to more remunerative pastures tomorrow are rewarded for being loyal, a grotesque parody of the word's meaning.

Decades before such stupefying parlance had infected Britain's national sport, when the game's finances were on another planet, Billy Liddell performed a massive act of good faith. Instead of receiving a loyalty bonus he gave Liverpool a bonus of loyalty.

Given his inspirational abilities, leadership and goalscoring, Liddell's rejection of a mouthwatering offer to take his talents and boots to South America and, instead, commit himself to Anfield must rank as a landmark decision in Liverpool history. Without the man who led their scoring charts for eight of nine seasons through the 1950s the club might have plunged perilously beyond the redemption inspired by Bill Shankly's arrival at the end of the decade.

Liverpool even faced the prospect of Third Division football in 1954–5 after being relegated from the top flight the previous season. But Liddell hit 30 League goals in that campaign to pull them up to finish eleventh in the Second Division, the lowest League placing in the club's history.

That Liverpool's fate was no worse had much to do with the turn of events in the close season of 1950. That summer saw the end of petrol rationing, the launch of the *Eagle* comic, the first broadcast of *The Archers* on BBC Radio and North Korea's invasion of the South, sparking the three-year long war in which British troops were among the 3.5 million casualties.

The football headlines centred on two stories. One was England's trip to the World Cup Finals in Brazil as Britain's sole representatives, Scotland refusing to go after finishing runners-up in the home championship. Their South American odyssey brought the most sensational result in England's history, a stunning 1–0 defeat by the United States at Belo Horizonte. Lining up in an England side that also included Alf Ramsey, Billy Wright, Tom Finney and Stan Mortensen, was Liddell's Anfield colleague Laurie Hughes, the first Liverpool player to appear in a World Cup match.

Centre half Hughes played in all three England matches – they beat Chile, lost to Spain and failed to qualify from their group – and was rated one of the few English successes. But the fact that he wore his country's No. 5 jersey at all was linked to the other major football story in the summer of 1950 . . . the Bogota Affair.

At a time when English football was still in the cloth-cap era – players who packed stadiums the length and breadth of the land were paid a maximum of £12 during the season and £10 in the summer – came exotic tentacles from Colombia, reaching out to seduce British players with offers that made South American football akin to El Dorado.

Agents acting on behalf of Bogota-based clubs Independiente Santa Fe and Deportivo Los Millonarios approached a batch of leading British players, including Billy Liddell, offering them lucrative deals to go out to play in the Colombian capital.

One of the British agents was Ephraim 'Jock' Dodds, former Everton centre forward and Scotland team-mate of Liddell. Born in Grangemouth, he had spells with Huddersfield, Lincoln City and Sheffield United before joining Blackpool in 1939 to become a prolific wartime scorer, including a double hat trick – one in a record two and a half minutes – in a seven-goal haul in a 15–3 defeat of Tranmere.

Dodds also collected a hat trick in a 5–4 win over England at Hampden Park in April 1942, when Liddell made his international debut, and he signed for Everton in November 1946, scoring 37 goals in 58 senior appearances before starting a second stint at Lincoln in October 1948.

After retiring in 1950 as he approached his 35th birthday, Dodds became an agent for Los Millonarios who, with Bogota neighbours Independiente, were members of a rebel league which had broken away from the Colombian FA and were outlawed by world body FIFA. Dodds fell foul of the Football League and the FA for his activities on behalf of the rebels and eventually walked away from the game to launch a series of business ventures in Blackpool.

English football was indignantly up in arms at this attempt by a pirate organisation to lure away its stars without paying even a transfer fee. But Argentinian professionals, including the legendary Alfredo Di Stefano and his future Real Madrid team-mate Hector Rial, had already exploited the opportunity to acquire riches from the rebels by joining the Colombian gravy train.

As the 1950 World Cup Finals approached, Stoke City centre half Neil Franklin asked the England selectors not to consider him for personal reasons. It was a shock request as Franklin had appeared in 37 consecutive internationals, comprising 27 official postwar England games and ten unofficial matches prior to that.

Liverpool's Bill Jones took over Franklin's No. 5 jersey in England's World Cup warm-up wins in Portugal and Belgium with his Anfield colleague Hughes stepping in when the tournament got under way in Brazil.

By then, Franklin's situation had become clear. He had accepted the Bogota offer and, with his Stoke colleague George Mountford, became the first of the British mercenaries to head off with their families to Colombia, both of them signing for Santa Fe where they teamed up with Argentinian star Rial. The following month the exodus grew when Manchester United's talented and charismatic winger Charlie Mitten also joined Santa Fe after being offered a massive financial package. His decision went down like a lead balloon with his Old Trafford manager Matt Busby.

'We were on tour in the United States when Franklin and Mountford pioneered the Bogota trail so I decided to get my players together to warn them of the consequences of accepting these big money offers,' Busby recalled.

' I told them: "If you accept you are bound to be in trouble with your club, with the Football League and with the FA. In addition, you might find that Bogota is not quite the soccer Mecca you imagine it to be because nobody can guarantee that all these Colombian promises will be fulfilled."

'I wanted to keep my team intact and it was not idle talk, as was proved later when so many of the players who went to Bogota returned to England disillusioned about living conditions there.

'Charlie Mitten, however, was tempted and on the night before we were due to leave for home he told me that he had decided to take the plunge.

'We were enjoying a farewell drink in the Astor Club, New York when Charlie came over and said: "I can't refuse the offer that's been made to me. It's worth a signing-on fee of £2,500, plus £50 a week plus merit bonuses. So I'm going to Bogota."

'It was useless trying to dissuade him, although I tried hard enough. Eventually capitulating, I told Charlie that if he ever came back to England, as I thought he would, he would be finished as far as Manchester United were concerned.'

'Cheeky Charlie', as Mitten was nicknamed, signed for Santa Fe on 23 June 1950 for a financial package worth around £10,000, a fantastic sum in the era of the maximum wage in English football and more than he could have earned in fifteen years at Old Trafford!

Mitten, born in Rangoon, had once been mistakenly selected by Scotland because his father was serving in Burma in the Scots Guards. He made one wartime England appearance and, shortly after his arrival in Bogota, was selected to play for Colombia and helped them beat new World Cup winners Uruguay 3–1!

Shortly after Mitten's departure, two more British players followed – Wales international Roy Paul, then a wing half with

Swansea Town, and Everton full back Jack Hedley, who had been on the losing side against Liddell and Liverpool in the FA Cup semifinal two months earlier.

Paul and Hedley, along with Bobbie Flavell of Hearts, were recruited by Dodds. For them, though, it was a brief South American sojourn. They were back home a week later without kicking a ball for the rebels and complaining of unfair treatment. Continuing their careers in England, Hedley joined Sunderland and Paul, who captained Wales, moved to Manchester City and became a Maine Road star.

Another player well known to Liddell, his fellow Merseyside professional Bill Higgins of Everton, also followed the trail to Bogota. The former Tranmere Rovers amateur who played mainly as a centre forward but also wore Nos. 7, 8 and 11 in his 49 senior appearances for the Goodison club, made his League debut against Liddell in the Goodison derby of September 1946. Higgins joined the Millonarios club to become a team-mate of Di Stefano, who won championship medals in the rebel Colombian league in 1950 and 1952. But Higgins, his wife and young family never settled in South America and within five months they sailed home aboard the *Queen Elizabeth*.

Liddell was one of the prime targets of the Bogota agents. When the offer came, his widow Phyllis recalled, it was a highly lucrative package. 'I think it was estimated to be worth a total of around £12,000, which of course was a huge sum in those days,' she said.

'But in that era of the maximum wage players just accepted the situation as it was. It was something you never really thought about or talked about.

'For various reasons, primarily his loyalty to Liverpool, Billy dismissed the offer from Bogota. Also, our twins were very young, only months old. When news of the approach leaked out nobody wanted Billy to leave Anfield.

'That included our family doctor. It was funny, really. He wanted so much for Billy to stay that he told him one day: "It's not the place to go, Billy. The air in Bogota is very thin. Think of your family's health and wellbeing!"

'But he needn't have worried because Billy's decision not to go underlined what most people knew: that his commitment to Liverpool was a foregone conclusion.'

Liddell himself outlined the details of the package laid before him.

I was contacted by the English agent representing the Bogota clubs. The offer included a signing-on fee of £2,000 with top wages and hefty bonuses.

It was enough to make anyone consider the matter seriously and I certainly gave it a lot of thought. Perhaps if my twin boys had been four or five years old instead of only a few months I would have had an even harder decision to make.

The fact that the boys were so young finally decided me against accepting the offer. Later on, after hearing of the conditions in Colombia, I was jolly glad I'd decided to stay at home.

All the British players who went to Colombia returned home chastened by the experience and banned by the FA and Football League from playing in this country.

The football establishment, which even voiced ridiculous fears that the Bogota Affair threatened the future of the English game, closed ranks to freeze out the so-called mercenaries who, after all, had been guilty of nothing more than seizing an opportunity to gain greater reward for their talents and at the same time safeguarding the financial future for their families.

Their dreams might have disappeared like sand through their fingers but that did not make them the pariahs that they were cast as by the football authorities and some clubs. From today's perspective their reaction seems bizarre and unreasonable.

However, the world moved on, the Bogota Affair slipped from the headlines and the players' bans were eventually lifted. But Franklin, who was suspended for a year, never played for England again.

At the age of 28 Stoke sold him to Hull City for £20,000 in February 1951. He later played for Crewe and Stockport before going into non-League player-management prior to beginning a five-year spell in charge of Colchester United in 1963.

Franklin's former Stoke colleague Mountford joined Queen's Park Rangers in October 1952 while Higgins never played League football again. At the end of 1950, despite interest from Sheffield United and Luton Town, he signed for Bangor City, moved on to Bideford Town and eventually to Canterbury, where he ended his career as player-manager. Higgins and his family settled in the cathedral city where he entered the licensed trade and managed the Imperial Hotel for almost 25 years until his death in March 1981.

Charlie Mitten spent a successful season in Bogota before returning to England because of his family's homesickness. Had he stayed, he could well have joined Di Stefano and Rial in moving to Real Madrid, the two Argentinians being keen enthusiasts of Mitten's wing play.

Instead he was suspended by Manchester United and banned for six months by the English football authorities. But while many of the foreigners lured to Colombia left swiftly, blaming conditions, their relationship with the club or, simply, an inability by them or their families to settle, Mitten fulfilled his year's agreement, a fact even Matt Busby recognised.

'As I anticipated the Bogota emigration did not last long but it is to Charlie Mitten's credit that, unlike some others who went, he honoured his contract before returning to England to look for a job,' said Busby.

'My club could have done with him but they would never condone such a breach of disclipline and that is why Charlie was transferred to Fulham for a substantial sum of money.'

Mitten was also fined £250 and United sold him to Fulham in January 1952. He spent four years at Craven Cottage before becoming player-manager of Mansfield Town prior to taking charge of Newcastle.

Colombia rejoined the family of football nations when FIFA lifted their suspension in 1954, although Bogota's negative overtones for the English game resurfaced sixteen years later when international captain Bobby Moore was falsely accused of stealing an emerald and diamond bracelet in the Colombian capital during England's final preparations for the 1970 World Cup in Mexico.

For loyal Liddell and his colleagues, though, the mission at the start of 1950–1, after the anguish of Liverpool slipping away in the championship and losing the FA Cup Final a few months earlier, was to try to shake off their massive disappointment with success in the new season.

Alas, it was not to be. 'Although we still looked a reasonable side, as things turned out we were on the start of a downward path which, ultimately, led to the Second Division,' said Liddell.

> Sadly, after the Cup Final, our manager George Kay's health deteriorated rapidly, to the deep regret of all who knew him and appreciated his sterling service. He had worn himself out for Liverpool FC and it was no surprise when he resigned in January 1951.
>
> He had been in hospital for several months and was in a long time afterwards, gradually becoming weaker and weaker. The lads who visited him were terribly upset.
>
> At one time George had been a fine figure of a man, close on six feet tall and broadly built. But he lost weight to such an extent that he was less than seven stone when he died in April 1954 at the age of 62.

The 1950–1 season was personally sad for Liddell and his family. His father, James, the former miner who had been such a positive influence on his aspiring son, died in the January, leaving Billy to reflect:

> My mother and father made great sacrifices for me and nobody could have had more considerate parents. My father died shortly after my 29th birthday but I was glad that in his last few years, when he suffered much ill-health, I was able to repay him to some extent for all he had done for me.
>
> Our twins were less than a year old and after my father's death I brought my mother and younger brothers

and sisters to Liverpool, which meant all my family ties
were on Merseyside.

Liverpool's fortunes on the field that season were hampered by a
succession of injuries to Albert Stubbins. Even though the centre
forward scored five in the Football League's 6–3 win over the
Irish League at Blackpool in October, he was restricted to 23
League appearances and six goals for Liverpool, for whom
Liddell was again top scorer with fifteen.

Laurie Hughes, too, was absent for almost half the programme
with cartilage damage which, together with Jack Froggatt's
England emergence and, eventually, Billy Wright becoming
automatic choice, ended his international career.

Apart from four appearances by Joe Cadden, the Scot signed by
Liverpool after playing against them in America, fellow England
international Bill Jones stood in for Hughes at the heart of a
Liverpool defence whose last line also changed.

Wales goalkeeper Cyril Sidlow was displaced by Russell
Crossley, a player he had recommended to Kay in the knowledge
that his own Anfield career was nearing its end. Its close came in
the home clash with Newcastle in November 1950 when Sidlow
conceded four goals in ten minutes spanning the half-time interval
as Liverpool crashed 4–2, after Liddell had put them ahead from
a penalty. Sidlow moved on to New Brighton while his protégé
Crossley, who had gone to Anfield in 1947, shared the Liverpool
goalkeeping job with wartime-signing Charlie Ashcroft for four
seasons.

The winter of 1950 also saw the debut of inside forward Jack
Haigh, recruited from Gainsborough Trinity. But like Cadden,
who made only five senior appearances for Liverpool before
joining Grimsby in June 1952, Haigh's Anfield career was a short
one, embracing only eleven games and three goals prior to his
£4,000 move to Scunthorpe in August 1952.

Liverpool suffered an alarming run of ten games without a win
from September to early December 1950, a winter of discontent
which left their fans fearing relegation. Liddell, though, brought
some smiles back to the Kop faithful when he restored Liverpool

to winning ways with the game's only goal against Chelsea at Anfield, on a day when the side was stripped of injured captain Phil Taylor, Stubbins and Jones.

Under the headline 'Liddell Escaped Once – Scored', the *News of the World*, who were advertising Christmas trees for 3s 6d, reported: 'In the 70th minute Liddell for once shook off Bathgate and from the edge of the penalty area won the game with a mighty right-foot shot which touched the underside of the bar before flashing into the net.'

The win left Liverpool in mid-table on nineteen points from as many games and seven points off the bottom, a position filled by neighbours Everton who drew 3–3 that afternoon at Aston Villa. Everton ended the season propping up the First Division and were relegated, but Liverpool managed to lift themselves into ninth place. They could have finished higher but for two defeats and a draw in their final three games, the last of them a 3–1 reverse at new champions Tottenham.

Liverpool's FA Cup experience, however, was dismal. The previous season's finalists crashed out at the first hurdle in a shock 3–1 defeat at Norwich, the last Cup tie of Kay's managerial reign. A planned eve-of-match theatre visit by Liverpool at their Great Yarmouth base was cancelled because of a flu epidemic.

But it did not prevent them catching a cold at Carrow Road against opponents leading the Third Division South and unbeaten in 22 successive matches. After a goalless first half, thanks to some defiant goalkeeping by Cup debutant Crossley, Norwich hit three goals in the last 27 minutes. A late reply by Jack Balmer did nothing more than make the scoreline marginally better than on Liverpool's previous Cup visit to Norwich, a 3–0 defeat at the same third-round stage in 1937. 'Losing at Norwich, after playing at Wembley only nine months earlier, was a real come-down for us,' admitted Liddell.

There were further disappointments for Liverpool as Kay's tenure in charge ended bleakly. A brace of goals from Jimmy McIntosh sent them plunging to a 2–0 home defeat by struggling Everton. A week later they lost 1–0 at Charlton thanks to a foreign player whose signing on amateur forms was a masterstroke by the London club's boss, Jimmy Seed.

Although Swedish striker Hans Jeppson had captained his country in the World Cup the previous summer, after scoring on his debut in a win over England in 1949, he was in London studying business when Seed swooped.

When Jeppson signed for Charlton on 6 January 1951 they were battling against relegation, but when he left twelve weeks later, at the end of March, they were safe. He scored nine goals in eleven games, including winning strikes against Sheffield Wednesday (on his debut), Liverpool and Chelsea. He also hit two in a 3–2 win over Wolves and four in a 5–1 friendly match win over West Ham and his exploits earned him a lucrative move to Italian club Atalanta, for whom he turned professional for an £18,000 signing-on fee.

In English football, too, money made the front-page as well as back-page headlines. Sunderland broke the transfer record by splashing out £30,000 to sign centre forward Trevor Ford from Aston Villa but it was surpassed within months.

Just before the March deadline Sheffield Wednesday paid Notts County £34,500 for Jackie Sewell, which made him literally worth his weight in gold at 1951 prices. There was no glittering outcome for Wednesday, though. They were relegated on goal difference.

Anfield hopes were centred on the new era ushered in by the March appointment of Don Welsh as Liverpool's new manager. 'Following George Kay's resignation the directors were assisted by trainer Albert Shelley in selecting the team until Don's arrival,' Liddell recalled.

'Don had been a popular wartime guest player at Anfield as well as an outstanding Charlton Athletic star for many years. After giving up playing he became manager of Brighton, who were then in the Third Division South.'

Liverpool did at least manage to extract some revenge over Arsenal for their FA Cup Final defeat a year earlier when they went to Highbury for a League fixture in April 1951. Albert Stubbins recalled it as a game that brought great personal satisfaction for Liddell.

Said Stubbins: 'Alex Forbes was possibly the oustanding player of the 1950 Final even though he kicked Billy about a bit at Wembley – and that's an understatement! The next time we went to Highbury, Forbes came into our dressing room before kickoff.

'He said to Billy, who was a Scotland colleague of his: "I've got an autograph book here, Willie, which I'd like you to sign. You'd better sign it now because we won't be speaking later!"

'The inference was that he was going to give Billy another hard time. But Billy didn't react or make any comment. He wasn't the sort of man you could take a rise out of. Billy simply smiled, signed the book and gave it back to Forbes.

'An excitable or anxious sort of person might have been put off his whole game through something like that. But not Billy. No way. He was totally unruffled. He went out and gave his usual high-class display and we won 2–1.'

Although the season brought Liddell little joy at club level, his fortunes with Scotland were much brighter, despite his country's first home defeat by a foreign nation through Ernst Melchior's goal in Austria's 1–0 win at Hampden Park in December.

Scotland swept to the home championship, winning all three matches. Liddell scored in a 3–1 win over Wales in Cardiff, played his part in a 6–1 rout of Northern Ireland at Hampden and scored again in a thrilling conquest of England at Wembley.

Liddell and England's Wilf Mannion accidentally collided and clashed heads in the eleventh minute of the Wembley duel. Both players needed treatment. Liddell managed to resume but Mannion was unable to continue and was stretchered off suffering from what proved to be a fractured cheekbone.

England's ten men fought valiantly – even taking the lead through debutant Harold Hassall – before goals from Bobby Johnstone and Lawrie Reilly put the Scots in front. Liddell, shaking off the effects of his painful early collision to produce a menacing display on the left flank, swooped to score Scotland's third after Bert Williams dropped a Billy Steel cross.

It was a goal that proved decisive with England reducing the arrears through a superbly lobbed goal from Tom Finney, but

Scotland resisted the home side's grandstand finish to secure a 3–2 victory.

The following month Liddell left with Liverpool on an eye-opening end-of-season tour of Sweden in which they played five games, winning four and losing one, the Scotland star scoring five goals.

But it was the lifestyle that made an impression on him. 'Although the war had been over five years, food in England in 1951 was not as plentiful or varied as it had been in pre war days and what we found in Sweden made everybody's mouth water,' said Liddell.

We flew to Sweden on a charter aircraft, re-fuelling en route, and when we sat down for our first meal in our Stockholm hotel it was at a long table literally loaded from one end to the other with the most appetising food you could imagine.

There were at least a dozen different kinds of tinned fish – sardines, anchovies, herrings, smoked salmon, crab, lobster and so on – as many different varieties of cold sausage, meat pastes of all kinds, boiled ham curled up in little rolls, tongue, chicken, various cold meats, meat pies and a host of other things.

We all tucked in with gusto and, when the table had been more or less cleared, sat back and said what a splendid meal we'd had. But that was only the appetiser, the *smorgasbord*! Then the real meal began, starting with soup, fish and then a fifteen-minute rest.

During that time the waiters handed round cigarettes for those who smoked, followed by steak and chips with mushrooms and ending with fruit salad and ice cream, cheese and biscuits and coffee.

We discovered that the Brazilian team Flamengo, said to be the richest club in South America at that time, were also staying in our hotel and they came to our first tour match against AIK, which we won 7–0.

Before the game the Brazilians, who were on a seven-match Scandinavian tour, gave us a glimpse of their skills with some exhibition stuff. They could do almost anything with the ball except make it talk! Some of their feats put them in the music hall juggling class.

However, when it came to competitive football they weren't quite so outstanding, as we saw when they played Malmö. Their skill was unquestioned but when it came to finishing off their moves, they were not nearly as good. Moves to fix a game between us and Flamengo came to nothing because of the commitments of the two clubs.

We played Malmö two days later and our satisfaction in winning 4–1 was spoiled by Eddie Spicer's ill luck in breaking his leg early in the second half. He was taken to hospital and was well cared for.

A young lady biochemist at the hospital, who was from Merseyside and whose father had been a lifelong Liverpool supporter, saw to it that Eddie had plenty of company, bringing in anyone who could speak English to talk to him.

Hilding Albrekson, the former Sweden tennis player and chairman of the tennis section of the AIK club, was so concerned about the possibility of Eddie having to be left behind when we were due to move on to Norrköping that he wanted to take him to his own home, engage a qualified nurse to look after him and fly with him back to London!

As things turned out his wonderful offer was not necessary because Eddie's break was a simple fracture and he was able to return home by himself the day we left for Norrköping which, as the country's cotton capital, was the Manchester of Sweden – but very different from the Lancashire city.

Most of the main streets were tree-lined – like Southport's famous Lord Street – and there were scores of flower beds everywhere, all ablaze with masses of tulips. Another difference was the complete absence of smoke.

My hotel room was on the seventh floor, high above all other buildings, with a view extending about twenty miles in all directions. And over the whole of that area there was not a solitary plume of smoke anywhere. That was what struck me most forcibly.

Our visit was made even sweeter because not only did we beat Norrköping 1–0 before a crowd close on 20,000 but we learned that it was the first time the home team had been beaten by any English touring side in thirteen postwar matches.

It was a good win for us. Norrköping were an excellent team with two Swedish internationals in their ranks in Lindberg and Holmquist. From there we moved on to Gothenburg and won 5–3 against a team representing the city's three major clubs. Former Swedish international Sven Rydell told me that Liverpool were the best postwar team he had seen in his country.

Our hopes of making it five wins out of five were dashed in our last match, a second game against Malmö. This time they beat us 2–1 but it was a game I felt we should have won.

The launch of the 1951–2 season, Welsh's first full campaign in charge, came as the country celebrated the Festival of Britain, which ran from May to September, and also came to terms with some ground-breaking humour with the first BBC broadcasts of *The Goon Show*.

The admission charge to watch League matches was raised by threepence to 1s 6d and clubs also flirted with floodlit football, even though the FA refused to sanction them for first-class matches. On 19 September, Arsenal beat Israeli side Hapoel Tel Aviv 6–1 in a floodlit friendly at Highbury, believed to be the first official game under lights since 1878.

But it proved to be a less than illuminated season for Liverpool.Three successive Liverpool wins spanning late August and the start of September were followed by five matches without a victory.

The general election in late October saw Winston Churchill defeat Clement Attlee and return as Prime Minister and a 26-year-old candidate called Margaret Roberts fail to win a seat. Some 28 years later, as Margaret Thatcher, she would follow Churchill's path to No. 10.

Hours after the election Liverpool and their fans suffered a painful result of their own when West Brom went to Anfield and won 5–2, ramming in three second-half goals. It was the start of an eleven–game First Division run which brought Liverpool only three wins and over the season they collected only twelve victories, split equally home and away. But nineteen draws – then a top flight record – dispelled any relegation threat as Liverpool finished a mediocre eleventh. Liddell was disappointed.

Our League displays that winter were undistinguished. The team spirit of a few years earlier seemed to have evaporated and we were unable to win anything like the usual proportion of games at Anfield.

The crowd gave us their normal solid encouragement but it didn't have the customary effect. A newcomer to the team that season was right winger Brian Jackson, signed from Leyton Orient while still in the Army, with Don Woan leaving Anfield in part exchange.

I was still playing principally at outside left but Albert Stubbins continued to be plagued by a succession of injuries and made only thirteen appearances, his place mainly filled by Jack Smith, a Birkenhead lad who'd been a professional only a few months when he was drafted into the team.

Willie Fagan was now at the veteran stage and at the end of the season, in which he made only three appearances, he left for Weymouth as player-manager. Jack Balmer played only twice but with nobody of the same calibre to take the places of these three stalwarts of the early postwar years it was not surprising that we were slipping.

Yet the Liddell magic was still evident. His goal in Liverpool's match at Huddersfield on 29 December 1951 was hailed by sportswriters as 'the shot of a lifetime'. The *Liverpool Echo* reported:

When Jimmy Payne was brought down just outside the penalty area, the Huddersfield defenders formed a wall expecting the usual Liddell drive. But Liverpool changed their plans. Liddell hung back and Kevin Baron calmly rolled the ball to him.

The Scot took a few short steps forward and the ball flew like lightning into the Terriers' net. It hit a stanchion and rebounded as far as the penalty spot. Not a Huddersfield player had time to move. Goalkeeper Mills looked bewildered and the crowd stood in stunned silence.

The home side had scored earlier through Jim Glazzard and it was that man Liddell who played a leading role in the goal that eventually took Liverpool to a 2–1 victory. This time his shot struck Len Quested and dropped for Payne, who thumped the ball into the net.

The nation was plunged into mourning less than two months later with the death in February of King George VI, a popular monarch whose passing prompted worldwide public grief.

But as life gradually regained normality, the return to action of Stubbins prompted a remarkable response on Merseyside when his comeback in a reserve match against Everton after a five-month absence drew a crowd of 18,511 to Anfield in February 1952.

The following month Stubbins was restored to first-team duty and got back on the scoresheet at West Brom when Liverpool recovered from 3–0 down with less than half an hour to go to prise a point. Liddell, Bob Paisley and Stubbins all scored between the 62nd and 64th minutes.

A week later Liverpool won their first home League game for almost six months with a 3–0 defeat of Newcastle, Stubbins striking twice against his former club. 'My first was a shot from a tight angle into the roof of the net and my second was from close range after a goalmouth scramble,' recalled Stubbins.

'Only a great save by Newcastle keeper Bobby Simpson, when he pushed my left-foot shot round the post, denied me a hat trick. I was up against the great Frank Brennan that day and he was the first centre half to congratulate me when I scored. He came over to me and said: "Well played." I never forgot that.'

In the FA Cup that year Liverpool beat Workington and Wolves at home before losing at Burnley in the fifth round. For the third successive season Liddell was top scorer with nineteen goals from 40 League appearances. It was a magnificent feat for a winger, especially as no other Liverpool player even reached double figures in the scoring chart.

Little wonder that the manager of every opposing club began his team talk with ideas on how to stop 'The Flying Scot'. In contrast, Liddell was hardly a tactically driven player and was prompted to observe:

Much is said and written about tactical planning in football and pre-match schemes to wipe out the opposition's hopes. Without detracting from the value of some of them much of it is just eye-wash.

But, for once, in the Cup tie against Wolves, which drew Anfield's record attendance of 61,905, a tactical plan paid off handsomely. When our team was announced my name was, as usual, at outside left and Cyril Done's at centre forward.

We knew that whatever schemes Wolves might contrive would be based on that formation. But Cyril and I received our instructions and when we lined up for the kickoff Cyril was on the left wing and I was in the middle.

It didn't seem anything major but I think it temporarily upset Wolves' plans and made them reconsider what to do to clamp down on our attack. And it was during the crucial few minutes when they were readjusting that we did the damage.

I don't know what Billy Wright's thoughts were when he saw me lining up at centre forward but people told me afterwards that he had a puzzled look! The surprise paid off, for Bob Paisley scored a goal in the first few minutes which was just the spur we wanted.

When Cyril Done got a second soon after, I was doubly pleased because it was my idea he should be in the team. Our plan had been discussed in the week by our chairman, George Richards, Don Welsh and myself.

Another player's name was mentioned as a subject for the switch but I suggested that Cyril was better suited for it. It was one of the very few times in my career that I was asked for my opinion on team selection.

Although Wolves pulled a goal back through Jimmy Mullen after 72 minutes Liverpool were worthy 2–1 winners of a game that thrilled the record crowd – paying record gate receipts of £6,607 – and in which Liverpool's tactical masterstroke earned fulsome praise from the press.

The *Empire News* declared in a big back-page headline: 'Liddell switch a Welsh inspiration'. Match reporter Tony Stevens enthused: 'Cup hunter Don Welsh is a manager who believes in pre-match planning. Stan Cullis thought of telling Billy Wright to mark Billy Liddell so Don went one better and produced a winner.

'Liddell, in the No. 11 jersey, lined up at centre forward with Done on the left wing and Welsh's one-man band immediately called the tune. Before centre half Chatham's look of surprise had died and Wright had rearranged his plans Liverpool struck with the speed of cobras and were two up in nine minutes.'

The *Sunday Chronicle* was equally effusive. Under the heading 'Two "Wrongs" Made Them Right' the paper reported: 'Liddell at centre forward gave Liverpool terrific punch at the start of the game. Liddell gave a pass to Williams and turned the return centre towards Paisley, who shot through a crowd of players and into the net.

'Then they got a second goal when a centre by Balmer from the right misled Chatham and Done's shot, which first struck the forearm of goalkeeper Parsons, bounced into the back of the net.'

But there was to be no repeat of the journey to Wembley two years earlier. Despite toning-up preparations of brine baths and massage at a Cheshire hotel, Liverpool lost 2–0 at Burnley in round five. Bill Morris put the Turf Moor side ahead after only two minutes and former Anfield player Les Shannon sealed his former club's fate just before the interval.

The first full season of Britain's new Elizabethan era, the 1952–3 campaign, failed to change Anfield fortunes. The world witnessed the dawn of the jet age, with BOAC's first passenger service between London and Johannesburg taking to the sky at Heathrow.

There was, however, no takeoff for Liverpool. In a year which saw curtain up on Agatha Christie's record-running show *The Mousetrap*, the club were about to begin a long period on the backstage of English football.

As Al Martino's 'Here In My Heart' became the first No. 1 in the newly created record charts, Liverpool planted hopes that they were also bound for a high position by posting seven wins, three draws and only two defeats in their opening twelve games.

Liverpool were still without injured Laurie Hughes but Eddie Spicer made his comeback after a year's absence in their first match – a 1–1 draw at Preston – which was memorable for the fact that those usually clinical finishers Liddell and Tom Finney both failed to score from penalties. Liddell sent his kick wide, one of only two occasions in which he missed the target in his 44 penalties in senior peacetime football. He twice hit a post, had four kicks saved and scored from 36.

Charlie Ashcroft's save from Finney was to prove hugely significant eight months later when Preston and Arsenal topped the First Division, each with 54 points and identical records of 21 wins, twelve draws and nine defeats. Yet Preston lost out on the title by a tenth of a goal – a goal average of 1.41 to Arsenal's 1.51.

Liverpool were to have no such lofty issues to concern them. Anfield aspirations evaporated in a dismal 14–game run between October and January which brought only one win. Amid this gloom, Liddell and his colleagues also found themselves lost in a Northeast fog in the FA Cup.

They were drawn against lowly Gateshead of the Third Division North, a tie for which Roy Saunders made his debut at left half, behind Liddell, in place of injured Bob Paisley.

Referee F B Coultas allowed the game to go ahead at Redheugh Park on a glue-pot pitch in swirling fog, although the 15,000 spectators, like the players and the press, could see only fleeting glimpses of the action.

Gateshead had what they claimed was a legitimate goal disallowed in the 73rd minute but the reprieve for Liverpool was short-lived. Six minutes from the end Ian Winters met a corner and headed past Russell Crossley to secure a shock home victory and inflict one of the most embarrassing defeats in Liverpool history.

'If you asked me what took place in that game I couldn't tell you,' Liddell admitted.

> The pitch was as bad as any I ever played on. It was almost like a ploughed field in places and it was impossible to play decent football.
>
> Not that I'm advancing that as an excuse. Gateshead fought hard and deserved to win but I couldn't tell you what took place for the simple reason that the thick fog made it impossible to see beyond 40 yards.
>
> A couple of miles away at St James's Park the game between Newcastle and Swansea was abandoned after eight minutes. It was a farce playing under such conditions. But they were the same for both sides and certainly had nothing to do with our defeat.

Liverpool's exit coincided with Isthmian League side Walthamstow Avenue's elimination of Stockport to become the first amateur club to reach the fourth round since Corinthians in 1929. Gateshead went on to reach the quarterfinal, in which they lost to Bolton. It was their last taste of glory before being voted out of the Football League in favour of Peterborough seven years later.

Just three weeks after Liverpool had said an embarrassing goodbye to their FA Cup hopes for yet another season there was to be a shock and sad farewell to a grand lady of the sea. Merseyside and the world at large were stunned by a fire which destroyed the famous liner *Empress Of Canada*, burned out in her berth at Gladstone Dock. The cause of the fire was said to be a discarded smouldering cigarette-end in a cabin and the remains of the vessel were eventually broken up in an Italian shipyard.

Liverpool's task was to cling onto their top-flight status in a season that had seen the emergence of winger Alan A'Court, forward Louis Bimpson and full back Ronnie Moran as well as Roy Saunders. Along the way they conceded ten goals in their two meetings with future champions Arsenal, who won 5–1 at Anfield and 5–3 in the Highbury return in April, a result that began an alarming closing sequence for Liverpool. They had lost four of their previous five games before going into their final fixture, at home to Chelsea, still facing relegation, as Liddell recalled.

When we came to that last game it was a toss-up who would go down with Derby County, who were already doomed. It rested between us, Stoke City, Chelsea – who had another match to play – Manchester City and Sheffield Wednesday.

But if ever the Anfield supporters helped their team win a game it was that day. We'd taken only three points from the previous nine matches – six of which had been away – and although our determination to make a fight of it was strong enough our confidence was not exactly at its highest level.

We were without Albert Stubbins, who'd played only five times all season, and in attack we had Sammy Smyth, a Northern Ireland international who had been signed from Stoke for £12,000, and Louis Bimpson, a big, bustling lad who was always a great trier.

Louis got our second goal against Chelsea late in the game after Bill Jones had put us ahead in the first half. Ever ready to fill any breach Bill had been switched from full back to inside forward. Our 2–0 win took us to the 36-point mark and the safety of seventeenth place. Stoke, beaten 2–1 at home by Derby, went down – with Derby.

We struggled desperately for points away from Anfield that season, winning only four and drawing two of our away games. It was our home displays which saved us from relegation, even though they were nothing very brilliant at times. But it was a lucky escape for us.

Liverpool's luck, though, was about to run out.

Chapter Nine

Into the Wilderness

The jaws of relegation opened and finally consumed Liverpool in 1954 to confirm the worst forecasts of pundits and public alike, who accused the club of lacking foresight and making inadequate transfer market investment in the team.

Their great star Liddell had performed outstanding feats in the previous four seasons when, despite playing as a winger, had been top scorer each year with League totals of eighteen, fifteen, nineteen and thirteen goals respectively. But the unfair workload of carrying the team's salvation and the passions of the Kop was too much of a burden even for his talented shoulders as he was shuffled betweeen four of the five forward positions in 1953–4, scoring only seven goals.

Supporters vented their spleen in the letters columns of the newspaper sports pages, with one correspondent declaring: 'I am sorry for Liddell pulling his best out with four inferior forwards.'

Liddell's brilliant versatility was such that it prompted a remarkable situation that reflected the bizarre nature of the directors picking the team, a procedure which persisted at Anfield until 1959.

Peter Robinson, recruited from Brighton to become Liverpool secretary in 1965 and later their long-serving chief executive, revealed: 'Apparently the board met one night to select the side and after switching players here and there they named the team.

'It was only after it had been announced that they realised, to their horror, that they had accidentally left out Liddell. Because he could play anywhere they'd forgotten to put him in a position and the directors hurriedly had to go back and pick the team all over again, this time with Liddell included.'

There was a massively more significant consequence of this selection process, one which delayed the Anfield revolution under Bill Shankly by eight years and probably robbed Liddell of the chance to conclude his illustrious career in the top flight of English football under the management of his fellow Scot. After the retirement of George Kay in 1951, and prior to Don Welsh's arrival, the Liverpool directors, alerted by Shankly's management style at Carlisle, invited him to Anfield and asked him to take over.

'They sent for me and offered me the manager's job,' said Shankly. 'The only snag was that the manager didn't pick the team. The directors did that. So I didn't take it. I said to them: "If I don't pick the team what am I manager of?" I went back to Exchange Station and got the train home.'

So instead of taking an express back to the peaks of English football, Liverpool chugged down a branch line to a destination of relegation and eight seasons languishing in the old Second Division.

Yet Liddell's quality remained constant, his unselfish contribution of class and consistency making him a public idol of the highest esteem. Prior to buying a car, Liddell would travel by public transport. The impact of coming face to face with their hero remains a cherished memory for a host of his admirers. One of them, former sports journalist Paul O'Brien, recalled in a letter to the *Liverpool Echo* in March 2003: 'We lived off Edge Lane Drive and one of my boyhood thrills was to see the great Billy Liddell on the top deck of a 6a tram travelling from his Bowring Park home to training at Anfield.

'He used to change to the 26/27 at Durning Road. He was always chatting to the Reds fans, who were not slow to grab the chance to sit next to a soccer hero.'

In May and June of 1953, Liverpool made another tour of the United States and Canada with Liddell again proving a trans-atlantic star, as he had been five years earlier. He scored thirteen goals in Liverpool's ten games, including a hat trick against Chicago All Stars, and his frequent appearances at centre forward were a harbinger of things to come at Anfield.

Sadly for Liverpool the extension of their unbeaten record on North American soil – they won nine and drew one match, against Young Boys Berne, in which Liddell scored the equaliser – was in stark contrast to their fortunes in the forthcoming domestic season.

The summer of 1953, which saw Elizabeth II crowned as queen on 2 June as news came through that Hillary and Tensing had conquered Everest, saw the departure from Anfield of Albert Stubbins. He returned with his family to his native Tyneside where he played for a spell with non-League club Ashington prior to a coaching stint in America, before going into football journalism.

Even though Sammy Smyth and Louis Bimpson top-scored with thirteen goals each in the 1953–4 campaign, the club's failure to adequately replace Stubbins, and the likes of Fagan and Balmer, took its toll. Indeed, since the £12,500 signing of Stubbins in 1946 the only transfer expenditure, other than nominal fees, comprised £7,000 on Ken Brierley from Oldham in February 1948, £6,500 to sign Brian Jackson from Leyton Orient in November 1951 and the £12,000 paid to Stoke for Smyth.

That was a total of just over £25,000 in more than six years, at a time when the British transfer record for a single player was the £34,000 Sheffield Wednesday had paid Notts County for Jackie Sewell in March 1951 and when deals of £20,000 and upwards were frequent.

And despite regular crowds topping 45,000 the club's reluctance to open the purse strings extended to the stadium itself, which was becoming dilapidated and prompted Shankly to describe it as a 'slum' when he was belatedly appointed manager in December 1959 and learned there was not even piped water to flush some of the toilets!

But in midwinter of 1953, when the relegation writing was on the wall, boardroom panic set in and Liverpool suddenly splashed £37,000 on four players in a ten-day December spree. Half back or centre half Geoff Twentyman cost £10,000 from Carlisle, goalkeeper Dave Underwood £7,000 from Watford, while inside forward John Evans and full back Frank Lock arrived for a combined £20,000 from Charlton on Christmas Day, making their debuts 24 hours later in a goalless home duel with West Brom.

In February another new face arrived, defender Tom McNulty costing £7,000 from Manchester United. But it was all too late. The five newcomers were unable to salvage Liverpool's cherished top-flight status which they had enjoyed for almost half a century.

Their 3–1 Wednesday night win over Portsmouth, with Liddell scoring the third goal, was a deceptive launch to the season for the Anfield faithful. Liverpool lost five and drew three of their next eight games, managed only five wins by the turn of the year and lost their first fourteen away games, including a 1–0 third-round FA Cup defeat at Bolton.

Their first away win did not come until 7 April – a 2–0 win at Manchester City – and, added to Liverpool's three-month run without an away win from the previous season, it set an unwanted all-time club record of 24 games, spanning fourteen months, without a win on opposition soil.

The season also saw Liverpool's longest-ever run without a League win, a dismal fourteen-match sequence. After beating Blackpool 5–2 on 5 December their next win did not come until 3 April, a 4–3 victory over Sunderland, and the club record 97 League goals they conceded that season was the worst in all divisions of the English and Scottish Leagues.

'My memories of 1953–4 are all disappointing ones,' was Liddell's unsurprising verdict. 'For some time, in the words of the press, "the writing had been on the wall" at Anfield. Our steady descent over the previous five years in the League table had been causing considerable anxiety to the club's directors as well as supporters.' He continued:

We had progressively declined from eighth place in 1950 to ninth, eleventh and then seventeenth, and in the absence of strengthening signings it seemed that we would be faced with an even harder struggle to keep out of the Second Division.

Letters poured into the newspapers proposing all sorts of remedies. Everybody had ideas as to who should be signed and listed star players the club should have gone out and signed.

The Liverpool board had made innumerable attempts to sign players the previous season and continued to do so in the autumn of 1953 though it was not until December that they had any luck.

Until then we'd been doing fairly well in our home games – apart from an early 5–1 defeat by Preston – but we were having a shocking time away. Although the forward line was scoring more goals than the majority of teams in the bottom half of the table, the defence were conceding far too many.

It became increasingly obvious not only that the rearguard must be strengthened as quickly as possible but that if really outstanding and experienced stars could not be bought, the club would have to go for the next best.

But before any newcomers arrived we were beaten 5–1 at Portsmouth. This, after conceding those five against Preston, five at Chelsea and six at Charlton, to say nothing of a couple of fours and threes, obviously made Don Welsh cast around for some method of plugging the gaps.

I didn't play at Portsmouth due to a pulled muscle but the manager asked me how I felt about playing at full back in the next game – against Manchester United at Old Trafford. It was to be the start of a sad sequence of events.

Once or twice in the past I'd played at full back for part of a game when somebody was injured and, from what I'd been told, had shaped fairly well. But while I was always ready to take up any position which was to Liverpool's advantage I had no desire to become a full back permanently.

I told Don how I felt and that if he wanted me to play there, I'd do my best but I didn't think it was a good move from the club's point of view. Although he referred to it once or twice more I was relieved to see my name at outside left as usual when the team was posted on the dressing-room notice board.

Yet, as things turned out, I ended up playing left back for 75 minutes of the game. The match at Old Trafford marked the debuts of two of the new signings, goalkeeper Dave Underwood and Geoff Twentyman, who was selected at left half.

When Dave ran out to collect the ball early in the first half he crashed in a heap with Eddie Spicer and United's centre forward Tommy Taylor. Eddie didn't get up on his feet like the other two and, cruelly, it turned out that he had broken his leg in the collision.

It was the second time he had suffered that misfortune. But, unlike his break on the tour of Sweden three years earlier, this injury ended his career prematurely. Dave, naturally, was most upset at what happened to Eddie but it was nobody's fault. It was an accident. Sheer bad luck.

I was captaining the side that day and thought that instead of shuffling the team around too much, it would be simpler if I took over at left back after Eddie had been carried off. So, for a sad reason, I did play full back after all – and our ten men lost 5–1.

As well as the club's five new signings, Barry Wilkinson, then an eighteen-year-old lad in the RAF and previously with Bishop Auckland, made his senior debut during the season and Alan Arnell, who was in the Army, came in for a few games at centre forward before I was asked to take over there for a time.

Despite the changes we couldn't get away from the relegation zone and with Manchester City, Sunderland and the two Sheffield clubs showing signs of improvement our position became increasingly precarious.

Middlesbrough were also in trouble and we sealed their fate by taking all four points by winning both our Easter games against them. But we were destined to accompany them into the Second Division, our relegation being assured when we lost 3–0 at Arsenal on 10 April.

The game had another sad feature because Arsenal skipper Joe Mercer, who still trained with us and was a popular figure with our lads, broke his leg and had to hang up his boots. Arsenal had won the championship the previous season when Joe had been advised to retire at the top.

The call of football, however, had been too strong for Joe who, at 39, felt he could give his club another season of good service. He was only a few matches from the end of the League programme when he played against us and collided with his team-mate Joe Wade in repelling one of our attacks.

It happened after about half an hour and I was only a couple of yards away from the incident. Even if I hadn't heard the ominous crack of bone, I'd have realised from the agonised expression on Joe's face that he'd been seriously hurt.

Just like Eddie Spicer's misfortune this was another pure accident and even as Joe was being carried off, I think he must have realised that was the last time he would play League football.

Despite the pain he was suffering Joe courageously lifted himself on one elbow on the stretcher and waved to the Highbury crowd. I also overheard him telling Joe Wade not to worry. That was typical of him.

Two days after Liverpool's fateful Arsenal defeat – 'The visitors were like clay in the hands of the potter,' wrote one reporter – a new sound emerged as Bill Haley recorded 'Rock Around The Clock', Britain's first million-selling disc, featuring in fourteen films and recorded in 35 languages.

For Liverpool, though, the top flight clock that had ticked at Anfield since 1905 finally stopped as they finished bottom with a meagre 28 points although, remarkably, their 68 goals scored was seventeen more than tenth-placed Cardiff who provided one of Liddell's enduring memories.

The Welsh club were the visitors in Liverpool's penultimate home game that season. When their goalkeeper Ron Howells injured a hand, full back, Alf Sherwood went in goal and soon found himself facing a Liddell penalty. But the Wales defender acrobatically saved the spot kick and a shot from the rebound to ensure that Cardiff went home with a 1–0 win and Liddell's praise for their stand-in keeper. 'It was the finest penalty save I ever saw,' said Liddell.

'If Alf had not been such a splendid full back I'm sure he could have held down a place with any team in goal. He performed as though he'd spent all his life there!'

Compounding the relegation agony for Liverpool was the return of city rivals Everton to the First Division, the Goodison club being promoted after three seasons in the Second.

The fact that Everton's promotion maintained Merseyside's unique record of staging top-flight football ever since the League's formation was scant consolation for Liverpool who also mourned the passing of George Kay who died in April, following his long illness, at the age of 62.

Four men who had played under Kay's management ended their Anfield playing careers as Liverpool slipped into Division Two – captain Phil Taylor, Bob Paisley and Bill Jones were given free transfers while the unfortunate Spicer succumbed to injury. Taylor and Paisley both joined the backroom staff with Jones also continuing to serve the club in a scouting role after a spell as player-manager of Ellesmere Port Town.

'There is going to be some hard thinking in the boardroom,' wrote Bob Prole in his *Liverpool Echo* column under the pseudonym 'Ranger', as he took stock of Liverpool's demise. 'On this form the Anfielders have much reconstruction to do.'

Sadly for the Kop faithful, the board failed to put the building blocks in place. Roger Bannister had just run the first sub-four-minute mile but there was to be no sprint back to the top flight for Liverpool, no quick fix.

'We were in a poor way,' declared Laurie Hughes, who took over the captaincy from Taylor as Liverpool embarked on Second Division life in 1954–5. 'Great players had left and weren't replaced,' he added.

Over the next six years most of the players recruited, while honest, hard-working professionals, were neither expensive nor inspired signings. The arrivals over that period comprised: inside forward Antonio (Tony) Rowley from Birmingham for an undisclosed fee; centre half Alex South (from Brighton, £5,000); right back John Molyneux (from Chester, £4,500); defender Dick White (from Scunthorpe, fee undisclosed); goalkeeper Tommy Younger (from Hibernian, £9,000); wing half Johnny Wheeler (from Bolton, £9,000); right winger Tony McNamara (from Everton, £4,000); inside forward Jimmy Harrower (from Hibernian, £11,000); right winger Fred Morris (from Mansfield, £7,000); goalkeeper Bert Slater (from Falkirk, exchange for Tommy Younger); centre forward Dave Hickson (from Everton, £10,500); and left half Tommy Leishman (from St Mirren, £9,000). Liverpool also signed South African goalkeeper Doug Rudham on amateur forms in October 1954. He turned professional the following year.

'With Liverpool in the Second Division after so long in the highest class of football it goes without saying that the club's aim was to get out as quickly as possible,' said Liddell. 'But, as so many others previously had discovered, it's far easier to drop down than get back to the First.

'Our initial campaign in the lower sphere didn't start very encouragingly with only three points from our first seven games and we never looked like possible promotion candidates.'

Such was Liverpool's form there were even real fears that they could slide towards a relegation battle to stay out of the Third Division. They failed to win a League away game until February, registering ten defeats and two draws, prior to a 2–1 victory at Fulham.

'Frank Lock lost his place at left back to be followed by Ronnie Moran and several young players were blooded in the team but we never struck the right blend for any length of time,' said Liddell.

Early in the season I was switched from outside left to centre forward. We'd started with Louis Bimpson leading the attack but big Louis didn't quite fit the bill, despite his earnest efforts, and the manager, Don Welsh, asked me how I felt about taking on the job.

My answer was the same as always. That I was willing to play practically anywhere so long as I got a game. But this time, compared with when I was asked about playing at full back, I felt I had a reasonable chance of succeeding as I'd played there before occasionally and I knew the ropes.

If goals are anything to go by, I didn't do too badly. In the 29 League games in which I wore the No. 9 jersey I scored 27 goals and 30 in all in my 40 appearances in our initial Second Division campaign. Nine of my goals were from penalties, the taking of which I had developed into something of an expert!

Liddell, indeed, was the supreme catalyst of the club. Shrugging off his deep disappointment at being omitted from Scotland's 1954 World Cup Finals squad, his magnificent response to playing down the middle for Liverpool made him their League top scorer for the fifth time in six seasons and earned him the job permanently. He also won a Scotland recall – at outside left.

But he was at centre forward for the nadir of Liverpool's descending fortunes at Birmingham on 11 December 1954 when they were demolished 9–1, the heaviest defeat in the club's history. The team line-up was: Rudham; Lambert, Lock; Wilkinson, Hughes, Twentyman; Payne, Anderson, Liddell, Evans, A'Court.

If it was a trauma for the entire club and its followers, it was a shattering experience for young Rainhill-born Alan A'Court, who had gone to Anfield from Prescot Cables and whose chance on Liverpool's left wing had been presented by Liddell's switch to lead the attack.

'I was barely twenty and I'd never known anything like it,' admitted A'Court, still feeling chilled at the recollection of Liverpool's sad winter's tale at St Andrews. 'When we got back to Merseyside I wouldn't even go home. I stayed sulking at my auntie's!

'The pitch at Birmingham was wet on top and rock hard underneath and we were slipping and sliding all over the place. But that was no excuse. It was the same for both sides.

'We went 3–0 down in the opening fifteen minutes before Billy Liddell pulled one back for us. We conceded another goal before half-time and let in another five in the second half. But I still say Billy's was the best of the ten goals that day!

'He kept his balance beautifully on that treacherous surface, turned like an ice-skater and hit a screamer past England goalkeeper Gil Merrick into the top corner of the net. But the result knocked me flat.'

A'Court recovered to become a Liverpool stalwart. He made 381 appearances and scored 63 goals in a career that extended into the Shankly era. He also won five England caps and a place in the 1958 World Cup squad in Sweden.

He was also thankful to have been a team-mate of Liddell's. 'Billy was superb as a role model,' said A'Court. 'It was a privilege to have played alongside him and great to follow in his footsteps. He was quite a conservative type of fellow but he had a good sense of humour and liked a laugh. It was easy to see why people used to call the team "Liddellpool".'

Liverpool took time to remove the bitter taste of the Birmingham debacle. A week later they crashed 4–1 at Doncaster prior to mixed Yuletide fortunes. Liddell gave the Kop fans in a crowd of under 25,000 the welcome gift of seeing him score four goals, which included a penalty, in a 6–2 Christmas Day defeat of Ipswich.

But 48 hours later the Suffolk club turned the tables with a 2–0 win at Portman Road, Liverpool's last action of 1954. The new year, though, brought some cheer to Anfield as the team marched through January unbeaten, winning four and drawing one of five League and FA Cup games . . . and the outcome of the last of that quintet was sensational.

Home wins over Derby and Blackburn in the Second Division, in which Liddell scored a total of three goals, were accompanied by Cup progress at the expense of Lincoln City, who drew 1–1 at Sincil Bank and lost in the Anfield replay by the game's only goal struck in extra time by John Evans, who had also scored in the first match. That narrow win earned Liverpool a fourth-round derby trip to Everton, with the bookmakers making the Anfield team distinct outsiders in the belief that the Goodison club would avenge their 1950 semifinal defeat by their local rivals.

Liverpool, after all, were languishing in the Second Division, without an away win since the previous April, while Everton were sixth in the top flight.

'We were very much the underdogs,' recalled Liddell.

We had failed to win an away game up to then that season while Everton were doing quite well in the First Division and were strong favourites.

They'd just done a Christmas double over Wolves, winning 3–1 at Molineux and 3–2 at Goodison against the club who were the glamour side of the time after beating some of Europe's top clubs. So the tie looked a certainty for Everton. But certainties in football have a nasty habit of coming unstuck.

To prepare our lads for the game, manager Don Welsh took them away for a few days toning-up in Blackpool during the week, although I couldn't go because I had to stay behind to do my accountancy work for Simon, Jude and West.

The shock events of that Saturday, 29 January 1955 are weaved permanently into Mersey derby folklore, the result providing the biggest upset in the history of the Everton–Liverpool duels which span three different centuries.

The team line-ups, in their 2–3–5 formations, were:

Everton: Jimmy O'Neill; Eric Moore, George Rankin; Peter Farrell (captain), Tommy (T E) Jones, Cyril Lello; Eddie Wainwright, Wally Fielding, Dave Hickson, Harry Potts, Tommy Eglington.

Liverpool: Doug Rudham; Ray Lambert, Ronnie Moran; Roy Saunders, Laurie Hughes (captain), Geoff Twentyman; Brian Jackson, Eric Anderson, Billy Liddell, John Evans, Alan A'Court.

Referee: Arthur Ellis (Halifax).

A crowd of 72,000, paying receipts of £10,715, saw Liverpool captain Laurie Hughes win the toss and opt to defend the Gwladys Street end as the tie swung into action at 2.45 p.m.

A week earlier television viewers had witnessed snooker's first-ever official 147 maximum break, achieved by British champion Joe Davis, but the break watched by disbelieving Goodison spectators was not in the script.

With eighteen minutes gone, rank outsiders Liverpool went ahead through Liddell, whose brilliance shone through an afternoon of ecstasy for Anfield fans and sheer agony for Evertonians. When Brian Jackson crossed, Liddell beat centre half Tommy Jones to meet it and fire a blistering left-foot shot into the corner of Jimmy O'Neill's net.

Home hopes briefly flickered twice, when both Dave Hickson and Harry Potts planted the ball into the Liverpool net, but on each occasion the offside flag had already been raised and their efforts were correctly ruled out. In between those two incidents Liverpool doubled their advantage from a 29th-minute Geoff Twentyman free kick.

Left back Ronnie Moran, who would complete almost a half-century of service to Liverpool in many roles, was then a month away from his 21st birthday and revealed that his side's second goal was reward for their pre-match homework:

'We unlocked the Everton offside trap with a set piece we'd worked on in training. Everton had a habit of rushing out when defending long-distance free kicks in the hope of catching opposing forwards offside.

'So when we took the kick, Eric Anderson ran through from a deep position to catch them out. Both Eric and Johnny Evans went for the ball but Eric managed to pass to Alan A'Court, who came in on the left and scored with an angled shot from about eight yards out. It was a crucial goal for us.'

Early in the second half Liverpool skipper Hughes was injured in a tussle with Hickson. He was able to resume after treatment but only as a limping passenger for the remainder of the match.

'I got a right clattering in that game but the best you could hope for was the magic sponge,' said Hughes. 'There were no substitutes in those days so instead of being taken off I was switched to outside left with Alan A'Court moving inside, Evans operating at centre forward, Geoff Twentyman taking over at centre half and Billy Liddell dropping to left half. But we won – and, as captain, I was overjoyed!'

The enforced reshuffle heaped even more credit on Liverpool's display in general and Liddell's in particular. 'When Hickson beat Twentyman and advanced on goal with only Rudham to beat, Liddell appeared from nowhere to take the ball off his toe,' the *Liverpool Echo* reported.

'Liddell was certainly inspirational, leading by example, correcting his colleagues' disposition whenever necessary and all the time being in the centre of the action.'

There was powerful opposition testimony to Liddell's effectiveness as an emergency wing half. 'I latched on to a pass in that Cup tie and I was going forward on the attack when suddenly I didn't have the ball any more,' recalled Everton inside forward Wally Fielding. 'I looked round and saw that Billy Liddell had taken it away from me with one of the greatest tackles anyone ever made on me.'

Liverpool, who according to one press observer 'never made two moves when one would do', found the simplicity and directness of their play reaping further dividends in the 57th minute. Winger Brian Jackson beat George Rankin and unleashed a twenty-yard angled shot that O'Neill failed to hold, and Evans punished the keeper by tucking home an easy chance to make it 3–0 and extend his record of scoring in all three of his side's Cup games that season.

Evans scored again in the 75th minute, heading in a Jackson cross, to make it 4–0, a final scoreline prompting gulps of incredulity way beyond Merseyside.

'It was beyond the power of the police to do anything about the hundred or so eager Liverpool fans who swarmed onto the field as the final whistle went,' declared one match report.

High in the Goodison stand Phyllis Liddell could not contain her glee.'My wife was so excited that she threw a box of chocolates in the air and never saw them again,' related Billy.

'It was a truly great day for us. We turned the form book upside down and ran Everton off their feet. In doing so we gave our delighted supporters ammunition for their arguments with Evertonians over the respective merits of the two teams.'

Liddell's team-mate Moran concurred. 'It was the best thing that had happened to Liverpool for years,' he said. 'But there were no prolonged celebrations in those days. After waving to the supporters at the end we got changed and made our own way home.

'I think Billy and Laurie Hughes were the only two players in our squad who had cars and after that great win over Everton I walked down to Sleepers Hill to get the No. 18 tram to Seaforth, then caught the bus home to Crosby. The Liverpool fans I met on the way were delighted.'

So delighted in fact that Merseyside's pubs and clubs echoed that weekend to the strains of triumphant Kopites singing their victory songs, which included this salute to the Cup-tie scorers:

> Hey diddle diddle, hey diddle diddle,
> Two from Evans, one from Liddell,
> And one from A'Court on the wing,
> That's how the Reds got in the swing,
> Hey diddle diddle, hey diddle diddle,
> And all inspired by Billy Liddell.

Another ditty was sung in special tribute to Liddell, which went thus:

> Who makes the full backs and the half backs run?
> Who hits the ball like it's fired from a gun?
> Who makes the Kop yell, yell, yell?
> It's the one and only Billy Liddell.

In contrast, a cloud of gloom descended on Everton and their supporters after a result that Goodison manager Cliff Britton sportingly admitted was fully justified.

Among the downcast Evertonians was a schoolboy who hero-worshipped Dave Hickson and film star Alan Ladd. The same youngster was to become the owner of the Goodison club and Britain's top theatre impresario. 'That Cup tie was the first derby match I ever saw,' recalled Bill Kenwright. 'I was only nine and

I queued up all night to get a ticket. Then we lost 4–0. I was heartbroken.'

Goalkeeper Jimmy O'Neill was no less disappointed. 'It just wasn't my day,' admitted the Republic of Ireland international. 'I crashed into a post and hurt my head trying to save one of the Evans goals.

'After the game I had to spend some time with friends and relatives who had come over from Ireland. I was feeling very low and, grateful though I was for their support, I was glad to see them go home.'

The FA Cup result was announced to a stunned audience at Liverpool's Shakespeare Theatre, where George Formby was appearing in pantomime, but the Goodison triumph had a bigger spin-off for Liverpool in their League programme than in their Cup campaign.

'The win over our old enemies gave us a tremendous psychological boost, particularly away from home, and we won five and drew one of our remaining nine Second Division away games,' said Liddell.

However, Liverpool's home pairing with Huddersfield Town in the FA Cup fifth round was to bring no repeat of their heroics at Everton. The First Division visitors snuffed out Kop dreams of glory by winning 2–0 on a treacherous Anfield pitch which had a covering of snow masking icy patches.

A warning had come from Liddell the day before the game when he said: 'I hope I won't be regarded as being discourteous to Everton by saying that we expect a harder struggle than we had in the last round.'

Huddersfield kept Liverpool waiting for four minutes before taking the field for the kickoff and their performance ensured that the Anfield club's long wait for Cup success would also be extended. The Yorkshire club employed short-passing containing football while Liverpool attacked directly and urgently, although Liddell's yards-long slide in the opening minutes was indicative of the perils of the conditions in an era three years before Everton pioneered undersoil heating and more than forty before it became a standard facility in top-flight English football.

Johnny Evans shot wide from Liverpool's best chance early in the game and after a goalless first half Huddersfield went ahead five minutes after the interval. Albert Hobson, despite losing his footing as he shot, saw the ball curl beyond Charlie Ashcroft and into the net off the inside of the far post.

Liverpool's desperate attacking, which saw Liddell switch to the left flank in a bid to prise an opening, went unrewarded and Huddersfield secured victory seven minutes from the end. Jim Glazzard seized on Brian Frear's pass to hit an angled shot which Ashcroft touched but failed to stop.

'Once more, Liverpool's Cup hopes have proved castles in the air,' wrote Ranger in the *Liverpool Echo*. 'They slid away into oblivion on Anfield's ice-rink surface almost as quickly as some of the players' feet from under them.

'For over half a century Liverpool have been reserving a place on their sideboard for the Cup. They can now stick a vase of flowers there until next year – forget-me-nots for preference.' But it would be another decade before that yearning was satisfied, under a manager called Shankly, recruited from Huddersfield.

Late in the 1954–5 season – when 80-year-old Sir Winston Churchill resigned as Prime Minister and was succeeded by Sir Anthony Eden, who went on to win a General Election – Liverpool went through an eight-match spell spanning March and April in which they conceded ten penalties, without being awarded one!

Their opponents scored from nine of the spot kicks, two of them dispatched by former Liverpool centre forward Cyril Done to help Port Vale to a 4–3 win. Liverpool drew four and lost two of the first six games of those eight matches, but away wins at Middlesbrough and West Ham and a home draw with Birmingham – thanks to a Liddell brace, one a penalty – ensured they would finish in a club-record low eleventh place in the Second Division.

Liverpool brought down the curtain on the campaign with a 6–1 hammering at Rotherham in the last match, with four of the Yorkshire side's goals coming from Scottish outside left Ian Wilson. Liddell scored Liverpool's goal in the last minute to take his season's haul in League and FA Cup to 31 in 44 appearances.

As well as his four goals against Ipswich he scored a hat trick in a 4–1 home win over Fulham, when he collected his 100th League goal from open play sandwiched between two penalties.

The four FA Cup goals Johnny Evans scored that season – during which he became the first postwar Liverpool player to be sent off with his dismissal at Lincoln – made him the club's top overall marksman with 33. His haul included all his side's goals in the 5–3 home League win over Bristol Rovers in September to become the first Liverpool player to score five in a senior game since Andy McGuigan in 1902. The feat was subsequently achieved by Ian Rush in 1983 and Robbie Fowler in 1993.

During the summer of 1955, Europe and its wider implications was on the agenda of world leaders and the football authorities. The Eastern Bloc nations, headed by the Soviet Union under its new leader Nikita Khrushchev, signed the Warsaw Pact to ensure the continuation of the Cold War. The Iron Curtain alliance also embraced Czechoslovakia, Poland, Romania, Hungary, Bulgaria, Albania and East Germany. Meanwhile, eighteen of Europe's top football clubs, including English champions Chelsea, met in Paris at the invitation of French sports newspaper *L'Equipe* to set up a new European Cup competition.

However, English insularity prevailed in all its glory. The Football League's management committee asked Chelsea to 'reconsider' their decision to participate, citing the extra fixture burden as their reason, and the London club duly withdrew. In contrast to this blinkered English stance even Iron Curtain nations took part, while Hibernian carried Scotland's flag to the semifinal and a £25,000 profit.

A year later Liddell's friend Matt Busby defied the League and led new English champions Manchester United into the second European Cup tournament to pioneer a new era for the English game, one which was to bring tragedy and triumph to Old Trafford.

Liddell was appointed Liverpool captain for the 1955–6 season, which was preceded by his second selection for the Great Britain team that met the Rest of Europe in Belfast in August, a week before the new domestic campaign began. It was a supreme tribute to Liddell's talents that despite playing Second Division football he should share with fellow winger Stanley Matthews the distinction of retaining his place in the team representing the cream of the United Kingdom – two months before winning his last Scotland cap.

At Liverpool, though, the season did not begin smoothly, as Liddell described:

We didn't get off to a good start and, having been appointed captain, I was especially disappointed. By early October, with a quarter of our fixtures played, we were thirteenth in the table.

We seemed to have no possible hope of promotion – something that certain supporters didn't fail to rub in. But we buckled down and gradually we improved. Johnny Molyneux, a strongly built right back signed from Chester during the close season, struck up a splendid understanding with Ronnie Moran.

Johnny made his debut in our fifth game and another new-comer later that season was centre half Dick White, signed from Scunthorpe. Dick had a great sense of humour and he produced solid, consistent displays although it would be another two seasons before he became a first-team regular.

Dave Underwood took over in goal from Doug Rudham and we started climbing the table steadily. By mid-April we had a good chance of finishing runners-up to gain promotion but, unfortunately, we failed to stay the pace in the last few weeks. Lowly Doncaster beat us at Anfield, to complete the 'double' over us, and we lost at Fulham and Lincoln City.

Although we had a run of three straight wins, over Port Vale, Rotherham and Bristol Rovers, we gained only six points from our last six matches. That left us, frustratingly, in third place, four points behind second-placed Leeds and seven behind Second Division champions Sheffield Wednesday.

I ended up as top scorer with 27 League goals, three of them from the penalty spot, and long before the season's end

Above: Down the generations: a very young Billy Liddell with (*from left*) his father James, his grandfather and great-grandfather in a family portrait from the 1920s.
Courtesy of the Liddell family.

Right: Embarking on life's journey: Phyllis and Billy Liddell on their wedding day in July 1946.
Courtesy of the Liddell family.

1939-40.

Player's Name	✓	Address	Position	Date Signed	Date of Birth	Wages S.	W.	Amount Paid	Received	
Riley (1)	A.J.	T.A. 455 Wallis. Breck Rd. Liverpool	Goal	18/8/25	1905. 34	6	8.	NIL. S.A.		
Kemp (2)	R.	T.A. 6 Rosemore Gardens "	Goal	8/12/36	15/10/1912.	6	7-8	"		Died 1940 22 Nov -23 in
Bramsby (3)	E.	1 Sheldon Ave. Chester.	X Goal	24/3/39	age 22.	3	3.-	free.		
Cooper (4)	J.	T.A. 17 Anderson St. Liverpool	R.T.B.	4/17/34	1905. 35	6	8.	£6700 Footb		
Harley (5)	J.	9 Inman Rd. Anfield	R.B.	30/4/34	Feb 1917.	6	8	NIL. Hospital		
Ramsden (6)	B.	T.A. 42 Liverpool Rd. Little Crosby	4.3.	7-3-35	Nov. 1917.	6-6	6-8	NIL.		
Peters (7)	K.	T.A. Kings Rd. Aigburth	L.B.	4/5/36	1915.	4-4	5-7	NIL.		
Lambert (7)	R.	116 Thomas Hollis Rd. Walton	9.H.	18/1/36	1912.	5	5-6	NIL.		
Busby (8)	Jn. T.A.	42 Bosebury Ave. Waterloo	R.H.	11/5/36	Aug 1909.	6	8	£800 - H. City		
Bush (10)	T.A. J. W.	31 Oakfield Rd. Anfield	9.H.	31-3-32	Feb. 1914.	6	8	NIL.		Shrewsbury Loan.
Rogers (11)	J.	12 Scott St. Fairfield	X 9.H.	15-5-33	April 1910.	6	8	NIL.		
Jones (12)	T.A. J.	4 Bosmore Rd. Anfield	L.H.	15-3-38	Feb. 1912.	4-4	5-7	NIL.		
Rosedale (13)	T.A. J.	302 Bosmore Rd. Anfield	9.H.	25-2-37	June 1919.	5	5-6	adop.		
Paisley (14)	R.	30 Lovers Lane Waterloo	L.H.	9-5-39	1919.	5	5-6	adop		
Spicer (15)	B.	52 Allington. Grassendale	L.H.	4-16-39	age Liverpool	5	5-6	NIL.		
Freaxenbergs (16)	B.	73 Lonbury Rd. Anfield	O.R.	11-9-53	Nov. 1911.	6	8	NIL. S.A.		
Jones Ruth (17)	ARMY.	11 Camp Sandforaugh	O.R.	10-3-38	June 1918.	5-6	5-6	£1050 Wrexham		
Liddell (18)	W.	108 Bosmore Rd. Thingwall	O.R.	17-4-39	Jan. 1922.	3	4-5	£100-75		
Taylor (19)	T.A. P.	31 Oakfield Rd. Anfield	O.L.	4-5-36	Sept 1917.	6	8	NIL. Hospital		
Eastham H. (20)	T.A.	31 Oakfield Rd. Anfield	I.F.	27-2-36	June 1917.	6	6-8	£1000. + Kent Leb.		
Eastham S. (21)	ARMY	1h Camp	X F.I.H.	9-5-38	age. 26	5	5-6	£1025 Blackpool		
Hagan (22)	T.A. N.	116 Arthur Ave.	I.F.	13-10-57	Feb. 1918.	6	8	Army.		
Balmer (23)	T.A. J.	43 Southside Down. Deal Bdy.	I.F.	25-9-35	Feb. 1916.	6	8	£600. Dublin		
Van Den Berg (24)	W.	110 Priory Rd. Anfield	O.L.	18-10-37	March 1918.	6	8	NIL.		Local
Shafto (25)	T.A. J.	123 Sellstrong Rd. Anfield	9.F.	8-10-37	Nov 1919.	5	5-7	too		headsdestining
Kinghorn (26)	T.A. W.	101 Priory St. Liverpool	O.L.	9-5-38	age 23	6	8.	NIL.		Queens Park
Stone (27)	T.A. C.	68 Arthur Rd. Last Derby Green	I.F.or 9.F.	Dec 1937	Oct 1920.	3	4-5-6	NIL.		Bootle boarding school
Paterson (28)	T.A. B.	Anfield	I.F	30-5-37	Dec 1916.	5	3-67	£500		Llandine £9
Patterson (29)	T.A. B.	30 Bosmore Par. Anfield	X 9.F.	11-6-37	Tues 1918.	3-4	4-5-6	£100. L		Childwine
Jones W (30)	T.A. N.	110 Priory Rd. Aigburth Green	L.F	9-9-38	Aug 1921.	3-4	4-5-6	£600		Morfield or Little Bank Rd
Cumming (31)	T.A. N.	57 Avenue St. Bootle Liverpool	X O.L.	6-3-39	age 21	4	5-6	£015		Knowsley St. Bootle

Opposite: A section of Liverpool FC's playing staff wages sheet for 1939–40, which shows that Billy Liddell was on £4 to £5 in the winter and £3 in the summer. It is shown in the right-hand column of Liddell's entry that the club paid Lochgelly Violet a total of £175 to sign him.
From author's own collection.

Above: In tune: Billy and his wife Phyllis enjoy a sing-song at home with twins Malcom and David.
Courtesy of *Liverpool Daily Post & Echo*.

Above: Champions: the Liverpool title-winning side of 1946–7. Billy Liddell is second from right (*front row*) with Bob Paisley (*standing*) immediately behind.
From author's own collection.

Above: On the FA Cup trail in 1950. Back row (*left to right*): Phil Taylor (captain), Ray Lambert, Laurie Hughes, Cyril Sidlow, Bill Jones, Bob Paisley, Eddie Spicer, Albert Shelley (trainer). Front row: S R Williams (chairman), Jimmy Payne, Kevin Baron, Albert Stubbins, Willie Fagan, Billy Liddell, George Kay (manager). Courtesy of *Liverpool Daily Post & Echo.*

Below: Royal moment: Liddell is presented to King George VI at Wembley, prior to the FA Cup Final against Arsenal. Courtesy of *Topham.*

Above: Autographs of the
Liverpool squad 1949–50 (Billy
Liddell's, *bottom right*; his brother
Tom' s, *top left*).
From author's own collection.

Left: Billy Liddell (*left*) with Dave
Horridge Senior as guest of
honour at the West Derby Darts
League awards night at the Jolly
Miller pub in Liverpool, in 1954.
Courtesy of the Horridge family.

Top: The programmes for Great Britain's games against the Rest of Europe in May 1947 and August 1955.
From author's own collection.

Above: Billy Liddell (*front, second from left*) pictured in the 1955 Great Britain squad. Courtesy of The Irish Football Association.

Right: Wonder wingers: Scotland's Billy Liddell (*centre*) and England's Stanley Matthews (*left*), the only two players to have appeared in both postwar Great Britain teams, chat to Roy Paul of Manchester City and Wales.
Courtesy of the *Daily Herald*.

Above: The famous 'equaliser that wasn't' against Manchester City in a 1956 FA Cup replay. Billy Liddell fends off Dave Ewing's challenge and his shot is heading past Bert Trautmann in the City goal. But referee Mervyn Griffiths (seen with arm upraised, ending the match) disallowed it, saying he had blown for full time seconds earlier.
Courtesy of *Liverpool Daily Post & Echo*.

Below: The line-ups in the Worcester City match programme for the FA Cup tie in January 1959 when Liverpool omitted Liddell from the team and suffered a humiliating defeat by their non-league opponents.
From author's own collection.

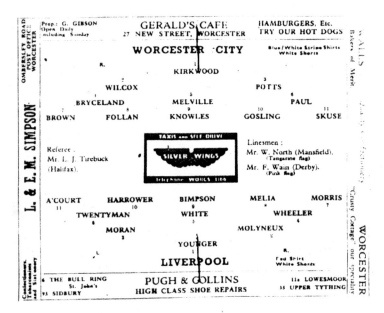

BILLY LIDDELL TESTIMONIAL MATCH

LIVERPOOL v. INTERNATIONAL XI

AT LIVERPOOL FOOTBALL GROUND, ANFIELD
WEDNESDAY, 21st SEPTEMBER, 1960
Kick-off 7.15 p.m.

Souvenir Programme—Sixpence

Left: The front cover of Billy Liddell's testimonial match programme in September 1960.
From author's own collection.

Below: Ferenc Puskas (*left*) kisses the air stewardess, watched by Billy Liddell (*at back*), after the legendary Hungarian flew into Liverpool's Speke Airport for a charity game in May 1967.
Courtesy of *Liverpool Daily Post & Echo.*

Below: Liverpool Re-United ... Phyllis Liddell *(front left)* with former Liverpool players and wives. Others in the picture are *(left to right)* former Anfield manager and captain Phil Taylor, Ray Lambert, Laurie Hughes, Bill Jones, Jimmy Payne and Eddie Spicer.
Courtesy of the Liddell family.

I'd decided that the centre forward berth suited me and also helped the team.

With new, young team-mates it was difficult to play an unorthodox wing game without upsetting the balance of the forward line so the switch to the middle meant I was always in the thick of things.

I could move around as I pleased and there was plenty of work to do, which was something I always liked. Although you get closely marked by defenders when you play centre forward I tended to find more space to work in. Although my favourite position remained outside left I enjoyed wearing the No. 9.

During the autumn and winter of 1955 Liverpool managed to secure their share of the back-page headlines while the front pages brought news of Princess Margaret's announcement that she would not marry divorcee Group Captain Peter Townsend, the launch of ITV by Lew Grade and Britain's attempts to counter terrorism in Cyprus.

In November, Liverpool swamped Fulham 7–0 at Anfield, with Liddell collecting two of the goals on a day when all five forwards scored in a match for the first time since the war, Johnny Evans, Alan Arnell, Alan A'Court and Jimmy Payne also on the mark along with left half Geoff Twentyman.

A few weeks later Liddell hit a sizzling hat trick in a 5–2 home defeat of Nottingham Forest, all three of his goals coming at the Kop end in the second half. The only goal of the opening 45 minutes came when Evans lobbed an early shot over Forest goalkeeper Harry Nicholson.

Shortly after the interval a former local schoolboy star, who had joined Liverpool's ground staff as a fifteen-year-old, celebrated his senior debut with a goal. It launched inside forward Jimmy Melia on a career that brought him England honours and even greater recognition as the white-shoed manager of Brighton who took Manchester United to an FA Cup Final replay in 1983.

The first of Liddell's treble did not come until the 51st minute and Forest shocked the Anfield crowd by scoring twice in 60 seconds with Jim Barrett getting both goals, the first from a penalty after Ronnie Moran had handled. But Liddell soothed his side's anxieties by capitalising on the loose ball after Nicholson blocked an Evans shot and claiming his second goal of the match. The Scot completed his hat trick with a brilliant last-minute header.

Rookie Melia was soon under Liddell's spell, recalling: 'I was in the army doing my National Service at Catterick barracks when I was chosen to make my debut against Forest and Billy laid the ball on for me to score.

'He was just unbelievable. At that time there was a massive playing staff. There were about fifty professionals. It was far too many and it was just crazy. But Billy was something else. A fantastic player.

'There is nobody in the modern game who could equal him. He was a living legend to the fans and did everything for the team. He took the penalties, free kicks, corners – and scored most of the goals!

'I remember a game against Bristol City at Anfield when we got a penalty. Even though Billy was playing, the boss had told me to take it as I'd already scored from a penalty in a game when Billy was injured. So I put the ball on the spot and suddenly the whole of Anfield started booing me!

'I could hear Liverpool fans saying "the cheeky little b— taking the penalty when Billy's out there!" I could hardly believe it. I blasted the ball into the net, thinking that would at least win the crowd over. But they carried on booing me! It just showed the amazing esteem Billy was held in.'

The valiant commitment that so endeared Liddell to the public was evident later that same season of 1955–6 when he sustained a gashed head from a collision with Doncaster centre half Charlie Williams in a Good Friday game at Belle Vue.

Liddell had to leave the field to have three stitches inserted in the wound. But fifteen minutes later he was back to complete the match, which Liverpool lost 1–0. 'He took quite a nasty blow but that didn't bother Billy,' recalled Ronnie Moran, Liverpool's left back that day. 'He just got stitched, had his head bandaged and

came back out again. The man Billy collided with, Charlie
Williams, later became a comedian and appeared on television.
He didn't play like a comedian that day, though!'

Liddell was forced to miss the home game against Bristol City
next day but turned out two days later on Easter Monday, still
sporting his head bandage, to captain the side in the return fixture
with Doncaster, which the Yorkshire club won 2–1.

By a quirk of fate, in the home clash with Doncaster the
following season, in January 1957, Liddell was carried off on a
stretcher for the first time in his senior career after a tussle near
the corner flag with visiting left half Jim Kilkenny.

'We both went up for a high ball, our heads met with a terrific
bump and we both fell to the ground like logs,' Liddell recalled.
'I was unconscious so it was only later that I learned that Jim had
also been taken off.' He went on:

Neither of us resumed and Jim came out of it worse than me
– he had to have six stitches, while I had to have three. That
evening my wife Phyllis and I were among a small party of
friends who had booked seats for the Liverpool Empire
panto, in which my old friend Ken Dodd was appearing.

When we went into his dressing room at the theatre Ken
didn't miss the chance to have a laugh at my expense, saying
that obviously my skull must be very thick because I'd
needed only half the stitches Jim Kilkenny had done!

Like Frankie Vaughan, Russ Hamilton and other show-
business friends of mine, Ken has always been a keen
football follower. For a while he was a vice president of
Liverpool Supporters Club and, when his engagements
allowed, was a regular at Anfield matches. Frankie Vaughan
was just the same. He loved to come into our dressing room
and have a chat with the lads.

He came to one of our matches at West Ham with Anna
Neagle, with whom he starred in films. Anna and her
husband Herbert Wilcox were keen West Ham fans and
Frankie joked that he didn't know whether it was wise for
him to cheer for us. As things turned out we drew 1–1.

However, Liverpool's failure to recapture their top-flight status, by finishing third and missing promotion by one place and four points, was no laughing matter and cost manager Don Welsh his job at the end of the season. He was succeeded in May 1956 by Liddell's former team-mate Phil Taylor, who stepped up from chief coach to take over as manager.

But three months earlier the events at Anfield on a winter's afternoon added another remarkable and ironic layer to the legend of Billy Liddell.

Chapter Ten

Seconds Out

Liverpool's FA Cup campaign in 1956 was fuelled mainly by the goals of Billy Liddell. It would end with a flashing shot from the great Scot that was, quite literally, counted out to ensure arguably the most agonising climax the Kop has ever endured and an indelible entry in Anfield history.

Two fierce Liddell shots in the span of a minute dispatched Accrington Stanley in the third round at Anfield before Liverpool took two attempts, including extra time, to dispose of the challenge from another Third Division club, Scunthorpe United.

Only a last minute Liddell goal at Anfield saved Liverpool from the deep embarrassment of being knocked out by the lowly visitors who were managed by Merseyside-born Bill Corkhill, once a Liverpool reserve-team player, and whose team included Jack Haigh and Mervyn Jones, who had made sixteen first team appearances for Liverpool between them.

Watched by a crowd of more than 53,000, Haigh helped to shock his old club by lofting the ball into the area where Laurie Hughes could only misdirect the ball to John Gregory, who fired past Dave Underwood and put Scunthorpe in front after 22 minutes. Liddell applied the finish to a brilliant run by Alan Arnell to equalise and send the teams in level at half-time and when Jimmy Payne blasted in a Johnny Evans cross from Liddell's free kick, early in the second half, everything pointed to Liverpool securing an expected victory. Scunthorpe had other ideas.

Two goals from John Davies in the 75th and 76th minutes – the first a long-range shot that flew past Underwood and the second after the keeper had mishandled a Jack Brownsword cross – stunned Anfield as Scunthorpe went 3–2 in front. The exit door was gaping for Liverpool as the contest moved into the last minute. Then, in one final home attack, right-winger Jimmy Payne found space to deliver a centre. Liddell met it to head past Peter Marshall for his second goal of the game that preserved Liverpool's lifeline and sent the tie into a replay.

The renewal of combat at the Old Show Ground was equally tense and tight. Liddell put Liverpool ahead after nineteen minutes, when he raced onto a long clearance by John Molyneux and sent Marshall the wrong way, but ten minutes later Scunthorpe were awarded a penalty by referee Kevin Howley after a Jones cross hit Molyneux's arm. Brownsword's weak spot kick was saved one-handed by Underwood, diving to his right, only for Scunthorpe to wipe out Liverpool's lead when Davies headed in a Jones free kick shortly after the interval for his third goal of the tie.

With seconds of normal time remaining Liddell almost staged a repeat of his late headed strike in the first match. But Marshall denied him with a great save to send the battle into extra time in which Liverpool came out on top 2–1 through a 109th-minute goal scored by Arnell after Liddell headed on Alan A'Court's centre.

'It was touch and go, Scunthorpe put up a tremendous fight,' said Liddell, whose side's victory earned a fifth-round trip to First Division Manchester City.

The Maine Road match was preceded by a blizzard, yet more than 70,000 spectators packed into the stadium to see the action on a snow-covered, uneven rock-hard pitch. It ended goalless, although Liddell had a foretaste of things to come when he put the ball into the City net only for his effort to be disallowed because of a linesman flagging Jimmy Payne offside.

So the tie resumed on Wednesday afternoon, 22 February, 1956, in front of a 57,000-plus crowd who generated receipts of £6,978. The team line-ups were:

Liverpool: Underwood; Molyneux, Moran; Saunders, Hughes, Twentyman; Payne, Arnell, Liddell, Evans, A'Court.

Manchester City: Trautmann; Leivers, Little; Barnes, Ewing, Paul; Spurdle, Hayes, Johnstone, Dyson, Clarke.

Referee: Mr B M Griffiths (Newport).

Anfield, like the Manchester pitch four days earlier, was cloaked in snow, but the conditions could not detract from City's quality and their precision moves contrasted with the quick thrusts and sudden bursts of Liverpool.

The game marked the return to Anfield of City's celebrated goalkeeper Bert Trautmann, the former German paratrooper and prisoner of war who had given a remarkable exhibition there five months earlier when he appeared for a Lancashire Select XI against a combined Liverpool/Everton team in Eddie Spicer's benefit match. Some of his saves were breathtaking.

In the Cup replay he found fortune smiling on him and City despite the fact that they were the classier side, their narrowest escape coming when Trautmann failed to gather a Roy Little back pass, sparking a desperate scramble that ended with Bill Leivers dangerously heading over from under his own bar.

Following a goalless first half, Alan Arnell warmed the chilled Liverpool fans by putting the home side in front after 52 minutes, side-footing a Johnny Evans header from Geoff Twentyman's free kick out of Trautmann's reach. But it was an advantage that lasted only a dozen minutes.

Molyneux's challenge on Roy Clarke gave City a free kick from which their captain Roy Paul found Liddell's Great Britain and Scotland colleague Bobby Johnstone. His great dribble set up Jackie Dyson for the Lancashire cricketer to equalise.

Liddell's menace attracted double cover on the Liverpool No. 9 from Paul and Dave Ewing, the latter earning boos from home fans for some over-physical treatment of the Anfield hero.

Johnstone crowned an impressive display by creating the opportunity for little Joe Hayes to score a second City goal with a minute left. Just as some spectators began to head for home, Liverpool broke up a City attack in their own goalmouth and Evans headed the ball up the field where it was collected on the halfway line by Liddell, who sped forward across the snowbound surface. Liddell described what happened next.

I made a bee-line for the City goal with Dave Ewing in hot pursuit. The roar of the crowd was terrific and I knew there was so little time and that this was our last chance. I managed to shake off Dave and when I got into the penalty area I let fly with everything I had as Bert Trautmann came out.

The ball flew into the Kop net and the crowd went wild. But when I turned round I realised the 'goal' had not been given. Apparently, the referee Mervyn Griffiths had blown the whistle but I hadn't heard it and City's defenders hadn't.

The referee said he had blown his whistle as I was running with the ball and told press men that he had blown fifteen seconds before I put the ball in the net. I made it a policy never to argue with referees but I could have done that day.

He was pictured with his arms extended as I was about to shoot and how long he'd stood like that I don't know. But I was not far from him when I began my run and I told him that even allowing for the snow it would not have taken me fifteen seconds to get from the halfway line to the penalty area.

I would have thought my 'goal' was nearer five than fifteen seconds too late. But referees have a job to do and until they have x-ray eyes to see what happens on their blind side, and some at the back of their heads to spot what goes on behind them, there are bound to be occasions when their decisions are questioned.

Confusion reigned at Anfield that afternoon. Even though the players and officials shook hands and walked off the pitch the majority of fans stayed in the ground expecting extra time.

Only after a public address announcement – jeered by the Kop – that Liddell's strike had been counted out by the referee and that City had won did the crowd begin to disperse into Anfield's wintry environs.

Sharing the sense of anguish among Liverpool supporters was Phyllis Liddell. 'I can still see the scene now, of Billy running down the pitch and putting the ball into the net,' she recalled. 'Naturally, we were all delighted but then there was the hollow realisation that it had been disallowed. I burst into tears. I think it was the only time I cried at a football match.'

Another spectator, Tommy Almond, declared: 'I was behind the Kop goal when Billy let fly with a tremendous shot. I saw the ball bulge the net as the referee, from the halfway line and making no attempt to keep up with the play, blew his whistle and raised his arm to signal what we thought was a good goal.

'The referee was from Newport, South Wales and the City captain, Roy Paul, who was also captain of Wales, also came from South Wales. Two of the first to leave the field that day were the two Welshmen, who actually had their arms around each other's shoulders laughing their heads off as they went off.'

In an era long before video facilities and regular televised football the one piece of hard evidence capturing the famous incident was provided by a picture taken by *Liverpool Daily Post & Echo* chief photographer Neville Willasey. It showed referee Griffiths signalling full time as the ball left Liddell's boot. But the question of timing was left hanging in the air tantalisingly, never to be fully answered and stoking debate down the decades.

Today, when large chunks of stoppage time are an accepted part of the game, Liddell's late strike would probably have counted . . . but would it have endured so long in the memory or have the cachet of what transpired to be the glorious closest of close calls? I think not.

City's win denied Liverpool the tasty morsel of a sixth-round Cup derby against Everton, who met a similar fate to their Mersey neighbours by losing 2–1 at Maine Road. City went on to Wembley where they won the Cup with a 3–1 defeat of Birmingham in which Trautmann emerged as one of the old stadium's heroic figures.

The blond German keeper, who had just become the first overseas player to be voted Footballer of the Year by England's football writers, dived at the feet of Birmingham's Peter Murphy and held onto the ball despite receiving blows to his head and neck which knocked him unconscious. After being revived he played on, only to suffer another collision five minutes later. Again, he got up to complete the final fifteen minutes of the match and climb Wembley's 39 steps to receive his medal from the queen.

It was not until three days later that the full extent of Trautmann's bravery unfolded when X-rays revealed that he had finished the Final with a broken neck. Amazingly, it did not finish his career. He resumed action for City just before Christmas and five years later was back at Anfield to keep a special date for Liddell in his testimonial match.

The departure of Don Welsh at the end of that 1955–6 season and the elevation of former captain and wing half Phil Taylor, who had made almost 350 senior appearances for the club, from coach to manager, was a staging post in Liverpool history. Wales full back Ray Lambert's retirement meant that only Liddell and Laurie Hughes remained of the postwar championship and Cup Final squad.

New boss Taylor added to his resources by signing goal-keeper Tommy Younger from Hibernian for £9,000, to displace Doug Rudham, and wing half or inside forward Johnny Wheeler for a similar amount from Bolton, with whom he had won an England cap.

It was the summer when America dropped its first hydrogen bomb from an aircraft over Bikini Atoll in the Pacific and the Suez crisis began after Nasser's seizure of the canal.

Somewhat more heart-stirring – except perhaps for Australian cricket – was Jim Laker's demolition of the tourists' batting. Playing for Surrey at The Oval in May 1956, the off-spinner became the first English bowler for 78 years to take all ten Aussie wickets, for 88 runs. Then in July in the Test at Old Trafford, Manchester, he performed the unequalled feat of taking all ten of Australia's second innings wickets and nineteen in the match for a total of 90 runs.

For Liverpool fans, though, it was to be another season when their promotion dreams were exploded yet again. Liddell recounted:

After our improvement the previous season, when we finished third, there were optimistic hopes in the board room and the dressing room and among our supporters that 1956–7 would see our return to the First Division.

But we were pipped on the post. We didn't start too encouragingly, which was one of our weaknesses, but came with a real flourish at the end by winning our last seven home games. We also improved our away record, taking twenty points from five wins and ten draws.

If only we could have turned just two of those drawn games into wins we would have been promoted. Although we never had any hope of overhauling Leicester City, who led almost throughout the season, we ended only one point behind runners-up Nottingham Forest.

Although I started the season again at centre forward, and had been scoring fairly consistently, injuries to Brian Jackson and Louis Bimpson left the club in a bit of a quandary about the outside right position.

So Phil Taylor switched me to the right wing, knowing I'd had plenty of experience playing there. I played seventeen successive games wearing the No. 7 jersey and another at inside right – a position for which I hadn't the slightest liking – before being restored to centre forward.

I still managed to end up top scorer for the seventh time in eight seasons. I got 21 League goals, the closest to that being Johnny Wheeler, Alan A'Court and Alan Arnell who each scored ten.

Included in Wheeler's total was an unusual hat trick, scored in the last nine minutes against Port Vale at Anfield on his fifth Liverpool appearance. It ensured a 4–1 victory for his new club, who had equalised through Liddell early in the second half.

For left winger A'Court it was the season when he made his England Under-23 debut against France at Bristol in the game in which the brilliant Doncaster Rovers teenage forward Alick Jeffrey broke his right leg in two places to end his international career before it had hardly begun. The youngster, discovered by his club manager Peter Doherty and earmarked by Matt Busby to join Manchester United, did make a comeback of sorts but broke his other leg playing for Skegness Town two years later.

A'Court was more fortunate. He had seven Under-23 outings

and won five full caps, including three games for England in the 1958 World Cup Finals in Sweden, a tournament in which a seventeen-year-old called Pelé burst onto the global stage to help Brazil win the coveted trophy with two goals in the 5–2 win over the hosts in the final.

Liddell celebrated his 400th League appearance for Liverpool with a 2–0 home win over Bury on 22 December 1956 in which he scored one of the goals from the penalty spot. Sadly, the fates conspired to deny the Liverpool captain a large crowd on his landmark day. Just five days earlier petrol rationing had been imposed, due to fuel shortages caused by the closure of the Suez Canal and the Iraq oil pipeline. Subsequent public transport cuts and thick fog on the day of the match restricted the Anfield attendance to 18,754.

It was a Christmas when Merseyside acted as a transit camp for thousands of Hungarian refugees en route to Canada and America after fleeing in the wake of Russian tanks rolling in and crushing their brief, desperate attempt to shake off the Soviet yoke.

Liverpool's football fortunes matched the dank, dark winter when they crashed out of the FA Cup at the first hurdle in a mud-bath at Third Division Southend. An early goal from Jim Duthie and a late strike from Jim Thomson after Wheeler had equalised wrote another painful Cup chapter for Liverpool, for whom goalkeeper Tommy Younger was star man.

'There'd been a lot of rain all week and the Roots Hall pitch was an absolute quagmire,' said Liddell. 'It was impossible to play good football on it and we never really got going. It was a bitter pill to go out again at the hands of another Third Division club but on the day there was no disputing that Southend were the better team.'

Within days of Liverpool's ignominious Cup exit the country had a new Prime Minister, Harold Macmillan succeeding Sir Anthony Eden. But as the door to Downing Street opened to its new incumbent in a blaze of flashlights another door opened, unheralded, into a smelly city centre basement in Liverpool.

The newly opened Cavern Club in Mathew Street – its name inspired by the Paris jazz club *Le Caveau* – originally staged

jazz and then skiffle. But it would be in the vanguard of a
popular music revolution, driven by the beat of four young men
called The Beatles, themselves admirers of folk hero Liddell.
The seeds of their union were sown just six months later, in
July 1957, when the paths of Paul McCartney and John Lennon
first crossed at a fete at St Peter's church hall in Liverpool's
Woolton district.

A few miles away at Anfield the revolution necessary to
restore Liverpool FC to its former glories was still some years
distant, and 1957–8 brought a frustratingly similar story of
the team keeping their fans on tenterhooks but again missing out
on promotion.

This time they finished fourth, three points behind Second
Division champions West Ham, two behind runners-up Blackburn
and one behind third-placed Charlton. Liddell, as usual, could
hardly have done more to inspire Liverpool, finishing top scorer
for the eighth time in nine seasons.

Five of his 22 goals came against promoted Blackburn, both in
Liverpool's 2–0 home win in November and a hat trick in the 3–3
draw at Ewood Park in February, to bring his haul to eleven in his
last eight League meetings with the Lancashire club, a series that
yielded a total of 38 goals.

'Liddell was the hero,' reported the *Liverpool Echo*. 'He scored
a second-half hat trick, with two shots and a header, and fought
like a demon for every ball.'

A week later Liverpool were back at Blackburn in the sixth
round of the FA Cup, a path on which they had embarked by
avenging the previous year's third-round defeat by Southend –
but only just!

They had to rely on a Ray Smith own goal to snatch a 1–1 draw
at Anfield and it was not until eleven minutes from the end of the
Roots Hall replay that Dick White scored an equaliser before
Tony Rowley's goal secured a 3–2 win.

Northampton Town were then despatched 3–1 at home –
Liddell's blistering right-foot volley opening the scoring – before
Bobby Murdoch's goal on his Cup debut gave Liverpool a 1–0
win at Scunthorpe in round five.

So Anfield Cup ambitions had once again been ignited when they made their swift return to Ewood Park following their 3–3 League thriller, after which a prophecy made to Liddell came true, as he explained:

As we walked off the pitch at the end of the League match Matt Woods, the former Everton centre half who'd played so well for Blackburn, came over to me to congratulate me on my hat trick. But he added that I wouldn't have the same luck the following week. Unfortunately, he was right.

I'd far rather have switched my hat trick to the the Cup tie, in which we were handicapped by an early injury to inside left Jimmy Harrower, who'd been signed from Hibernian for £11,000 the previous month.

Jimmy had to have his right thigh strapped by our trainer Albert Shelley in the opening quarter of an hour and could move only at half speed for the rest of the match. Even though we took the lead through Bobby Murdoch, a Merseyside lad who first joined us an amateur, Blackburn scored two late goals and won 2–1.

Thus the gloom descended again on Liverpool's FA Cup aspirations, although the previous autumn the club had opened a new, illuminated football era which had been long delayed through the obstinate refusal of the football authorities to embrace it.

Even back in the nineteenth century Everton, then known as St Domingo, had helped pioneer floodlit football by playing under arc lights to earn the nickname of 'The Moonlight Dribblers'. In 1949 non-League Merseyside club South Liverpool were among the first in Britain to install floodlights. But it was not until February 1956 that the first ever Football League game under lights was staged between Portsmouth and Newcastle (on the same day as Liddell's famous 'goal that wasn't' against Manchester City).

Three months previously Wembley staged its first floodlit game, an international between England and Spain, and both Liverpool and neighbours Everton decided to invest in this exciting new development. As a grand switch-on at each ground the Mersey rivals staged a two-match home and away meeting, with the winners lifting a trophy provided by Liverpool County FA to mark its 75th anniversary.

First Division Everton were at home in the first leg on Wednesday 9 October 1957, the overdue arrival of floodlights classically illustrated by the fact that five days earlier the world's first space satellite, Sputnik 1, was launched by the Soviet Union.

The *Liverpool Echo*, its enthusiasm overflowing, declared in a ten-page souvenir special: 'Enough electricity to last an ordinary house for six months will be used at Goodison Park tonight. The most soccer-minded city in Britain will be eager to pass judgement not only on their teams but on the modern miracle that is floodlit football.'

The game drew an attendance of 58,771 with Everton winning 2–0, thanks to two goals from Eddie Thomas who, by special agreement in those pre-substitute days, had replaced injured Wally Fielding. Liddell missed the match through injury, seventeen-year-old Johnny Morrissey coming in and starring against the club he would join five years later for £10,000.

Three weeks later the second leg under the new Anfield lights pulled in a crowd of 46,724 and Liddell celebrated his comeback with two goals in a minute midway through the first half. Morrissey added a third shortly afterwards, but goals from Dave Hickson and Jimmy Harris reduced Liverpool's victory margin to 3–2 and by virtue of a 4–3 aggregate their rivals lifted the commemorative trophy, which is still on display at Goodison.

One feature of the match which struck Liddell concerned himself and rival captain Don Donovan, who had succeeded Peter Farrell as Everton skipper. 'Don, like myself with Malcolm and David, was the father of twins. I wonder if it's unique for that to be the case for captains of clubs in the same city. It's certainly highly unusual.'

Between the two inaugural floodlit games Liddell's wide playing repertoire, which extended to every outfield department, went close to including goalkeeping as well when Liverpool went to Derby County on Saturday 19 October 1957, the day after 15-year-old

Paul McCartney played his first gig with his band the Quarrymen at the New Clubmoor Hall, deep in the Merseyside suburbs.

Liverpool's succession of injuries and illness had forced them to name four captains in five games – the fourth of them, Geoff Twentyman, himself being carried off! – and when Liddell returned at the Baseball Ground after a seven-match absence with a pulled muscle he had a problem to solve.

I had a tricky decision to make as captain because our keeper Tommy Younger was injured and couldn't continue. At one time or another I'd played for Liverpool in every position except goal, having been chosen for all five forward roles and deputising for injured players in all the full back and half back positions.

Here was the opportunity for me to figure in my eleventh different berth and complete the 'set' because Tony Rowley, who I'd first asked to go in goal when Tommy was hurt, declined the job.

But on second thoughts I asked Ronnie Moran to take over, as I knew he was quite a capable goalkeeper in an emergency. He did so without a moment's hesitation and played a blinder, even though we lost 2–1.

I deputised for Ronnie at left back while injured Tommy, the first postwar Liverpool keeper to be taken off in a match, came back on to play centre forward.

Ronnie, who later succeeded me as captain after Johnny Wheeler had done the job for a year, was called up that season for the first of two Football League appearances. He was an extremely sound and capable full back and it always puzzled me why no further representative honours came his way.

He covered his goalkeeper in the way that Dougie Gray of Rangers used to do when I watched him in my younger days. I reckon Ronnie, by his splendid anticipation, saved Liverpool more times than any full back in my experience.

He prevented many goals by heading or kicking the ball off the line with the keeper beaten and if there was a better or stronger kicker of a dead ball than Ronnie Moran I would have liked to have seen him.

The 1957–8 season saw Liddell reach another glittering mark in his career when he surpassed Elisha Scott's League appearance record for Liverpool. At the time it was thought that the redoubtable Irish goalkeeper had played 429 games between 1912 and 1934. So when Liddell clocked up his 430th League outing for the club against Notts County, managed by Tommy Lawton, at Anfield on 9 November 1957 it was suitably heralded by the media and the club – and by Liddell himself – as the record-breaker.

However, subsequent statistical scrutiny revealed that Scott made 430 League appearances so, in reality, it was not until a week later that Liddell set a new club record, in a 3–1 defeat at Ipswich.

But in the belief that Liddell's outing against Notts County, in which he scored the third Liverpool goal in a 4–0 win, overtook Scott's total Liddell admitted:

The Press made so much of this milestone in my career that, for the first time in my life, I felt self-conscious as I ran onto the field before the match to great applause from the crowd.

Then, as the referee whistled the captains to the middle to toss up, the whole Notts County team came over and shook my hand, a nice gesture which the supporters seemed to appreciate as much as I did.

Obviously it was a match in which I was particularly anxious to score and I got my wish. When the match was over my old friend Tommy Lawton, the opposing manager, added his own congratulations to his team's and it was Tommy who was responsible for the great gesture by his players.

Liddell went on to make 492 League appearances for Liverpool in which he scored 216 goals. Only Ian Callaghan, who replaced his boyhood idol in the team, stands above the great Scot in the club records with 640 League outings between 1960 and 1978.

The 1957–8 campaign also saw Liddell score in a 2–2 draw at Craven Cottage, taking his career goal haul against Fulham to thirteen, a total he later equalled against Middlesbrough. His haul against Fulham included two penalties in a hat trick in September 1954. The double spot-kick success was not achieved again by a Liverpool player for twenty years, when Alec Lindsay scored from two penalties against Leicester in 1974.

Liverpool's home record in 1957–8 was impressive. They began with a 1–1 draw against Huddersfield but did not concede another Anfield goal until December in their tenth home match, a 1–1 draw with West Ham when Liddell's late goal secured a point.

They won seventeen, drew three and lost only one of their home games, but won only five on opposition territory, which included a 5–1 defeat at Charlton when Laurie Hughes made the last of his 326 appearances deputising for Dick White in a depleted flu-hit side. Gerry Byrne put through his own goal on his debut and only outing of the season. The nineteen-year-old former Liverpool Schoolboy made only a single appearance the following campaign and was eventually transfer-listed until his career was dramatically rescued by the arrival of a man called Shankly.

Liddell described the climax to the season:

At the beginning of March 1958 we were third in the table, five points behind West Ham and Charlton. Blackburn had a point less but two games in hand so we obviously had a good chance of finishing in the top two and being promoted if anybody slipped up.

Charlton did slip but West Ham and Blackburn didn't. Although we won seven and drew two of our last ten games we couldn't catch West Ham who finished top with 57 points.

Blackburn were second on 56, Charlton finished third with 55 and we were fourth, a point further away. For the third year running we'd secured a talent money place. But that wasn't any real consolation. We were very disappointed.

Overshadowing not only football but Britain's national life in 1958 was the Munich air disaster that tragically cost the young lives of so many of Manchester United's European pioneers and almost that of their manager, Liddell's friend and former Liverpool captain Matt Busby.

On Thursday 6 February the aircraft carrying the United party after their European Cup game at Red Star Belgrade crashed on the runway at Munich. Twenty-three people perished, including eight of the vibrant, awesome team built by Busby. The Old Trafford supremo himself was left critically ill and fighting for his life, a battle he would win and emerge from to lead his club to greater glory. The Munich tragedy stunned the nation and a minute's silence was observed at football matches throughout the country.

A decade later Busby saw another generation of United players become the first English team to lift the European Cup – just twelve months after Celtic had led the way for Britain – and the next English club to win it would be Liverpool in 1977, master-minded by the managerial genius of Liddell's former colleague Bob Paisley.

In the late 1950s European football was not even a pipe dream for Liverpool, trapped as they were in the Second Division, but the 1958–9 season was to be the club's last full campaign under Phil Taylor's management. It would prove eventful both for the club and Liddell, whose standing in the community – his tireless commitment to sport and youth development complementing his Corinthian values on the pitch – was recognised in 1958 when he was appointed a magistrate for the city of Liverpool.

'His selection was a tribute to the man, to his club and to the game,' enthused noted football historian Dr Percy M Young. 'The only other practising footballer to have been so honoured was Ray Middleton, the Chesterfield goalkeeper.

'One can only observe that such selection is realistic and imaginative and, in so far as the intention is towards the problems of youth, more likely to be efficacious than the promotion of other worthies whose frequent distinction is that they have none.'

Phyllis Liddell recalls clearly how Billy received the news of his magisterial selection: 'His appointment came out of the blue.

It was a real surprise both to Billy and to me but a great honour. One day he received a letter from the Duchy of Lancaster inviting him to join the Bench.

'Somebody had recommended him but we never found out who. Billy was, by nature, a very quiet, softly spoken person but we, the family, told him that now he had become a magistrate he would have to assert himself on the Bench, which he did.

'To do that, given his quiet nature, he must have had to dig deep into his personality and the same applied when he had to make himself heard when he gave talks, either to youth clubs or on after-dinner occasions.

'I'm sure his faith and his principles played a big part in helping him do that. He certainly succeeded because he was a magistrate for thirty years until he had to retire at the age of seventy.

'Being a magistrate as well as a famous footballer was, of course, highly unusual. One day Billy and I were walking down Lord Street in Liverpool city centre when someone shouted from the other side of the road: "Hi, Billy. Nice to see you. You remember me, don't you? You sent me down!" That really tickled us.'

Liddell, who served in both the adult and juvenile courts, brought to his duties some passionate beliefs about youth care and influence, saying:

There is a lot of concern about juvenile deliquency but I feel very strongly that in the big cities, and elsewhere for that matter, there are nothing like sufficient open spaces for the youngsters to let off steam and energy in harmless ways.

It's true that many children go off the rails through lack of parental supervision and guidance but many of those might not do so if they could play organised games under good conditions.

Often, as boys filed in to appear before the juvenile court magistrates, they used to recognise me and give a hesitant sort of grin as though to say: 'I cheer you on Saturday afternoons so don't be hard on me!'

I've been told that some of them even boasted to their pals about Billy Liddell's signature being on their probation orders! Boys will be boys.

However, Liddell was to find himself on a very different bench in traumatic circumstances, reduced to a spectator's role as Liverpool suffered one of the most humiliating experiences in their history.

The summer of 1958 saw the Litter Act come into force in Britain, the country's first parking meters installed in London's Mayfair and Columbia Records sign a seventeen-year-old vocalist called Cliff Richard.

Liddell was in the Liverpool party that made a five-match close-season tour of Spain, in which he scored three goals, and he gave an impressive display in Scotland in Liverpool's 2–2 draw with an Edinburgh Select side at Tynecastle Park, when he scored both goals.

'Liddell may be a yard or two slower nowadays but he still knows where the goal is in addition to spraying his passes most effectively,' declared the *Liverpool Daily Post*, which also reported that he played on after being concussed in a collision with a pitch-side photographer.

But Liverpool won only four and lost five of their first eleven games in the new season, a worrying period climaxed by a 5–0 drubbing at Bill Shankly's Huddersfield, a match Liddell missed through injury.

He returned a week later to help the side beat Lincoln City 3–2 at Anfield, with new winger Fred Morris, a £7,000 signing from Mansfield, scoring twice on the day that BBC TV's *Grandstand* sports programme was first transmitted.

Then came the bombshell. Liddell was dropped for the first time in his iconic Liverpool career, left out of their line-up at Fulham in the club's thirteenth game of the season on 18 October (the same month he was appointed to the Bench as a Justice of the Peace).

Louis Bimpson, in and out of the team since his signing from local non-League club Burscough in 1953 and who would join

Blackburn a year later and play in the FA Cup Final, took over
Liddell's No. 9 jersey. How ironic that the opposition should have
been Fulham, against whom Liddell had scored thirteen goals and
a club that vied with Middlesbrough as his favourite quarry.

Fans were shocked and angry at Liddell's exclusion, baffled at
the decision to drop their hero after he had scored nine goals in his
nine appearances so far that season, reaching his double century of
League goals in the opening week of the campaign. How, asked
Anfield supporters in the letters pages of the local papers, could the
club even contemplate ditching the man who had so often galloped
to the team's rescue like the cavalry in a western movie and whose
name had literally been synonymous with Liverpool?

Fate applied its own twist with Bimpson scoring the only goal
at Craven Cottage to inflict the first defeat of the season on
Fulham, who still went on to secure promotion, as runners-up to
Second Division champions Sheffield Wednesday. Liverpool's
victory in London sparked a surging run that brought fourteen
wins from sixteen League games up to early February. Liddell
remained out of the team and relegated to the reserves, for whom
he made twelve appearances that season, scoring four goals.

Across the Mersey, his absence from the Liverpool team stirred
lofty ambitions at New Brighton FC, who had been Football
League members until 1951 and had captured national attention in
1957 when, as a Lancashire Combination club, they reached the
fourth round of the FA Cup by beating Stockport, Derby and
Torquay before being overwhelmed 9–0 by Burnley.

New Brighton had set a record for fielding the oldest ever
League player when Scottish international half back Neil
McBain, then their secretary-manager, appeared as an emergency
goalkeeper against Hartlepool in March 1947 at the age of 51
years 4 months. So their eyes alighted on 36-year-old Liddell, a
spring chicken by comparison, in the belief that his signing as
player-manager would be a massive coup. Their audacious
approach to take the Kop hero across the Mersey was rejected
both by Liverpool and by Liddell who, contrary to some contemporary newspaper reports, never harboured an ounce of
managerial ambition at any level of football.

Meanwhile, for the first time in their postwar history Liverpool pressed on deliberately without Liddell, who displayed familiar graciousness in his response.

'Louis Bimpson got off to a good start after taking over from me at Fulham,' he said. 'But after scoring nine goals in twelve games he got injured and Alan Arnell was called on to play at centre forward.'

Yet another statistical aberration, similar to the one surrounding his surpassing the previous season of Elisha Scott's appearance record, kept Liddell on needless tenterhooks through the winter.

At the time it was believed that Everton's long-serving England goalkeeper Ted Sagar's senior Merseyside club record for most League appearances stood at 465. In fact, Sagar's total was later confirmed as 463 but Liddell, in the midst of media publicity prompted by the wrong figure, was unaware that he had already passed it, as he recalled:

After being left out at Fulham in October I played one game in November – a 2–1 home win over Bristol Rovers – which took my number of League appearances to 465 which equalled what was announced as Ted's total.

I wouldn't have been human if I hadn't been looking forward to my next League game so that I could overtake Ted. But I had to wait four months! My opportunity finally arrived in March. Alan A'Court, feeling less than fully fit, was rested for the Good Friday home game with Barnsley and I was recalled in my favourite position of outside left.

The great welcome I got from the crowd was unforgettable and I was very grateful to them. Like me, they believed I was about to break Ted Sagar's record and they gave me a tremendous reception.

The roar of appreciation from the majority of the 52,546 crowd for their returning hero, now 37, was to increase in volume. Jimmy Melia scored for Liverpool early in the match but there were only eleven minutes left with the game level at 1–1 and

Barnsley in command when Liddell took charge of events. Taking possession out on the flank he cut inside and unleashed an unstoppable shot that flew into the Barnsley net. 'No goal at Anfield was ever greeted with such acclaim,' said one observer, with only a touch of hyperbole.

If the Kop faithful were delighted with that strike, they were ecstatic four minutes later when Liddell drilled in his second goal of the match to secure a 3–2 win. Then he was denied a hat trick only when his flying header crashed back off the underside of the bar.

'I was a happy man when I trotted off the field that afternoon with the roar of the crowd ringing in my ears,' said Liddell, who retained his place for all but one of the remaining games, reverting to centre forward after A'Court's return and playing at inside right for the last two matches in place of Jimmy Harrower.

Why on earth he was left out in the first place must remain one of the most baffling questions in Liverpool history. Despite his long absence Liddell still finished second top scorer with an impressive tally of fourteen goals from nineteen League outings behind 21–goal Melia.

Had the directors not been foolhardy enough to drop him in the first place, Liddell might have supplied the firepower to help fourth-placed Liverpool bridge the seven-point gap between them and runners-up Fulham, which again cost them promotion.

'That was very disappointing,' Liddell admitted. 'I wanted to have another run in First Division football before hanging up my boots and another chance had slipped away.' Liddell was fated never to achieve that ambition of stepping once more onto the top-flight stage.

If the promotion failure was something to which long-suffering Liverpool fans had become inured, as well as the club's persistent FA Cup disappointments, nothing prepared them for the experience of 15 January 1959. Less than a fortnight after Fidel Castro overthrew the established powers in Cuba's revolution, Liverpool were the victims of a sensational overturn of football's recognised order.

Liverpool were drawn away to Southern League part-timers Worcester City and Liddell's exclusion from the team meant that his remarkable unbroken 40-match postwar FA Cup run had been ended. The tie was originally scheduled for Saturday 10 January, but a frozen pitch at St George's Lane forced a postponement. One travelling Liverpool supporter, writing under the pseudonym 'Kemlyn Kid', recounted his wasted trip thus:

'Being a non-League side we'd no idea where Worcester was but we all nipped off to Exchange Station and got on the football special. We all had our scarves, rosettes and rattles and were making a hell of a racket.

'The *Daily Mirror* was ranting on about giant killers just because they'd beaten Millwall in the second round but we'd won six League games in a row so we weren't too worried about little Worcester.

'The weather was horrible and the train cold and all you could see out of the window were the great billows of smoke from the steam engine pulling us. As soon as we got to Worcester and started to get off the train we got told the game was postponed. The pitch wasn't fit.

'We all had to get back on the train and go home. The game was now going to be played on Thursday afternoon. I couldn't go and Dad had run out of dead Grannies! So we had to wait for the *Echo*.

'Dad couldn't believe the score and I couldn't believe it. Worcester City had beaten Liverpool 2–1. It was the biggest humiliation we'd known. Dick White, a hero at Southend a year earlier, became the villain of Worcester and scored an own goal. He said that the ball ran off him into the goal and that was that.

'It was the biggest embarrassment of an embarrassing decade . . . a Cup Final defeat, losses against three sides from the Third Division in the FA Cup, relegation, a 9–1 defeat at Birmingham and in two seasons we let almost a hundred goals in. Dad said he'd never go again until we had a new manager.'

Liddell, who travelled to Worcester with the Liverpool party and helped trainer Albert Shelley stud the players' boots, could only watch as an anguished spectator as Worcester humbled their visitors from Anfield who, at the time, were still in contention for a return to the top flight of English football.

On a brown, bare surface devoid even of a blade of grass, the home part-timers, captained by Liverpool's former Manchester City adversary Roy Paul, carried out their manager Bill Thompson's plan to keep the ball on the ground to make Liverpool's defenders twist and turn.

That ploy and Worcester's direct style soon unhinged Liverpool who went behind after only nine minutes when visiting right back John Molyneux, attempting to turn a low cross back to Tommy Younger, succeeded only in turning it away from the Scotland goalkeeper. Although Dick White won the race for possession with Tommy Skuse he mistakenly prodded the ball into the path of the eighteen-year-old who gleefully fired into an unguarded net.

Liverpool improved – as their pride decreed they must – at the start of the second half with Geoff Twentyman hitting a post and home keeper Johnny Kirkwood saving twice from Alan A'Court and stopping another effort from Fred Morris. But with ten minutes left Worcester doubled their advantage when White's attempt to clear from Knowles went awry and the ball looped up off his foot and over the advancing Younger.

Three minutes later a Liverpool penalty, awarded for a foul on Louis Bimpson in a goalmouth scramble, was dispatched by Twentyman to cut the deficit. It was, however, merely academic. When the final whistle sounded the home fans went wild with delight and the local *Evening Times* declared: 'Worcester has never seen anything like it.

'Young boys and elderly gentlemen danced like dervishes side by side. What could be the cause of such euphoria? The building of a new bus shelter on the Droitwich road? A personal appearance at the local Spar shop by Alma Cogan?

'No, it was the remarkable performance of Southern League Worcester City in removing such an illustrious name as Liverpool from the third round of the FA Cup.'

A humorous follow-up was recalled by a caller to BBC Radio Merseyside's *Football Football Show* in January 2003. 'Bob in St Helens' told presenter Alan Jackson: 'The Worcester skipper Roy Paul revealed afterwards in an article in the *Empire News* that he had played with a hangover against Liverpool and that he had seen two Billy Liddells racing down the wing. When it was pointed out to him that Liddell hadn't been in the team, Paul replied: "That just shows you how much I'd had to drink!" '

But it was no laughing matter for Liverpool. Not since the early days of the twentieth century had Liverpool been knocked out by a non-League club, Southampton ejecting them 4–1 in 1902 and Norwich City winning 3–2 at Anfield in 1909.

The Worcester humiliation, compounded by another aborted promotion attempt, prompted the fans to vote with their feet. Liverpool's final home fixture, against Scunthorpe, was watched by a postwar low club League attendance of only 11,976.

The traumatic season, however, would prove to be a low-water mark for the club preceding a tidal wave called Shankly, whose sweep into Anfield would bring Billy Liddell's career full circle.

Chapter Eleven

Workload of a Legend

Was Clark Kent really the alter ego of Superman? Or was it William Beveridge Liddell inside that familiar costume righting wrongs and winning heroic acclaim?

The question is only slightly flippant because Liddell's demanding lifestyle was enough to send even the most dedicated business executive to the door of his psychiatrist seeking stress counselling. When you add his life as a football hero for club and country to his family responsibilities, his duties as an accountant and magistrate and his unstinting work for youth, the church and the community at large, plus his other sporting interests, it forms a workload that seems almost impossible for one man to shoulder.

Yet this kaleidosope of activity was undertaken with alacrity by the remarkable Liddell. 'It speaks volumes for Billy that he was such a great, consistent player while being, essentially, a part-timer,' exclaimed Sir Tom Finney, Liddell's great contemporary winger. Finney starred for Preston and England while running a plumbing business but pointed out: 'Whereas I managed to train every day Billy trained only twice a week. That's what I find incredible.'

Phyllis Liddell believes the momentum of it all just carried Billy along. 'I don't think he really thought about it,' she reflected. 'He just got on with it although I think he could have done with a few more hours in the day!'

Finney's comments identify something quite remarkable. If the contrast between the lifestyle of players from Liddell's era and their 21st-century football successors is a stark one, in Liddell's case it is a massive chasm.

There was no rotation of playing squads in Liddell's era. He was a man for all seasons and most matches and in 1959, nearing the end of his playing career, Liddell charted a typical week in his hectic life, one of wide-ranging demands beyond the comprehension of the modern, pampered Premiership player.

Some people's lives are so wrapped up in soccer that they never get away from it for any length of time. Nobody likes his football more than I do and if I'd not been lucky enough to earn a living at the game I'd have played as an amateur on every possible occasion.

I've always tried to put people in the picture regarding the life of a professional footballer by means of lectures to various luncheon organisations, youth clubs and so on – but it doesn't end there.

Often when my wife and I go out for a little relaxation I'm buttonholed by folk who insist on talking football interminably. They say variety is the spice of life and I fully agree. I think the variety I've been able to cram into my own life outside football has enabled me to put greater effort into the game than would otherwise have been the case.

I've never been in danger of getting bored with football, although I know some players who, if not exactly bored with it, have periods when they lose the zest which is necessary for a professional to keep on the top line throughout a long and arduous season.

Some players find the training routines particularly irksome. I think I would, too, if I hadn't got other interests. As it is, the training provides me with an opportunity to get away from ledgers and into the open air.

Conversely, I think the training I do and the football I play help me to give better service to my firm because I'm always physically fit – and that's a great thing for office workers.

In my early days as a footballer I had no need for a diary. I trained two mornings a week, played at weekends or in midweek matches, and went into the office for the remainder of the time.

Nowadays I have such a multiplicity of engagements that I'm obliged to write them down. This breakdown of a typical week gives people some idea of how my time is occupied.

Sunday: To many people, Sunday is the last day of the week and not of outstanding importance. I firmly believe it's the most important day of the week. After playing on Saturday it's a big temptation to stay in bed and I indulge this to a certain extent. But I'm up by 10 a.m. and on my way to Court Hey Methodist church by 11 a.m.

After lunch I revise the lesson for our youngsters at Court Hey Sunday School. For some years I was leader of the young people's class but nowadays take a smaller one in the junior school.

I'm very fond of children and never miss Sunday afternoon class unless we've been playing a match so far from home that it's impossible to get back in time.

After the children have gone I attend to my tasks as Sunday School treasurer. At one time my Sunday evenings were frequently occupied by attending sportsmen's services around Merseyside and often much further afield.

But with my sons growing up I prefer to spend the evening quietly at home with my family. After the youngsters have gone to bed Phyllis and I usually have friends in to discuss the ruling topics of the moment – football excepted, if I can manage to steer clear of it! As most of our visitors are church members religious topics get a good airing.

Monday: I rise about 8 a.m. and take the twins to school before going on to the office in Liverpool city centre. I usually spend my lunch hour in the company of friends from nearby shipping offices, most of whom support either Liverpool or Everton.

This is one place where I just can't get away from football argument. But it's all very light-hearted and lively. Sometimes I get my leg pulled unmercifully. I finish work at 5 p.m. unless something urgent demands that I stay later.

As a rule, Monday evenings see me with an engagement at a boys or youth club where I talk about my life as a professional footballer, show my souvenirs, international caps, medals, jerseys, programmes and such like.

Then I roll up my sleeves ready to answer questions. Question time is always lively and prolonged and, believe me, some of the questions the youngsters hurl at me would stump anyone!

Tuesday: The same early morning routine then on to the football club for training, which is usually done at our very fine Melwood training ground, where there are several pitches.

Lunch is provided at Anfield, after which I go on to the office for an afternoon's work. This programme is varied on two afternoons each month when I am on rota as a magistrate in the adult court. Service there varies from an hour up to three hours, according to the number or complexity of the cases to be heard.

Tuesday night is one evening which I keep free from all outside engagements so that I can take Phyllis to the theatre, cinema or a dance. We have similar tastes in plays, preferring thrillers, light comedies or good musicals.

Wednesday: This is usually a replica of Monday except that, occasionally, I'm invited to speak at luncheon club gatherings. My first job in the evening is to write my weekly article for the *Liverpool Echo* football edition. Then I get down to answering my correspondence, which is usually heavy and varied.

Thursday: The same as Tuesday except that the football training is changed. On Thursday it's usually lapping, sprinting and exercises, followed by a five-a-side match on the car park.

After lunch I go to the office for another afternoon's work. Occasionally, though, there's a change in the afternoon when I go to Alder Hey Children's Hospital and act as disc jockey for the WVS, putting on a record request programme for the young patients.

Thursday evening engagements vary, depending on the
calls of various organisations, such as the Liverpool and
District St. Andrew Society, of which I'm currently president.

Friday: This is an important morning for the twins, who
take their football kit for their weekly sports and soccer
afternoon at school, which is what they relish most of all the
week's activities.

By 10 a.m. I'm on the Bench in the Juvenile Court, a job I
find interesting, distressing and sometimes extremely
frustrating. I'm in the office on Friday afternoon – unless
we're travelling to an away game – and I spend the evening
quietly at home, catching up with more correspondence and
watching that 'one-eyed monster' television. I enjoy it but
I'm not its slave because I seldom have time to look at it.

Normally eight hours' sleep each night is as much as I
need but I try to get a minimum of nine hours the night
before a match – and sometimes more.

Saturday: How this is spent obviously depends on whether
we have a home or away match. But whichever it is I have an
extra hour in bed. At home, I often spend the morning
watching my twins play for their local Life Boys team.

I'm afraid the boys are far from being the leading lights of
their side and, though there is time yet for them to develop,
at present they give no sign of being the target of big club
talent spotters later on.

If they have the latent ability it will doubtless show itself.
If they haven't I won't worry. We can't all be professional
footballers and if they are better fitted for some other way of
making a living, they must follow their natural bent.

Opinions vary as to what is the best midday meal prior to
a match. In my own case it hasn't changed in all my years of
postwar football. In the RAF we had whatever was going
and, sometimes, we ate far more heartily than is regarded as
wise nowadays.

My own pre-match meal consists of one poached egg on
toast and a milk pudding. While some players would look
askance at that, I've always found it adequate.

When we're playing an away match I usually have steamed fish instead of poached egg. But I can't face up to anything like steak, which some players swear by.

For home games we report to Anfield not later than 45 minutes before kickoff. I'm usually the last to enter the dressing room, often because I'm waylaid by autograph hunters after parking my car.

I never refuse these eager youngsters unless it is absolutely unavoidable, such as when I'm dashing off to catch a train or to keep an appointment. I've got all the Liverpool youngsters 'trained' nicely now. They know they can get my autograph before the game and usually let me leave unmolested afterwards!

Since being appointed as a magistrate the ribbing I get from the team-mates for being last to report has taken a new form. One of them will see me come in and announce to the rest of the lads that 'His Honour' has taken his seat and all is well!

After the game I'm at the tail-end of the queue emerging from the bath. I like to stay in as long as possible and always finish off with a cold shower, no matter how bitter the day may be. Some of the lads don't always do that in the depths of winter but I've considered it an insurance against chills.

Saturday nights after a home game are usually spent with Phyllis at a cinema, theatre or private dance. After away matches we make the journey home, if it can be made the same night. Otherwise, it means travelling back on Sunday.

That is how my typical week is made up. Obviously there are changes from time to time, such as when the club decides we should go away for special training or relaxation.

There are also evening meetings of various social organisations cropping up at intervals which mean a change of schedule. Letter writing fills any spare time I have, particularly when I'm away from home. Long journeys allow me the chance for correspondence.

Now and again I've received abusive letters, occasionally very scurrilous ones, but they've been rare and they've never

worried me. But I've been incensed on the few occasions
that anonymous people have written to my wife, which is a
despicable thing for anybody to do.

If only people who send such anonymous letters knew
how Phyllis and I regard such communication, they'd save
the expense of buying a threepenny stamp.

But most letters are welcome and many make you smile.
One of them was unique. I received it after incidents of
football fans misbehaving at away games and a report that a
photograph of me had been stolen from a public house.

The letter read: 'Dear Billy, I am writing to say that I am
sorry for taking your photograph from that public house,
about which you may have read, but I hope it has not dis-
pleased you. I want to assure you that it was not hooliganism,
like there was after the game at Blackburn. I did it only
because I am one of your greatest fans and liked the photo so
much I could not resist taking it. But now I am very sorry.'

Unfortunately, the writer, presumably regarding dis-
cretion as the better part of confession, didn't give his name
or address, otherwise I'd have sent him an autographed
picture and got the original one back to return to the owner.

The worst experience I ever had with a 'supporter'
happened a few years ago when a man started ringing me
every Friday. He asked all sorts of impertinent questions,
such as whether the players were behaving themselves or
whether they'd been drinking.

Apparently, he didn't know that most of the lads are either
teetotallers like myself or never take more than a very
occasional glass of beer. At first, the calls were made
reasonably early in the evening. Then they started coming
through at midnight or after and the later they were, the more
tipsy the caller seemed.

After several weeks of this I informed the telephone
authorities and the police. As they were unable to trace the
source of the calls the Post Office changed my telephone
number which was made ex-directory. That stopped the
nuisance.

Half a century before the media frenzy over Posh and Becks underlined football's new money-driven celebrity status Phyllis Liddell had to contend with being married to a figure who was in constant public demand. 'In a sense it was like having a husband in show business,' she admitted.

'Invariably, if people knew Billy was at a certain place we would have to make arrangements to leave at least an hour before we were supposed to simply because we knew there would be a host of people who wanted to see him, shake hands with him or get his autograph.

'And if they'd had a few drinks, they'd come forward even more eagerly. I remember one occasion, as an example, when a golf captain and his wife who were friends of ours were standing waiting for us to leave a dinner-dance. I had to say to them: "I'm sorry, but you'll just have to make your own way because Billy won't refuse anybody and we'll be some time yet."

'There were several misapprehensions about Billy. One of them was the claim by some people that he was a lay preacher. He wasn't. He was steadfast in his faith but he never went round pushing it.

'What he liked doing was going to youth clubs to speak to the lads about team spirit and the way faith came into sport. I've known boys come to me and say: "We've never smoked or done this or that because Billy doesn't."

'That sort of thing, where Billy's example has influenced youngsters, sticks in your mind. He never rammed any of his views down people's throats. He never drank or smoked but never had any objection to others having a drink or a cigarette, like me for example!

'But Billy was a great role model. He liked to do the right thing. Although he was quiet I think he did appreciate what people thought of him. Everyone, it doesn't matter who they are, has at least a bit of ego. They've got to have, although it wasn't evident with Billy. Everything just rolled off him.

'Another misapprehension about Billy was that he lacked humour. That belief probably stemmed from his dour Scottishness. But, in fact, he had a great sense of humour. Perhaps he got that from his mother, who had a loud, infectious laugh.

'Billy used to appear in pantomimes I produced for the children at Court Hey Sunday School. We did all the traditional pantos such as *Jack and the Beanstalk*, *Cinderella*, *Snow White* and such like.

'We used to make the scenery in the garage at our house and Billy and his pal Alec McDonald, who he first met through the church and who became a close friend, used to appear in the pantos in various roles.

'At the pantos we'd have an audience of about three hundred kids, ranging from tots to teenagers, and they absolutely loved it. So did Billy and Alec! Alec, who was older than Billy, was a born comedian.

'We used to tell him that his talent was going to waste and that he should turn professional. He was such a funny man and often he'd have Billy and I and many others in absolute pleats.

'When we staged the pantos Billy's mother would watch from the front row and she'd laugh so loudly it would set off everyone else! She was the ideal person to have in the audience.'

Sport filled much of Liddell's time away from football, accountancy or charitable commitments. He played tennis as a club member and also in the summer when he and his family and a group of friends used to holiday at the Devon Coast Country Club, which was run by a company owned by former Liverpool chairman Billy McConnell.

'Billy had a wonderful eye for a ball,' said Phyllis. 'We both played badminton and in between matches we'd have a game of ping-pong. Billy occasionally played golf but, being a teetotaller, he wasn't a club man in the sense that he would socialise at the bar.

'Tennis, though, was a great love of his and we went to Wimbledon every year. Billy was in the know and always managed to get tickets. We were part of the furniture there and because we had friends living in Wimbledon we used to stay with them and walk from their home to the courts.

'Much of Billy's time was taken up with meetings connected with all his interests. When he sat on committees he didn't say very much but he would absorb a great deal and I'm told he made worthwhile suggestions.

'He was so quiet at home and didn't talk about what he was doing and, of course, he played for Liverpool despite training for only two half-days a week. People regularly asked where he found the time to do everything he did. Our boys David and Malcolm used to say: "My Dad does this, that and the other . . . and he plays football!" '

Malcolm revealed that his full realisation of the extent of his father's hero-worshipped status did not occur until recently – thanks to the Internet! 'It's funny because at the time you didn't think that much about it but it was brought home to me through the Friends Reunited website,' said Malcolm, who lives in Redcar with his wife Margaret and family.

'I looked up Ryebank Prep School in Huyton, which was the first school David and I attended, and there were people on that website saying that they'd had in their class two lads who were the sons of Billy Liddell.

'They said it would be like going to school today with David Beckham's son! That really brought things home to me and when I told David he was as gobsmacked as I was.

'As a youngster when I went shopping with my father in Liverpool virtually every other person would stop and say, "Hello, Billy" and he would always stop and speak to them. It was a continual procession of people but as a child you didn't really take it in that he was a famous footballer held in great esteem.

'When my father was at his peak as a player, I was only seven or eight and I was only months old and a babe in arms at the time of the 1950 FA Cup Final, although I do remember subsequently seeing Pathé News clips of the match.

'David and I later went to Quarry Bank Grammar School where our PE teacher used to remind us that John Lennon, who'd been at the school before us, used to deface his noticeboard with his funny little drawings.

'We both became PE teachers ourselves and, being quite tall, we did well at basketball and represented both Lancashire and Yorkshire counties, the latter by dint of the fact that we were resident in Leeds when we were training. I also played basketball in the National League for Sunderland and I still play tennis.

'Sport was always one of our great interests but I never really thought I would go into football because of the icon my father was. I felt it would have made it harder.

'Now, I sometimes wish I had! Even in the Third Division it would have been lucrative. But it was a conscious decision not to aim for a football career and I think David felt the same.

'When we went to Anfield to watch my father play we'd sit in the stand behind the directors' box. But as far as I can recollect I don't think we were afforded any great privileges. Football in those days didn't really cater for women and children. It was very much a male bastion rather than family orientated.

'We just accepted that my father played football but what did make an impression on me when we went to the match was the way the crowd responded to him and chanted.

'When I tell people that my father wasn't even a full-time player, and that he trained only twice a week, their jaw tends to drop. They can't believe it. It's unthinkable in football now and remarkable even then.

'At home I can recall my father's little black car – I can't remember the make or model – which my brother, my dad and I used to have to pull out of the small garage before we could get in it.

'On Saturday mornings when Liverpool were at home the meal in our house was always poached egg on toast, my father's pre-match meal. We all had it. I also remember being at Sunday school at the Methodist church and having the strange experience of hearing my dad talk about abstinence. The upshot was that my brother and I both signed the abstainer's roll, which for me has since gone by the wayside.

'My father was an incredibly modest man and I can never recall him shouting. He was softly spoken but he had a strong, moral sense of duty which obviously was part of his approach to serving as a magistrate. He was also an articulate man.'

Malcolm still follows Liverpool and his two sons Timothy and Andrew also have Anfield allegiances. 'I didn't have to spread that gospel,' he smiled. Twin brother David, who lives with his wife Jill and family in Castleford and keenly follows Liverpool's fortunes, recalls his father's sporting drive even after he had hung up his boots as a footballer.

'When we were on holiday my father would always take Malcolm and I to a pitch-and-putt course or a putting green and he was very competitive even there. He wasn't a regular golfer, it was something he never really took up, but in the couple of times I played with him I could see his great eye for a ball.

'Being the son of Billy Liddell the iconic footballer was always secondary to being the son of Billy Liddell the man. When people used to ask me what my dad did I'd reply: "He does this, he does that and, oh, he's a footballer!"

'My father was very involved with so many things, including boys clubs and youth groups, and he also appeared in the pantos my mother staged at the church hall. She played piano and produced the shows.

'There was an image of my father as a very dour man but he wasn't. He had a love of puns and plays on words. My great memory of my dad the footballer is of him having treatment at Anfield. He'd take Malcolm and I to the ground and we used to go into the treatment room with him.

'Albert Shelley and Bob Paisley were around then and it was all heat lamps and smells of embrocation. I have this vivid mental picture of Albert pummelling a player on the table – often my dad – with a cigarette dangling in his mouth.

'The gym as they called it then was nothing more than a small room with a couple of weights in it. The revolution in sports technology has been amazing. The treatment room was situated below what was then the paddock at Anfield and when you stood on the paddock terrace outside, there was a small, frosted-glass window.

'Unknown to the supporters that window was in the treatment room and the thought always used to strike me – if only the fans knew that through that little window their idols were stripping to their underpants and climbing on the table to have treatment!'

'I decided at an early age, probably eleven or twelve, that I wasn't going to attempt to follow in my father's footsteps into football. My father used to watch Malcolm and me play for the Life Boys team and said that he didn't think we were leading lights of the side.

'I realised that perhaps that was not the course my life was going to take. I was aware of the huge problems there could be attempting to follow a famous father into professional football. I did, though, enjoy basketball and managed to reach county standard, as did Malcolm who also played in the National League.

'My dad was very modest and was not one to talk about the games he'd played in, the goals he'd scored or the places he'd been. He was a man of few words and I can never remember him coming in after a match and talking about it.

'He must have had a kind of second personality, another persona separate from his home life, to enable him to give all his public talks and speeches. He said so little about football that I gleaned much of my information about his career from reading things about him.

'I was amazed to learn how much he'd done. All his press cuttings were stuffed in a suitcase so I decided, for my own benefit, to put a scrapbook together to chart his career.

'A few years ago we were on holiday in Brittany and I'd enrolled my son Steven, who was then eleven, for a football course. When we turned up, the young British student who was running it asked for Steven to register.

'Soon after, Steven came running back to me, a bit shocked, and said: "He knew who grandad was. When I told him my name was Liddell he asked me if I was the grandson of Billy."

'I think that brought home to Steven how famous my dad had been but it didn't end there. Amazingly, one of the questions in a quiz at that holiday centre was: "What nickname did Liverpool have in the 1950s? Answer: Liddellpool." I thought that was really ironic.'

Billy Liddell had already headed south and embarked on his football career when his family in Scotland celebrated the arrival of twins George and Rena, seventeen years younger than their famous brother.

George, still a keen Liverpool supporter and Anfield regular, recalled: 'Ours was almost like two families, with three older children and three younger ones. I used to go to Liverpool on visits to see Billy before the family moved down to Merseyside permanently in 1951 when I was eleven, the year after my father died.

'I remember as a boy being taken by Billy to Liverpool's Melwood training ground and having the great thrill of kicking a ball around with all the players before they went back to Anfield for baths and lunch.

'He was a great player who could play on either wing, down the middle or wherever they asked him and he could kick a ball with both feet. He took everything opponents dished out to him and he would certainly get knocked about a bit at times. But he was never violent, never retaliated and was never booked.

'To see him play was a marvellous experience and he's up there amongst the all-time greats. Unlike the international appearance money paid today Billy said that he'd play for his country for nothing.

'For him it was an honour to play for Scotland. He told me that he wouldn't change and that with modern football being more of a business than a sport he said he was glad he played in the era he did.

'I've got some great memories of him as a player, none more vivid than when I went from school to watch the famous FA Cup replay against Manchester City in 1956 when Billy's "goal" in the last few seconds was disallowed.

'I watched that match from the bandbox, which was situated just at the top of the steps leading out of the players tunnel, which was for the musicians providing pre-match entertainment.

'After matches Billy was always last out of the dressing room because he always had a cold shower after a hot bath. The younger players didn't bother but Billy always said it was good to have a cold shower to close his pores.

'Billy would sometimes have to go into the office to do some work at Simon, Jude and West on Saturday mornings and then, before he had his own car, catch a tram up to Anfield to play the match in the afternoon! Many people don't realise that he really was a part-time player.

'He used to take me to games and when he'd parked his car at Anfield he'd ask all the autograph hunters to form a line and he'd sign for every one of them. On occasions he would sign so many that someone would be sent from the dressing room to ask him to get changed because kickoff time was approaching!

'He was a very fit man and he used to upset his twin sons by beating them at squash when they were very nimble teenagers.'

George's twin sister Rena reveals that such is the legacy of her older brother's iconic status that she still gets introduced to people as Billy Liddell's sister, but insisted: 'It doesn't annoy me because he was such a lovely, unassuming fellow, with a dry sense of humour, as well as being a great footballer.

'Unfortunately, I didn't see him play very much. But I'm a regular at Anfield now and George's wife Betty and I share a season ticket. George and I used to take part with Billy in the pantomimes that Phyllis staged in Court Hey church hall.

'Phyllis really got everything going. She's a very talented lady, producing the pantos as well as playing the piano. She plays by ear and we've had some happy times.

'When we lived in Scotland we had a pedal organ in the house and we also took in lodgers. When Phyllis and Billy came up to see my mum she'd have a great time playing the organ and having sing-songs.

'I remember one of the occasions Billy came up to Scotland he gave a sermon at a church in Dunfermline with the theme: "Play up and play the game". He certainly lived that creed fully.'

Liddell played out his Corinthian career during the era of the maximum wage, the Professional Footballers Association succeeding in their campaign for its abolition in January 1961, just months before he hung up his boots and only weeks before the PFA's eloquent chairman Jimmy Hill suffered a career-ending twisted knee playing for Fulham at Everton.

Yet his thoughts as a player on footballers' earnings, which he committed to print in 1960, make fascinating reading. Compared

to today's massive salaries for Premiership players the figures
Liddell quotes seem barely credible in this post-Bosman,
freedom-of-contract age when a player like Michael Owen earns
more in a week than Dixie Dean did in his lifetime.

Yet Liddell, taking into consideration his celebrity status and
income from his accountancy profession, admitted he was one of
the more fortunate players of his era, declaring:

> Due to the foresight of my parents in insisting that I should
> work at something else besides football my future causes me
> no concern.
>
> And people like Billy Wright, Stanley Matthews, Tom
> Finney, Danny Blanchflower and others have probably, at
> times, drawn more from journalism, advertising and other
> sources than they have purely by playing the game.
>
> I've not fared too badly myself in this respect.
> Unfortunately, these additional avenues of financial reward
> are not available to all players and it is those who have the
> greatest claim to sympathy and improved conditions.
>
> A player on top terms with a Football League club earns
> £20 weekly during the season and £17 in the summer. First-
> team bonuses are £2 per point gained, with half that in the
> reserve side.
>
> On top of their basic wage and bonuses players can also
> earn talent money with the top clubs in the First and Second
> Divisions permitted to share out £1,100 between their
> players at the end of the season.
>
> Runners-up can divide £880 with decreasing amounts
> down to the fifth-placed club which is allowed to share £220.
> There's a lower scale in the Third Division, commencing
> with £550 for the champions and £220 for the fourth club
> while Fourth Division payments range from £330 to £55.
>
> In the FA Cup the bonuses start at £4 for a win in the first
> and second rounds, £5 in the third and increase to a winning
> bonus of £25 per player for those fortunate enough to emerge
> victorious at Wembley.

Here again, successful clubs are allowed to reward their players with talent money. The Cup winners can distribute £1,100 among their players and beaten finalists a total of £880.

Teams who reach the semifinal may reward their players up to a total of £660, those beaten in the sixth round £440 and those knocked out in the fifth round can pay an aggregate of £220. Starting in 1960–1 there will also be substantial bonuses and talent money in the League Cup.

At international level a player chosen for his country draws £50 for each match. England, on many occasions, have played eight or more games a season whereas Scotland, Ireland and Wales normally don't have quite so many. There are also inter-League and other representative matches for which top players can receive from £10 to £25.

Also, a professional with a leading club can look forward to a benefit of £750 after five years' service, which is equivalent to £3 per week added to his wages throughout that period. After five more years with the same club his second benefit is £1,000.

One problem with benefits that has caused considerable controversy for years is that League rules state only that clubs may pay benefits not that they must. So the player is at the mercy of his employers.

They can pay him less than the permitted maximum if they wish or even, as sometimes happens with struggling clubs, express regret that the state of their finances does not permit them to pay anything.

While that may be true it does not soften the disappointment of those whose lot is cast with the less prosperous clubs. I feel that something should be done for players who give loyal service to a club yet never get their due reward.

Talking of finance, I consider that by far the best innovation in the history of the game was the inauguration of the Provident Fund in 1948. Since then a fixed percentage of the total earnings of every player, ranging from ten to eight per cent, has been put away annually in a special fund.

The player doesn't contribute a penny towards it. All the money comes from the Football League. Players who were in the scheme at the start and are still playing League football may have anything up to £1,200 to their credit today.

The total amount becomes payable on the first January after the player's 35th birthday if he has ceased playing. If he's over 35 and fortunate enough still to be playing – as I was at that age – then he gets the money at the beginning of the year following that in which he ceases playing. This grant is not subject to income tax, which makes it even more acceptable.

Underlining, however, that everything is relative Liddell added:

Despite the constraints of players' contracts to talk of professional footballers as a whole as 'slaves' and the 'last bonded men in Britain' has always struck me not only as ridiculous but calculated to do their cause more harm than good.

I remember going to the Liverpool ground one morning just after the description was first used. As I parked my car at the end of a line of other vehicles belonging to my teammates a rather down-at-heel passer-by sneeringly remarked: 'The slaves don't seem to be doing too badly, mate. I wish I was one of them!'

But in case you construe that as meaning that all is well with professional football, and that the players have no grounds for complaint, let me emphasise that this is not so.

The player's contract as it stands today is definitely one-sided. He can sign for only one season at a time then has to wait before knowing whether he's to be offered another. The transfer system is also loaded against the player.

A man who for perfectly genuine reasons would like to change clubs can ask for a transfer but his club may refuse his request. Yet if they want to part with him they can put him on the transfer list without asking his views.

While a player has the last word in a transfer deal that
applies only to his choice from clubs who are prepared
to pay the fee on his head. It may be a very limited
choice indeed.'

The wisdom of Liddell's advice to aspiring youngsters with
football ambitions has not been diminished by the subsequent
revolution in football's structure and finances. Indeed, the
struggles of Nationwide League clubs to make ends meet, and
moves by clubs to cap wages, warn of the colder climate gripping
much of the national sport.

'I would advise every boy who wants to take up the game
professionally to follow my own example and finish his
apprenticeship or training in some other job before becoming a
full-time player,' said Liddell. He continued:

Then he can tackle football without any worry regarding
the future. He will enjoy his game far more with the
knowledge that if he fails, either because he doesn't make
the grade or is unfortunate enough to suffer serious injury,
he won't be thrown on the scrapheap with no other living at
his fingertips.

That is why I fully endorse the vocational training schemes
set up by the Football League and the Football Association to
help players prepare for work and life outside the game.

Those who do combine soccer with something else should
understand, however, that football must always be their main
employment and that nothing must interfere with it.

It isn't all milk and honey with a Third or Fourth Division
club. Yet, by comparison with many other ways of making a
living, even that has its attractions and advantages.

Richly deserved reward for Liddell's own loyalty to Liverpool
was witnessed by the nation's television viewers in September
1959 when he received a long-service benefit.

The BBC's *Sportsnight* programme screened the presentation
to Liddell of a cheque for £1,000 by Liverpool manager Phil

Taylor and chairman Tom Williams, taking his total benefits earnings to £2,500.

'He has scored 226 goals for Liverpool in 478 League games and the *Echo* said that worked out at almost £11 for every goal – even in these money mad days, with footballers wanting more than £20 a week, nobody can say that Billy doesn't deserve this,' observed the appropriately titled Liverpool FC Supporters magazine *Oh Liddell-pool We Love You!*, on sale at 1s 3d.

The writer added: 'Billy has earned more in benefits than any other Merseyside player ever and he's the hero of everyone who supports Liverpool. That's why we named our magazine after him.

'Everyone in our house stayed up to watch the television programme and see Billy get his cheque, even my sister who now likes someone called Marty Wilde. King Billy is our man of the decade.

'His goalscoring record through the 1950s has been nothing short of phenomenal. Had it not been for his magnificent tally of 30 League goals in 1954–5 who knows what might have been? We may even have fallen into the Third Division. Billy, we salute you.'

The front cover of the supporters magazine announced that main features in its next issue would be 'Players Demand £1 A Week Pay Rise', 'Admission Prices To Rise To Two Shillings' and 'Is Live Football On The Wireless Killing The Game?'.

Soon, though, they would have two other issues to discuss – the retirement of Billy Liddell and the Anfield revolution engineered by Bill Shankly.

Chapter Twelve

Revolution and Retirement

Time is a capricious being. It teases, tantalises and sometimes, as in the case of Billy Liddell and Bill Shankly, inflicts sheer torment. In the modern genre of 'What If?' hypotheses one of the most haunting in the entire, colourful history of Liverpool Football Club centres on these two legendary Scots, poles apart in personality but loved and revered by Kopites like no others.

The gods smiled on Anfield to shepherd both men through the club's gates but they snarled by preventing the pair working in harness for Liverpool, other than a brief period at the dawn of Shankly's revolution and the twilight of Liddell's career prior to retirement.

The club itself cannot escape aiding and abetting fate. Liverpool's policy of the directors being responsible for team selection led to Shankly abruptly rejecting an offer to become manager before Don Welsh was appointed in 1951. 'If I can't pick the team what am I manager of?' retorted Shankly.

Had Shankly taken charge at Anfield then he would have had at his disposal the fabled Liddell talents at their height. The calamitous relegation of 1954 and Liverpool's subsequent wilderness years would almost certainly have been avoided. The whole course of English football history might have been different.

'It was a great pity that Billy's playing career was drawing to a close when Shanks arrived as manager because he would have loved to have Billy in the team in his prime,' observed Ronnie

Moran, who spent almost fifty years at Anfield as player, coach and caretaker-manager.

'In fact, if Shanks had come a few years earlier, when Billy was at his peak, and sorted out the team and back-room staff things would have been very different.'

Later, after Liddell had hung up his power-packed boots, his knowledge, wisdom and wise counsel should have been utilised on the Liverpool board during the Shankly years. As a shareholder, Liddell's regular attempts to become a director by putting his name forward for election were always shamefully unsuccessful.

But why did the directors not co-opt their great servant onto the board? Liddell would have provided ideal support to Shankly and his managerial successor Bob Paisley, a long-time friend and former team-mate, and there would have been no question of his presence undermining the manager.

The reason Shankly himself was not made a director after his dramatic resignation as manager in 1974 was because Liverpool had seen how the giant shadow of Matt Busby's presence on the board at Old Trafford had overwhelmed successive Manchester United managers. They were determined not to allow that to happen to Paisley.

But Liddell was totally different. He had not been a manager and his self-effacing, softly spoken manner masked a wealth of knowledge which could have proved invaluable to Shankly and Paisley, both of whom were deep admirers of Liddell.

Phyllis Liddell reflected: 'Matt Busby used to say to Billy, "I've made my bed in management. I'm lying on it and enjoying it. But you'd never make a manager!"

'Matt thought Billy was just too nice to go into management – and he was right. The truth was that Billy never had any managerial ambitions. He had so much else going on in his life that he never even entertained the idea.

'But he would have liked to have been a Liverpool director. His name used to be put forward at the club's annual general meetings but he was never elected and, contrary to what some people believe, Billy never withdrew his name from the sheet.

'So I don't know the reason why he was unsuccessful in getting onto the board. There was obviously a reason but I don't know what it was and neither did Billy. I feel he would have made a very good and valuable member of the board. His presence would have been empowering not overpowering. He would have been there to offer sound, good advice and opinions.'

There was a deep mutual respect between Liddell and Shankly. They were in the same Scotland team – both of them scoring – when Liddell made his international debut in the 5–4 wartime win over England at Hampden Park in April 1942, the first of three international appearances they made together.

'Although it's classed as an unofficial international, many pundits rated the game in which I made my debut as the best ever between the "old enemies",' declared Liddell.

'I'll never forget scoring on my Scotland debut but I remember it, too, for the goal Bill scored. It was the winner and I'll never forget his delight and enthusiasm when the ball went into the net. His sheer passion and enthusiasm for the game was amazing.'

The praise was mutual. 'Liddell was some player!' exclaimed Shankly. 'He had everything. He was fast, powerful, shot with either foot and his headers were like blasts from a gun. On top of all that he was as hard as granite. What a player! He was so strong – and he took a nineteen-inch collar shirt!'

Just weeks after Liddell's memorable Scotland debut he and right half Shankly lined up together again – in Liverpool jerseys. Shankly, then with Preston North End, played as a guest in a 4–1 Liverpool Senior Cup win over Everton at Anfield on 30 May 1942. Shankly teamed up again with Liddell a week later as a guest in Liverpool's 3–2 home defeat by a Services team. But it would be more than seventeen years before the pair came together again in the cause of Liverpool FC.

The 1959–60 season was to prove a landmark campaign for both men. It was to be Liddell's last as a first-team player – apart from a single appearance the following season – and before the new decade dawned Shankly had been recruited at the second time of asking to rescue Liverpool from the well of mediocrity into which it had sunk.

As the curtain was about to lift on the season Liddell was paid a fulsome tribute by the massively popular *Charles Buchan's Football Monthly*. Alongside a front-cover colour action picture of Liddell in the August 1959 edition the magazine proclaimed him 'our choice as Footballer of the Year'.

Sadly, members of the Football Writers Association did not follow suit and Liddell was destined never to win the coveted award which, earlier that year, had gone to Luton Town's Syd Owen who was followed as the recipient by Bill Slater of Wolves.

Liverpool, in their wisdom, decided to omit Liddell from the team that opened the season at Cardiff City and lost 3–2 without a single visiting player getting on the scoresheet. Danny Malloy, Cardiff's Scottish centre half, charitably conceded two own goals, although some records credit Jimmy Melia with the first Liverpool goal.

The response by the Anfield board, who picked the team with the assistance of manager Phil Taylor, was swiftly to recall 37-year-old Liddell for the home midweek duel with Bristol City three days later. He took over the No. 9 jersey from dropped Louis Bimpson and did not disappoint.

The press eulogised Liddell's two-goal display in Liverpool's 4–2 win, with the *Liverpool Echo* describing him as the 'most loyal club man of all times and one of the greatest shots in the game'. The *Liverpool Daily Post* hailed him as 'the India-rubber man who makes a habit of bouncing back to stardom from the recurring threat of a quiet termination in the reserve team to a wonderful career'.

Liddell missed out on a hat-trick chance when Liverpool were awarded a second-half penalty. Despite the Kop chanting 'Give it to Billy' it was Jimmy Melia who took it and scored!

The Liddell comeback lasted four games until knee trouble kept him out of the September home clash with Scunthorpe. His absence meant that opportunity knocked for a former Stockton Heath player who had recently come out of the Army. Roger Hunt donned the No. 9 jersey on his debut and scored the second goal in Liverpool's 2–0 win.

The new boy stepped down to allow for Liddell's scoring return in a 2–1 home defeat by Middlesbrough three days later. Renewed injury problems, however, forced the Scot onto the sidelines again

for the next three games as Hunt returned in the No. 8 jersey he
was to make his own and in which his scoring exploits would
establish him as one of Anfield's all-time greats.

Liddell, who had scored four times in his five appearances to
then, teamed up with Hunt for the first time when he returned at
No. 7 in a remarkable 5–4 defeat at Swansea Town in October.
'Liddell's 480th League appearance for Liverpool was certainly
an occasion to be remembered,' wrote Reg Pelling in the *News
Chronicle*.

'After clashing many times with tough-tackling Swansea
skipper Harry Griffiths, Billy limped around for more than half
the game with damaged knee ligaments. He started at outside
right, had spells at outside left and centre forward and finally went
back to the right wing again.'

The knee damage consigned Liddell to a four-month spell out
of first-team action in which he missed sixteen Second Division
games and home FA Cup ties against Leyton Orient (won 2–1)
and Manchester United (lost 1–3). When he did return, the
1960s had been ushered in and Shankly had crossed the
Pennines to begin the task of reawakening the slumbering
Anfield club, gripped by mediocrity on the field and blighted by
a dilapidated stadium.

The previous summer had seen the departure of goalkeeper
Tommy Younger, Liddell's international colleague, who returned
to Scotland as player-manager of Falkirk, with Bert Slater moving
in the opposite direction in an exchange deal. Slater, small for a
goalkeeper at under 5ft 9in, was dropped after only three
appearances and Doug Rudham recalled to a side now captained
by Ronnie Moran after Johnny Wheeler had relinquished the job,
following a season as skipper.

But just three wins in twelve games through September and
October prompted Liverpool's long-suffering fans to vent their
anger and frustration and there were bouts of slow-handclapping
at matches.

Early in November, with Liverpool languishing 12th in the
table, the club made the dramatic £12,000 signing of centre
forward Dave Hickson from Mersey rivals Everton.

'I remember my first day at Liverpool,' said Hickson. 'Billy Liddell was the first person to come over and welcome me. I really appreciated that and I'll never forget it because he was such an idol, and deservedly so. He was one of the true greats of football. There's no doubt about that.'

The combative Hickson made a superb debut by scoring both goals in a 2–1 Anfield win over Aston Villa. A week later, at Lincoln City, he scored again, with Hunt also on the mark. But Liverpool's 4–2 reverse was a defeat too far.

Manager Phil Taylor resigned two days later, citing the strain and disappointment of fruitless promotion attempts as his reasons. He quit on the very day, 16 November, that *The Sound of Music* opened on Broadway. But the implications of his decision would be even longer running than the Rodgers and Hammerstein production. Just four days later Britain was one of seven nations that signed up to form the European Free Trade Association in a direct challenge to the original six members of the Common Market. For Liverpool, too, Europe was to be high on their agenda just a few years hence, even though it was beyond their furthest horizons at the time.

Taylor's exit left questions in its wake for many at Anfield. Liddell's close friend and former team-mate Bob Paisley, who had been promoted to first-team trainer at the start of the season, and Reuben Bennett, a craggy Scot who had been recruited as a coach less than a year earlier, and the rest of the back-room staff feared for their futures at the club under a new management regime.

Their anxieties were swiftly dispelled by Shankly. On 30 November he agreed to leave Huddersfield and become Liverpool manager, taking over on Monday 14 December. It was not only the start of a new week but a new era for Liverpool and, ultimately, English football.

Shankly's first act was to hold a meeting with the back-room team, which also included Joe Fagan, to assure them that their jobs were safe and that they would be members of his mission to reignite Anfield fortunes.

'I'll lay down the plans, you pick them up and we'll all work in harmony,' Shankly told them, adding in evangelical tones: 'We'll get the players we need and we'll make Liverpool great again.'

Thus, the Boot Room ethic was born. Shankly dispensed with 24 players over the next eighteen months but immediately withdrew one from the transfer list he inherited. Gerry Byrne would go on to play for England and achieve Cup Final immortality.

Shankly soon smashed Liverpool's self-imposed £12,000 transfer ceiling, a limit recorded in board meeting minutes, as new blood arrived in the form of Gordon Milne, Ian St John and Ron Yeats to blend with the developing talents of Hunt and a young winger called Ian Callaghan. The road to glory beckoned.

While the seeds of this exciting revolution were being sown, Liddell was out of action through his knee injury. But he observed the events with admiration for his compatriot's zealous determination to succeed.

'Bill brought with him to the manager's job the enthusiasm, drive, courage and energy he had shown on the field wearing a Scotland jersey,' said Liddell.

'As well as being a great driver of men he was also a players' man. It didn't matter whether it was a Cup tie, a League game, a practice match or a kick-around. Bill Shankly lived for what he was doing.'

Liddell's comeback was beaten by the elements, but not before he had once again grabbed the plaudits and the headlines. He made his return in the home game against Derby County on 6 February when Anfield was cloaked in fog. Play somehow lasted 71 minutes before referee Dennis Howell conceded defeat. He abandoned the game with Liverpool leading 1–0, a goal scored by Alan A'Court but created by Liddell. 'Not even the fog could deny the Kopites their joy and cheers for their great favourite, the one and only Liddell, on his comeback day,' Stanley Ford reported in the *People*.

'The "Anfield Express" obliged by laying on the seventeenth-minute goal for outside left A'Court but not that many of the 28,000 crowd saw anything of the scoring move.'

That applied, too, to the press box as Horace Yates revealed in the *Liverpool Daily Post*: 'There was a roar and I saw players congratulating Liddell and for a minute or so it appeared that the favourite of favourites at Anfield had celebrated his return with a goal.

'Only when an appeal was made to game-reader Bob Paisley, the trainer, sitting on the touchline, did we discover that Liddell had returned the ball to the middle for A'Court to meet it side-footed, with his right foot, for the scoring touch.'

With that unfinished game expunged from the records, Liddell officially made his first appearance under Shankly at Plymouth a week later, a game for which Liverpool took wing. They had broken new frontiers in domestic travel by flying to a League game for the first time for the match at Cardiff almost a year to the day earlier.

They did likewise for the duel at Home Park, boarding a Starways aircraft at Liverpool's Speke Airport for a charter flight to Exeter, then completing their journey by coach.

Liddell played at No. 7 in a 1–1 draw which extended Liverpool's unbeaten sequence to five games, after losing their first two under the new manager. He stayed in the side for a ten-game run, scoring what was to be his last senior goal for the club in a 5–1 home demolition of Stoke City in March.

Liverpool had now climbed to ninth in the table with matches in hand on all the clubs above them but, frustratingly, points were still frittered away. The two-goal half-time lead that goals from Hickson and Wheeler gave them at home against Huddersfield evaporated as Shankly's former charges hit back to draw 2–2.

It was an eventful afternoon for Liddell. Before kickoff he presented marathon-walker Wendy Lewis with a bouquet, and proceeded to set up Hickson's goal, burst a ball with one of his trademark thunderbolt shots and contrive to miss from the penalty spot with the chance to make it 3–0. Liddell, facing former Manchester United and England goalkeeper Ray Wood, saw his spot kick crash against a post, only his eighth failure in his 44 postwar penalties for Liverpool.

In their next outing, at Aston Villa, Liverpool lost an even more emphatic advantage. A majestic first-half display by Shankly's side against the Second Division leaders gave them a seemingly unassailable 3–0 interval lead, launched by Hunt's strike after home goalkeeper Nigel Sims could only fist out a fierce Liddell shot. Goals from Hickson and John Molyneux set up a happy half-time for Liverpool, their smiles broadening on the hour when Hickson made it 4–0.

At that point, the plaintive half-time appeal by Villa manager Joe Mercer appeared to have fallen on deaf ears. Dispensing with any tactical sophistication or jargon Mercer kicked the dressing-room tea urn and told his players: 'You got yourselves into this bloody mess now bloody well get yourselves out of it!'

Northern Ireland international winger Peter McParland led Villa's response with a solo goal after 66 minutes, and a brace from Bobby Thomson plus a Stan Lynn penalty put them level. If McParland had scored instead of spurning a last-minute chance Shankly's reaction would have been unrepeatable.

Liddell stayed in the side for the next three games – a 3–1 home defeat by Lincoln City, a 4–1 home win over Derby County and a 2–0 defeat at Leyton Orient – before handing the No. 7 shirt to debutant Callaghan for the home clash with Bristol Rovers on 16 April.

The youngster, who celebrated his eighteenth birthday six days earlier and had been a professional for less than three weeks, had an eye-catching baptism in the 4–0 win, but his performance was no surprise to Callaghan's hero figure Liddell.

'I was asked several times who would follow me in the Liverpool team,' Liddell recalled. 'I knew the club were scouting around the country looking to sign someone but I told people: "They've got someone at Anfield already, a youngster named Ian Callaghan."

'I told them that I'd played in the reserves with him twice and believed he would go on to become a credit to his club, the game of football and his country.'

Liddell's early assessment was spot-on. Callaghan's great journey took him to glory at home and in Europe, a place in England's 1966 World Cup-winning squad and also saw him over-haul Liddell's club record of most senior appearances and most League appearances in a career that spanned almost two decades.

After his debut Callaghan stayed in the side for the next game, a 3–0 Easter home win over Rotherham, before being rested for the following day's return at Millmoor for which Shankly recalled Liddell. The veteran Scot played his part in a 2–2 draw before stepping down again for Callaghan to play in the final two games of the season, wins over Ipswich and Sunderland.

The end of Shankly's first half-season in charge ended with Liverpool third, the fifth successive campaign they had finished in the top four. It meant Liverpool once more missed out on promotion, thus snuffing out Liddell's last hope of playing again in the top flight of English football. But at the age of 38 he was paid the compliment of being in Shankly's first retained list in which he cut the playing staff from 38 to 28.

Goalkeeper Rudham retired and returned to Johannesburg, long-serving defender Laurie Hughes hung up his boots to concentrate on business interests, while Barry Wilkinson and Fred Morris were transfer-listed and joined Bangor City and Crewe respectively.

The 1960–1 season, Liddell's last as a professional, was a time of galloping change, both globally and in sport. It saw the birth of the Football League Cup – devised by Football League secretary and anti-European Alan Hardaker. Football League action was first seen live on television in September when the Lancashire derby between Blackpool and Bolton Wanderers was screened. But the experiment was a one-off and more than two decades would pass before live TV League football became a regular event.

The young 1960s had already witnessed harbingers of fears to come. The Soviet Union's shooting-down of the American U-2 spy plane piloted by Gary Powers injected an even deeper chill into the Cold War into which a major figure stepped when John F Kennedy was elected United States president in November 1960.

In Liddell's adopted city of Liverpool the decision in May by Cavern Club owner Ray McFall to make Wednesday evenings rock'n'roll night was to transform the world of popular music. The Beatles and many other groups soon trod the stage of that

cramped city-centre cellar in Mathew Street and legends were
spawned to the drive of the Mersey Beat.

Liddell, meanwhile, approached the twilight of his career by
starting his last season in the reserves as Shankly's seniors
experienced a mixed start to the campaign. At the same time the
Olympic Games in Rome saw a young boxer named Cassius Clay
win light-heavyweight gold, while Anita Lonsborough, in the
200-metres breaststroke, and Don Thompson, the 50-kilometre
walker, won gold for Britain.

Liverpool's curtain-raising 2–0 home win over Leeds was
followed by a 4–1 defeat at Southampton and a 1–1 draw at
Middlesbrough which led to Liddell being recalled by Shankly to
senior action. He came in at No. 9 in place of Dave Hickson for
the return clash with Southampton at Anfield on Wednesday 31
August, the same day that the East Germans closed the border
with West Berlin.

It was Liddell's 534th senior appearance for Liverpool and
would also be his last, at the age of 38 years 234 days. He became
the club's oldest postwar player, a record that stood until his
compatriot Kenny Dalglish surpassed it when he played at the age
of 39 years 58 days in May 1990.

This was the Liverpool team (in 2–3–5 formation) for
Liddell's final first-team outing: Bert Slater; John Molyneux,
Ronnie Moran (captain); Gordon Milne, Dick White, Tommy
Leishman; Kevin Lewis, Roger Hunt, Billy Liddell, Jimmy
Melia, Alan A'Court.

Liverpool's heavy defeat at the Dell a week earlier, when they
conceded four goals despite Leishman giving them the lead, was
the first-ever League meeting of the clubs. Southampton made it
a double with a 1–0 victory on their first League visit to Anfield,
to deny Liddell a victorious farewell. They rubbed salt in home
wounds by returning in November to knock Liverpool out of the
new League Cup with a 2–1 win in front of the Kop.

Hickson returned to the side in place of Liddell, who reverted
to Central League football in the reserves but received richly
deserved acclaim in his testimonial match at Anfield on
Wednesday 21 September. The game, between Liverpool and an

International XI and refereed by the celebrated Arthur Ellis, drew a remarkable public response, reflecting Liddell's iconic status.

A 38,789 crowd turned up to salute their hero, a bigger attendance than all but three Liverpool home League games that season when the average dipped below 30,000, with only 13,389 watching the final home game against Stoke following another third-place finish.

The testimonial attendance, generating receipts of £6,340, illustrated the Kop's reverence for the heroic figure who had carried the club through its wilderness years. The Clan McLeod Pipe Band, led by Pipe Major Alex Queen, provided a suitable tartan flavour in tribute to Liddell by playing before the game and at half-time.

The Liverpool team was: Bert Slater; John Molyneux, Ronnie Moran; Johnny Wheeler, Dick White, Gordon Milne; Alan A'Court, Roger Hunt, Dave Hickson, Jimmy Harrower, Billy Liddell.

The international XI featured the return of Bert Trautmann, the German goalkeeper who had faced Liddell for Manchester City in the famous FA Cup replay at Anfield more than four years earlier. The team, playing in white jerseys, also included Jimmy Armfield (Blackpool); Joe Walton (Preston North End); Maurice Setters (Manchester United); Jimmy Dugdale (Aston Villa); Don Revie (Leeds United); Jimmy McIlroy (Burnley); Nat Lofthouse (Bolton Wanderers); Albert Quixall (Manchester United); and Tom Finney (ex-Preston North End).

The Liverpool chairman Tom (T V) Williams said of Liddell in an article in the testimonial programme:

I have known hundreds of footballers in my time, many of them wonderful players and loyal club men, but throughout my long experience I have never known a man I have admired and respected more than Billy Liddell, both on and off the field.

Since the days when he joined Liverpool as a sixteen-year-old amateur I have followed his career with the greatest interest and also watched the growth of his splendid character and personality.

In my official capacity I have been in much closer contact with him than most people and the more I have seen of him, the greater has been my admiration. Billy's ability as a footballer needs no recommendation from me.

His records and achievements speak for themselves. Never once throughout his long service with Liverpool has he given the club a moment's anxiety.

Whatever he has been asked to do he has done willingly and with good grace, content in the knowledge that even if it was occasionally not just what he would have preferred, it was for the good of Liverpool Football Club, which has always been his primary aim.

He has added much lustre to Liverpool's name by his sporting behaviour on the field, his high standard of play and his scoring exploits. Never have I seen Billy guilty of a deliberate foul, of arguing with the referee or anything else which would tend to lower the reputation of himself, his club or football in general.

Off the field he is just as much an example. He is a clean-living man who, without parading his religious beliefs, seeks to lead a true Christian life. Football has been good to him and, in turn, he tries to help others. He works hard for many church and charitable causes and gives pleasure to patients in hospital by making regular visits.

The welfare of young people is close to Billy's heart and his scope in this direction was considerably increased when he was made a Justice of the Peace, an honour which, as far as I am aware, has only once before been bestowed on a professional footballer still earning his living at the game.

Billy is a non-smoker and teetotaller but not a bigoted one. It is simply that neither relaxation appeals to him. From his pictures and demeanour on the field you might think he was a very dour person.

But I see him often when football duties are not on his mind and he has a light-hearted side to his nature of which many folk are not aware. Billy has been a credit to the game

throughout his long career. Football would be all the better
for many more of his stamp.

The bumper crowd who turned out for the testimonial saw an
entertaining contest which involved player switches and changes
of personnel. Liverpool, with Hickson bagging a hat trick and
A'Court also on target, won 4–2.

Liddell joined the ranks of the All Stars in the second half when
Swansea Town and former Liverpool right half Roy Saunders,
father of Dean, also went on and had the fans laughing with his
deliberate attempts to perform some fancy tricks.

But top of the bill belonged to Liddell and he almost brought
the house down when he scored against his own club, Lofthouse
collecting the other goal for the visitors.

At the end of the match Liddell walked off in triumph, the fans
crowning an emotional evening by cheering him all the way to the
players' tunnel, with both teams swelling the thunderous
applause.

The admiration was mutual. 'The Anfield fans were absolutely
fantastic, as they always have been as far as I'm concerned,'
said Liddell.

For so many of them to support me in my testimonial was
tremendous and the £6,000 I netted meant I was able to buy
a house. They've always been the best crowd in the game.
They are so knowledgeable and passionate.

To hear them in full cry when you're playing in front of
them is a feeling on which you can't put a value. It just fills
you with satisfaction and pleasure to know that with the rest
of the team you are providing entertainment and enjoyment.

I don't know whether the attitude of Liverpool supporters
is typical of crowds throughout the country but they usually
forgive a player the lack of any asset with the exception
of courage.

As soon as anybody shirks a tackle he is almost certain to
come in for barracking, even though he may be a brilliant
player on the ball. Not every player, of course, is blessed

with the physical attributes that permit him to dive into the tackle or throw his weight around.

I have sympathy for those players who are not cut out for that and I'm sure that many people, like myself, prefer to see players showing 75 per cent skill and 25 per cent power rather than the other way round.

But there is something special about the Kop supporters. On some grounds, if the visiting team gets the upper hand the heart seems to go out of the cheering. But not at Anfield.

If we go a goal down, it's invariably the signal for the Kop spectators to go into action with their famous roar. It's said by opponents to be worth a goal to Liverpool any time. The noise they produce literally forces their team back into the game.

At the end of December 1960, the farthing ceased to be legal tender in Britain but Liddell's Corinthian currency of sportsmanship never waned and was as evident in Liverpool's second team that month as it was on football's grander stages.

He was captain of the reserve team and in one Central League game he hit a typically thunderous shot which went wide and hit one of a group of youngsters sitting on an inner wall on the terraces.

'Billy forgot about the game and ran straight for the boy, vaulting the perimeter wall and staying with him until he knew he was alright,' recalled Stan Howard, a spectator that day. 'You knew he would have done exactly the same if it had been the World Cup Final. He was simply the best.'

In another Central League match that season Liddell was dangerously fouled and brought down by a Bristol Rovers player. There was a hush around Anfield as he received treatment with fans fearing he had broken his leg.

There were relieved cheers when he finally rose to his feet, but Liddell's first act was to plead with the referee not to send off the Bristol player. The referee responded: 'Billy, you have to apply the right punishment to someone found guilty in your court and I have to do the same as a referee.' So the offender was dismissed despite Liddell's plea.

As Liddell saw out his playing days in Liverpool reserves English football reached a financial watershed in January 1961 when the PFA, led by their chairman Jimmy Hill, won their long-running battle with the Football League by forcing the abolition of the maximum wage, which then stood at £20 a week during the season and £17 in the summer.

Threatening a players' strike, they also won their contract dispute, a victory confirmed in the High Court case brought by George Eastham, who wanted to move from Newcastle to Arsenal and whose self-termed 'slave contract' was deemed to be a restraint of trade.

It meant that the era of the £100-a-week footballer had dawned with Fulham chairman Tommy Trinder paying that three-figure sum to his England international Johnny Haynes. The average weekly wage at the time in pre-decimal Britain was £12 – with many a working man earning less – while a packet of 20 cigarettes cost the equivalent of less than 25p, a pint of milk 5p and a loaf of bread 7p.

Football's wages revolution also preceded the English game's first £100,000 transfer, the milestone being reached when Denis Law, who had been one of Shankly's charges at Huddersfield, moved from Manchester City to Torino. A year later he returned to England to join Manchester United for £115,000.

Just before Law's move to Italy his fellow Scot, Liddell, donned his boots for the last time as a Liverpool player, aged 39 years 109 days. The occasion was hardly auspicious for the Great Britain and Scotland star. It was a reserve fixture against Blackburn Rovers at Anfield in the Central League on Saturday 29 April 1961, just one week before League champions Tottenham beat Leicester in the FA Cup Final at Wembley to complete the twentieth century's first Double, watched by a crowd of 100,000.

Just 2,173 spectators turned up at Anfield but, fittingly, Liddell scored one of the goals in a 5–0 win with Willie Carlin bagging a hat trick and Alan Banks scoring the other.

Among the small crowd on that landmark day were John Culshaw and his brother. 'I can assure you that the goal Billy scored that afternoon would be in the top 10 of the great man's tally,' John recalled. 'Billy collected the ball on the touchline on the paddock side of the ground, near the players' tunnel, and made a diagonal run towards the Anfield Road goal.

'He was a couple of strides short of the corner of the penalty area when he unleashed a shot of unbelievable power, and the ball screamed – yes, screamed – high into the net. I tell you, the 2,000-odd lucky fans who saw that goal made more noise than 20,000.

'My brother and I were jumping up and down on the Kemlyn Road terracing like a couple of schoolboys. We are both in our sixties now but the memory of that goal has never dimmed and we still reminisce about it more than 40 years on.'

Liddell, though, got more than he bargained for. 'I played in the game and to Billy's great surprise we carried him shoulder-high off the pitch at the end with the crowd giving him a standing ovation,' recalled team-mate Ronnie Moran. 'Billy was a bit embarrassed but we felt it was the least we could do to mark his last game in Liverpool colours.'

Liddell looked back over his long career and picked his best British team, in the old 2–3–5 formation, drawn from men he had either played with or against. 'I tackled the task with some diffidence because I know how fraught it can be,' he admitted. 'Everyone has their own ideas and views. This side is purely my choice, based on my opinions and experience.' He began by choosing his goalkeeper and backs:

The goalkeeper is the most important man in any team. Unlike outfield players his errors are usually costly and often decisive. The candidates for my side include Jimmy Cowan, Harry Gregg, Frank Swift, Bert Williams, Jack Kelsey, Bert Trautman, Gil Merrick, Ted Sagar, Sam Bartram and Bill Brown.

'Swifty' had a marvellous temperament for a goalkeeper and he just snatches my vote from Bert Williams, his eventual England successor. When it comes to right backs I'm glad I never had to play against my Scotland colleague George Young, so big and powerful yet so clever and almost dainty in his movement.

Eddie Shimwell was a very close marker and a relentless

tackler. I never had a good game against him while Laurie Scott was one of the fastest I ever came up against. But I am choosing Johnny Carey at No. 2.

I played against him for Great Britain when he was right half in the Rest of Europe side in 1947 and he gave a wonderful exhibition. I always felt, though, that Johnny's best position was right back. He was a clever, intelligent player with splendid positional sense and split second timing of tackles.

At left back a number of distinguished players come to mind. George Hardwick played on classic lines, Bill Eckersley was not very big but a real terrier in the tackle while the Munich tragedy robbed England of Roger Byrne when he was in his prime.

Eddie Hapgood was close to the end of his career when I played against him and he still showed the wonderful form which made him a household name with Arsenal and England and he's my left back choice.

Next Billy considered his half back line:

There's a long list of possibles for the three wing half positions. England's Billy Wright could fill any of them. Despite his lack of size he could reach a fantastic height heading a ball and he was an extraordinarily strong tackler.

Another in somewhat similar mould is Jimmy Scoular, an inspiration to Newcastle, while Glasgow Celtic's Bobby Evans is the closest thing to perpetual motion I've seen at wing half.

There are other brilliant performers . . . Ronnie Clayton of England, Dave Mackay of Scotland and Northern Ireland's Danny Blanchflower among them. But in my opinion the finest of all was Matt Busby. Matt was never a robust player even though he had all the physical attributes.

He never needed to use them because his ball control and distribution were second to none while his positioning was such that he was always right in the game without ever seeming to exert himself.

At centre half I think first of that classic Welsh inter-national Tommy (T G) Jones of Everton. He always seemed in command of every situation without chasing about all over the place.

He attracted the ball like a magnet, never gave way to panic, and could invariably extricate himself from the most awkward-looking situation by playing football of the highest order.

Many a time I've seen Tommy dribble the ball out of a mass of opponents on Everton's six-yard line in the most nonchalant fashion, almost as if he was playing in a practice match. His goalkeeper Ted Sagar used to say that Tommy had caused him more grey hairs than any opponent!

Neil Franklin was another centre half who never needed to extend himself unduly while Stan Cullis was a dominant character on the field, a tower of strength to Wolves in the middle with a clever turn of footwork. Jackie Vernon was very difficult to beat in the air, as was Glasgow Rangers stalwart Willie Woodburn.

But I still think the most perfect footballer of the lot was John Charles, whose great talents took him to Italian club Juventus. John was ideally built, had control, heading ability, an excellent positional sense and was one of the most gentlemanly of players, a sportsman to his fingertips.

Although he could play well almost anywhere, I think his best position was centre half and that is where I have selected him in my team. Left half prompts memories of Joe Mercer and I have always felt that his greatest games were played after he joined Arsenal from Everton at the end of 1946.

Many people thought he was already over the hill but he proved them wrong. He was a great captain, a constant inspiration to his side and had a great deal to do with Arsenal's success in the early postwar seasons.

Other fine half backs include my Scotland colleague and later Liverpool manager, Bill Shankly, Alec Forbes, Ronnie Burgess, Jimmy Dickinson, Roy Paul and Tommy Docherty.

But the player I have chosen at left half is a man who

probably would have set up many new records had he not lost his life so tragically in the Munich disaster – Duncan Edwards. Duncan matured much earlier than the average player and with his skill, drive and splendid physique he looked like becoming one of the all-time greats.

Finally, Liddell turned his attention to his forwards:

Choosing my outside right brings me to the Stanley Matthews–Tom Finney question. Most people would be happy to put both in the team on opposite flanks and leave it at that – but I'm not dodging the issue.

Tom has won fame and glory in three forward positions – outside right, centre forward and outside left – but it was on the right that he first reached stardom. As well as Stan and Tom the choice also includes Gordon Smith, Willie Waddell and Jimmy Delaney.

Stan is the greatest crowd entertainer I have known. More plans have been made by defenders to stop him than for any other player – and very few have succeeded.

It always amazed me that so many people had studied him for so long and yet were still powerless to counter his wiles. He could bring the ball right up to the full back, feint to go through on the inside and then, as the back went into the tackle, Stan would lift the ball over his opponent's out-stretched foot and be away like a hare on the outside before the back could regain his balance.

That was only one of his countless ways of beating a man. Stan had all the other means at his disposal and nobody ever knew what trick he was going to pull out of the bag.

It was largely a matter of perfect balance, wonderful control, a body swerve which could get everybody going the wrong way and a remarkable facility for getting away at top speed from a standing start.

Stan was an individualist who could always, by his sheer ability, beat his man unaided, rarely needing the help of a colleague. His team-mates knew they could give him the ball

and not worry about what he would do with it. All they had
to do was wait until he opened up the way to goal for them.

Stan scored quite a lot of goals in his early days. After the
war he specialised in making openings for others. If football
was run on ice hockey lines, Stan would be the world
champion 'assister'.

Tom Finney had the same amazing ball control and body
swerve as Stan, the only difference being that Finney
operated more on his left foot and Matthews on his right.

The Preston man was often most dangerous when it
appeared he'd got too close to the dead ball line. His side
must have scored dozens of goals from this position as Tom
cut or chipped the ball back to a colleague lying handy
around the edge of the six-yard line.

Tom's versatility was proved on countless occasions and,
though he told me he preferred playing centre forward
towards the end of his career, I always felt he was at his
prime playing outside right.

He was most dangerous there because he didn't maintain
a touchline patrol as much as Matthews and when cutting
inside he was on his favourite foot and could let fly at goal.

Besides being a wonderful provider of chances Tom could
make and take them for himself and, because of this, I have
always thought he was more dangerous to play against than
Stan.

Tom was also a very good header of a ball whereas Stan
very rarely made contact with his head, preferring to position
himself so that he could get the ball at his feet.

While you may have gathered that I am pro-Finney, please
don't think I am anti-Matthews! That would be completely
wide of the mark. Both were supreme artists and I would like
both in my team. But what tips the scales in Tom's favour,
so far as I am concerned, is that he could score plenty of
goals as well as make them.

Then we come to the other flank and for some unknown
reason many people seem to think that the selection of
outside left is something of an afterthought. Yet, for many

clubs in postwar football it has been the hardest position of all to fill. Don't ask me why, unless kicking with the right foot comes more naturally to most players.

My left wing contingent includes Jimmy Mullen, Cliff Jones and Peter McParland, each from different British countries with differing styles of play but with the common denominator of being potential matchwinners.

My vote goes to Northern Ireland's McParland, an unorthodox winger with a wonderful turn of speed, a fierce shot and very competent in heading the ball. Coming to the inside trio up front it is strange how so many of the great inside forwards have been such small men.

I'm thinking of people like Jimmy Logie, Bobby Collins and Billy Steel, to mention just three. What they lacked in physique they compensated for in skill. Then there were the cheeky ball-players such as Alec Stevenson, Jimmy Hagan, Len Shackleton and Ernie Taylor, a great passer in Johnny Haynes and a fine shot in Bobby Charlton.

But the best pair of inside men I have played against or watched were Raich Carter and Peter Doherty in their Derby County days, which is why they are both in my team. I played with and against them in wartime representative games, which added considerably to my experience.

Peter could do anything with a ball and was adept in exposing the weaknesses of the opposition and opening up the defence. Raich was more direct though he, too, provided plenty of opportunities for his team-mates.

When it comes to centre forward I prefer one of the spearhead type who can round off the work of the rest of the forwards, men like Nat Lofthouse, Tommy Lawton and Jackie Milburn, one of the fastest centre forwards of my time.

Another fine centre forward was Tommy Taylor, at his peak when he died in the Munich Disaster, while my Scotland colleague Laurie Reilly always seemed to have endless energy. Roy Bentley and Trevor Ford are two others I admired.

John Charles, of course, was a brilliant centre forward – but he's in my team at centre half and even the great Welshman can't play in two positions at once. My vote goes to Lawton, who was beautifully built for the role and used to ram the ball into the net with his head in a manner even Bill [Dixie] Dean couldn't surpass, which is the highest possible praise.

So here is my team of all the talents: Swift (Manchester City); Carey (Manchester United), Hapgood (Arsenal); Busby (Manchester City and Liverpool), Charles (Leeds and Juventus), Edwards (Manchester United); Finney (Preston), Carter (Sunderland and Derby), Lawton (Everton, Chelsea, Arsenal and Notts County), Doherty (Blackpool, Manchester City and Derby), McParland (Aston Villa). I think you will agree that it looks formidable.

Liddell's great contribution to Liverpool brought him one of the Football League's first long-service statuettes, awarded only to players who had completed twenty years with one club.

While Liverpool and their supporters were still reflecting on the retirement of the great man, another Scot signed for the club just ten days after Liddell's final outing in the reserves. Ian St John was refused entry to Goodison by a steward when he arrived at the Everton ground on the evening of 9 May to make his debut for Shankly's side in the Liverpool Senior Cup, following his £37,500 capture from Motherwell. 'I'd only just arrived on Merseyside and nobody knew who I was,' explained St John. They soon did.

Shankly's new centre forward scored a hat trick in Liverpool's 4 – 3 defeat and he and Ron Yeats, signed soon after from Dundee United for £30,000, proved catalysts in the process that brought promotion the following season and, ultimately, championship glory and the club's first-ever FA Cup triumph.

Shankly's reignited Liverpool completed an amazingly swift journey from fantasy to fact. In 1959 one young Kopite wrote: 'I wonder if Liverpool will ever play in that European Cup thing that Real Madrid always win. When we have a kick-about on the rec [recreation ground] Liverpool always win the FA Cup and the European Cup and Billy Liddell always scores the winning goal.'

In August 1964 Liverpool went to Iceland to face Reykjavik for their first taste of European Cup combat as Liddell admitted: 'I would love to see them win it one day. I want them to become the first British club to do so.'

The main part of Liddell's dream did come true, even if it required a patient wait. Shankly, who in a three-year span lifted Liverpool from playing League games against Scunthorpe to European duels with the likes of Inter Milan, Anderlecht and Cologne, went desperately close at his first attempt when his side controversially lost to Inter in the 1965 semifinal.

Although Celtic in 1967 and Manchester United a year later were to place the first British pennants on the prestigious trophy, Liddell was thrilled to see his long-time friend and former team-mate Bob Paisley lead Liverpool to an amazing three European Cup triumphs in 1977, 1978 and 1981 and Joe Fagan add a fourth in 1984.

'Bill built a great side and completely transformed the club.' Liddell reflected, adding:

'It was a team effort on and off the field, involving the boardroom, the manager, the training and coaching staff and, of course, the players.

Many teams have been bullied or driven to success but the Liverpool team under Bill was inspired to greatness by the magnetism of the manager and his sheer will to succeed.

When he retired in 1974 it was a massive shock to me as it was to everyone else. But how fortunate the club was to have a man like Bob to call on to take on the task of following Bill, a job that many people believed was an impossibility.

As a player Bob was a great team man, winning the ball for his colleagues and never seeking individual acclaim. But when he talked about the game he revealed a very shrewd football brain.

He didn't miss much. He retained things and learned from them and he also became an authority on injuries and their treatment. When he was appointed manager, this vast store of knowledge stood him in good stead and he later became a director.

Bob was with Liverpool in various capacities for more than half a century and when you think of what he achieved he must be the club's greatest servant.

After his retirement from football, Liddell was appointed assistant permanent secretary and bursar (finance) of Liverpool University's Guild of Undergraduates. He was a hugely popular figure with the students and he stayed in the post until stepping down in August 1984. 'Billy enjoyed working with young people and they could relate to him,' said Phyllis Liddell.

Merseyside's rise as football's capital in the 1960s, due to the rival deeds of Liverpool and Everton, was matched by the explosion of Scouse music and humour with Gerry and the Pacemakers, the Searchers, Cilla Black, Ken Dodd and Jimmy Tarbuck among many others joining the Beatles in the vanguard of the nation's entertainers.

Often, the lines between football and showbiz were blurred, as Liddell demonstrated with a 'Treble Scots' stint on stage at Liverpool's Royal Court Theatre. Phyllis still smiles at the memory. 'It was the opening night of a Ken Dodd show and Billy, Ian St John and Ron Yeats went on stage, holding guitars, surrounded by the lovely Bluebell Girls,' she recalled. 'My granddaughter Sarah was only seven at the time and when we got some pictures of Billy on stage I said to her: "There's nana – one of the dancers!" For years Sarah believed I was one of the Bluebells!'

Billy filled a more familiar role in May 1967 when he played in a charity match with a host of other stars, pride of place going to the Hungarian legend Ferenc Puskas, captain of the 6–3 conquerors of England at Wembley in 1953.

It was a warm reunion as he and Liddell had been on opposite sides when Scotland lost 3–1 to Hungary at the Nep Stadium in front of a 102,000 crowd in May 1955, Puskas later joining Real Madrid following his country's uprising. Liddell went to Liverpool's Speke Airport to welcome Puskas, who arrived to a battery of flashbulbs and a glass of champagne at the foot of the aircraft steps! Puskas, in a typically generous gesture, had travelled after agreeing to play for free in the match which was in aid of Bankfield House Community Centre in Liverpool's Garston district, a cause also readily supported by Liddell whose work for youngsters included his chairmanship of the Merseyside Youth Association Football League.

Match organiser Brian Taylor revealed: 'I wrote to Real Madrid asking if Puskas might play and amazingly we received a telegram from the man himself which read: "Received your letter of 7th. I only wait you send me plane ticket. Puskas." We had the telegram framed.'

Other celebrated players had also agreed to turn out in the fundraising event, which was staged at South Liverpool's Holly Park and billed as 'Billy Liddell XIV v. Ferenc Puskas XI'.

This was the Liddell line-up: Bert Trautmann; Willie Cunningham, Wright (unidentified); Hugh Kelly, John Charles, Bill Slater; Billy Bingham, Jimmy McIlroy, Dave Hickson, Alan Hampson, Billy Liddell.

Puskas's starting team was: Albert Dunlop; Jones (unidentified), Jimmy Tansey; Malcolm Allison, Dave Ewing, Jackie Kelly; Willie Moir, Harold Hassall, Johnny Hart, Ferenc Puskas, Bill Perry.

It was an absorbing game which Liddell's side won 5–3 with Puskas, the man known as the 'Galloping Major' following his army service, scoring all three of his team's goals to thrill a substantial crowd. Puskas, who scored 83 goals in 84 appearances for Hungary and 35 in 37 European games for Real Madrid, showed he had lost little of his touch despite having reached his 40th birthday the previous month.

The magical Magyar put his team ahead from the penalty spot with Billy Bingham equalising. Mick Metcalf, former Wrexham and Chester inside forward and once an Everton amateur, was one of several substitutes used during the game and made an impact by putting Liddell's side in front. But Puskas restored equality with a spectacular, trademark banana shot and the teams were level at half-time.

Just two minutes into the second half, in which former Everton, Blackburn and Tranmere goalkeeper Harry Leyland took over from Trautmann, Liddell's former Anfield team-mate Hickson struck to put his side ahead before Puskas hit another equaliser. Hickson was on the mark again to regain the advantage, which was extended when the brilliant, versatile Wales star John Charles, who had switched from centre half to centre forward for the second half, hit a fifth for Liddell's side.

No official attendance figure was published but organiser Taylor recalled: 'There were more people locked out of the ground than there were inside! To see stars like Puskas, Liddell, Charles and company certainly caught the public's imagination.

'Puskas wasn't too mobile but he had a fantastic shot. I'd never seen power like that before. He could bend a ball like the Brazilians. I think we raised more than £1,000 as a result of the match – a huge sum of money for a small youth club in those days.'

Billy continued to play the occasional game and turned out for a magistrates' team which eventually persuaded him to put his boots away for good and restrict his football to garden kick-abouts with his grandchildren. 'I got one of my worst injuries in football when I broke my cheek bone playing for the magistrates' team, ' he revealed. 'It was all getting a bit rough so I decided to pack it in and concentrate on my tennis.'

Liddell's respect and admiration for Ian Callaghan, the winger and later midfielder he so accurately tipped for stardom and who adhered to a similar code of sporting behaviour, led to him joining Callaghan's testimonial committee in 1977.

The committee, which planned and organised Callaghan's testimonial match between Liverpool and a Lancashire Select XI as well as a variety show at Liverpool's Empire Theatre, also included comedian Jimmy Tarbuck and another former Liverpool star, Geoff Strong. I was chairman and I can vouch for the value of Liddell's wisdom and advice at meetings which we held at the former Liverpool Press Club in the Adelphi Hotel.

Liddell, who was at outside left when Callaghan made his reserve-team debut at leeds in the 1959–60 season, reflected: 'To be on Ian's committee and help organise his events was the least I could do. Elisha Scott held Liverpool's League appearance record when I started playing and I was honoured to overtake his total.

'Now Ian has surpassed my record and I'm delighted that it's a player and person of his calibre that has done so. He deserves all the accolades and medals he's collected over the years. He's never been in trouble on or off the field, he gets on with the game and he never ever gives anything less than 100 per cent.'

At the same time as Callaghan was writing new entries in the Anfield record books, a youngster growing up in the Aigburth district of Liverpool landed a job as a paperboy for a local shop. One of his deliveries was to the Liddell household. Hyder Jawad eventually became a journalist, writing for the *Liverpool Echo* and ghost-writing John Aldridge's *My Story* before becoming chief football writer for the *Birmingham Post*.

'My dad came over from Iraq in 1964, the year he first stood on the Kop, and he soon got to know about Billy Liddell and told me all about him, too,' said Hyder. 'My dad became a Liverpool fan and, because of that, so did I.

'He took me to my first match at Anfield when I was six. It was Liverpool against Stromsgodset in the European Cup Winners Cup in 1974. We won 11–0. So it was a good debut for me!

'I remember getting a copy of *Shoot Annual 1978* which had a double-page spread on wingers and there was a big picture of Billy Liddell, taken in action in 1946. So I walked to Billy's house, about five minutes away, to ask him if he would kindly autograph it for me.

'We had got to know where he lived from other people living in the neighbourhood and I went with my pal, Darren Griffiths, who grew up with me in Stratford Road and who is now Everton Football Club's press officer.

'We were both football daft and we read and bought anything we could find about the game. I was only about ten and when we knocked at Billy's front door I remember the amazing feeling I had when he opened the door.

'Perhaps I didn't really believe he lived there until he did open the door. It was just mind-blowing to meet a legend like him! It was like, wow! This was Liverpool's history in front of my very eyes.

'Obviously, I'd never seen Billy play but I knew all about him. You don't have to spend long in Liverpool to learn about Billy Liddell. I was tongue-tied at meeting him. But he was great. He signed the photograph for me – and I've still got it.

'From about 1980 to 1984 I worked for Davenports, the

newsagents, on Aigburth Road, Liverpool, and I used to deliver papers to Billy's home. I remember on one occasion when I arrived with the paper Billy came to the front door wearing a kilt. I got the impression that he was a really proud Scotsman.'

During his career with Liverpool and Scotland Liddell made indelible impressions in many parts of the world and that also applied to his short spell as a wartime guest player for Irish League club Linfield. In 1982 he was guest of honour at Belfast's Jumna Street Linfield Supporters Club at a reunion of former players. Liddell was accompanied that night by Frank Baker and Syd Peppitt, formerly of Stoke city, and Sunderland's George Wright, who were also wartime Linfield stalwarts.

Two days later Liddell was a top-table guest at the Northern Ireland Football Writers Association dinner, on what was to be his last visit to Belfast. 'But Billy kept in touch with his friends in Northern Ireland whose only regret was that he hadn't been able to make more than two appearances for Linfield,' said celebrated Ulster-based football writer Malcolm Brodie.

'Linfield's ground, Windsor Park, was a memorable venue for him. He scored twice for Scotland there in their 3–2 Victory international win over Northern Ireland in February 1946 and he also played there for Great Britain in 1955.

'Billy Liddell's name, like that of Newcastle United legend Jackie Milburn, who was a player-coach at the club in the late 1950s, will forever be part of the story of the Blues, the name Linfield are known by in Ulster.

'Linfield's tradition, professionalism and business acumen are the envy of many. The club and its supporters recall with pride, "The great Billy Liddell played for us". He will always be warmly and affectionately remembered in Northern Ireland.'

His name resonates, too, in Hungary, as Phyllis Liddell explained. 'Billy and I went on holiday there shortly after the collapse of Communism. We were on a coach admiring the lovely city of Budapest when the Hungarian tour guide announced: "Ladies and gentlemen, we are now passing the Nep Stadium, where the famous Puskas played."

'When we got off the coach another member of the party told

the guide: "There's someone else on this bus who played at that stadium. His name is Billy Liddell, of Liverpool and Scotland." The woman guide went home and told her husband, who was English and a Manchester United supporter.

'He, of course, knew about Billy and the upshot was that the tour guide told us that whenever future tourist groups passed the stadium (since renamed the Ferenc Puskas Stadium), she would announce: "This is where Puskas *and* Billy Liddell played."'

Liddell had long taken a keen interest in Liverpool FC Supporters Club, contributing articles for their handbooks, attending functions with Phyllis and eventually becoming their club president.

It was in that role in January 1982 that he had the pleasure of officially handing over a Sunshine Coach for handicapped children after fundraising efforts by the supporters brought in the £5,500 needed to buy the vehicle.

He gave much of his time to charity and youth causes and in 1986 received the National Association of Boys Clubs Gold Award, honouring his thirty years' service to the association, as well as being presented with certificates in recognition of his work for the Merseyside Youth Association and the YMCA.

In addition to those causes, his work at the university and his duties as a magistrate, Liddell was chairman of the Littlewoods 'Spot The Ball' panel, which also included former Everton greats Joe Mercer and Brian Labone, later supplemented by Ian Callaghan.

In November 1983 Liddell was among the celebrity guests at an unforgettable gala dinner in Anfield's Trophy Room, organised by the Football Writers Association to honour Bob Paisley, when the guests also included Matt Busby, Joe Fagan and other former colleagues of Liddell's in Jack Balmer, Cyril Sidlow, Eddie Spicer, Bill Jones, Ray Lambert and Phil Taylor.

Also present were then Everton manager Howard Kendall and his predecessor Gordon Lee. I had the privilege of compering the evening and introducing Liddell as one of the speakers, his address paying special tribute to Paisley's ball-winning capabilities. 'Bob supplied a lot of my ammunition,' he told the gathering, which represented a cross section of people involved in British football.

When he reached seventy Liddell had to retire as a magistrate, a post he had held since 1958 that eventually saw him become the father of the Merseyside bench. His service was dedicated and distinguished, winning the respect of the legal profession, court workers and public alike.

His physical fitness, too, had a spin-off in the court buildings with the lift boys revealing that they were sometimes left with aching legs. 'I was a fifteen-year-old lift boy at Liverpool Magistrates Court and I always used to run up the stairs with Billy – or Mr Liddell as we had to call him – because he refused to use the lifts!' said one.

The day after Liddell's seventieth birthday in January 1992 he went to watch Liverpool's home game against Luton Town accompanied, as usual, by Phyllis, both of them Anfield season-ticket holders. As part of his birthday celebrations he made a pre-match visit to the dressing-room area to say hello to players and back-room staff, including John Barnes, a fellow member of that disappearing breed called wingers.

'John's a great winger but his style is a lot different from mine in my day,' Liddell reflected. 'I was a natural right-footer playing on the left wing and always had a good view of goal when I cut inside. John's a natural left-sided player and very clever with it.'

Yet both men were superb exponents of wing play, a largely lost art lamented by many long-term football observers. At the peak of his career in 1952 Liddell, one of the supreme flank men, presented in *The FA Book for Boys* some valuable and thought-provoking advice to any youngster aspiring to keep the flame of wing play burning:

Far more attention is paid to the role of the modern wing-man than was customary in the case of his father and grandfather. In years gone by the sole purpose of a wing-man, as his name implied, was to collect the ball, take it down the wing, and then put over a cross for his inside colleague to finish off the job. The old type of wing-man was expected to put in a lot of practice to perfect his art of centring a ball to a particular spot, and he seldom worried about shooting at goal. Nowadays a winger must have all the attributes of his predecessor *plus* an ability to cut in towards the centre and have a shot.

This change came about with the advent of the stopper centre-half. The winger began to find that his crosses to the centre were being intercepted; the chances of the centre-forward being able to score from a pass were also reduced. But before saying something about how you can best position yourself to score when the opportunity arises, let me deal with the winger's additional task of making goals for the other forwards.

Some of the commonest mistakes committed by inexperienced wingers occur when they are approaching goal from an angle. In Fig. 1 the outside-left has the ball and sells the dummy to the right full-back. Being inside the penalty-area he decides to have a shot at goal himself, but the ball ends up outside the side netting, and a good opportunity is wasted. If, on the other hand, he had carried the ball nearer the goal and had drawn the centre-half towards him, he would have created an open space and an easier chance for his team mates, perhaps the centre-forward or outside-right, to shoot successfully.

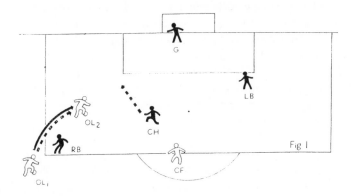

The centre-forward, being in front of goal, can divert his shot in many more different directions – it is not exaggeration to say that most goals are scored from the centre of the goal mouth.

If your colleagues are not in position, you would of course be justified in having a shot yourself. If so, aim for the far side of the net, for three reasons: (1) the goalkeeper may be able only to push out your shot towards one of your other forwards; (2) your shot may travel wide and enable your opposite winger to apply the finishing touch; (3) the ball has more chance of being deflected into the net by an opponent as well as by one of your own team.

Tom Finney is one of the greatest experts at creating openings for his colleagues from the goal-line. Apart from his extraordinary knack of being able to beat a man either on the inside or the outside, he knows what to do next. Tom is not one to hug the touchline, but makes straight for the goal-line, thus making it awkward for the centre half who does not get the chance to tackle him.

When Tom reaches the goal-line or thereabouts, he has usually drawn a man towards him. He then chips the ball back towards the centre, so that the centre forward or inside left can run onto it and have a shot. This is shown in Fig. 2, in which you will note that the other winger is lying handy, not too near the goal-line and not too far away from the play, so that he can pounce on the ball if it is crossed behind the inside men or flashed across the face of the goal.

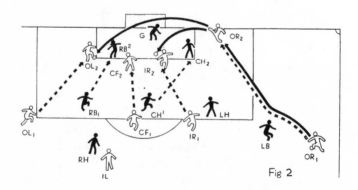

Fig 2

A winger must get into the habit of thinking well ahead and foster an awareness of his team-mate's positions. I learned this to my cost and with a considerable amount of embarrassment when I was still a schoolboy. It had started to snow during the game and it became difficult to see the lines, but I got the ball on the right touchline and started haring down the wing with it. I beat two men and kept on steadily with my eyes glued to the ball, the snowflakes driving in my face. I cut in towards goal and, when I thought I had gone far enough, chipped the ball inside for my colleagues. Imagine my surprise and shame when I suddenly realized that I had passed over to the wrong side of the goal-line without seeing it and without hearing the referee's whistle! From that moment on, I became a good deal less absorbed in my own prowess and realised the importance of remembering my team-mates before it was too late.

Now for some more complicated movements in which the winger may be presented with opportunities to take a shot at goal himself. The scheme shown in Fig. 3 depends for its success on a large element of surprise. The movement starts in your own half of the field, often quite near the penalty-area. In this case the outside right has the ball and is about ten or

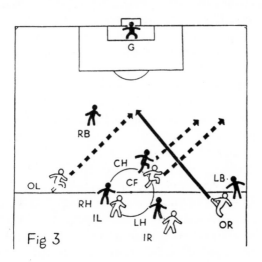

Fig 3

twenty yards from the halfway line. His inside man is lying square with him, waiting for the pass inside the half back, and allowing the centre forward to move to the wing.

The centre forward tries to get behind the full back and, as the opposition would not like him to have a free hand if the ball is put over the full back's head, usually draws the centre half with him. When the outside right sees that the centre half is being drawn out of the middle, he sends a long fast drive down the field. Most people would expect the inside left to take up the centre forward's position, but he would have the right full back and the right half to contend with. But the other winger has only the full back to cope with, and if he is on his toes and the ball is placed in the right spot, the surprise and speed of his dash forwards can often lead to a goal. If the defence is to be caught on the hop, the three men involved, the two wingers and the centre forward, must act simultaneously.

Let us now see how the winger can cooperate with his centre forward. When a ball is cleared from your own penalty-area up to the centre forward, the latter usually tries to bring his inside men into the game by nodding the ball down to them, and then turning quickly for the through ball down the middle *à la* Jackie Milburn. This is fine with short balls or hanging balls, when the centre forward can get up high enough to control it, but it is difficult with a hard, fast ball or a high ball near the centre half.

It is best then to help the ball on its way down the middle of the field by flicking it over the centre half's head. There is usually quite a space before the full backs are reached, and this opens up the way for either wing man to dart through after the ball. Once the ball is past the centre half, the way to goal is open and a speedy winger with good ball control can bring the move to a successful conclusion. But once again remember the need for perfect timing and understanding. If the winger goes too soon, he may get off-side. If the centre forward does not know when his wingers are going to run ahead, he may find himself heading the ball behind them instead of in front.

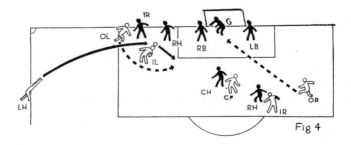

Fig 4

To end, here is a move (Fig. 4) which gave my team many chances last season. The ingredients needed are a player who can get up well to head a ball and a half back who can throw a good length ball. The left half throws a long ball to the inside left, standing near the goal line, and the outside left starts running towards goal. His aim is to meet the ball as it is headed down by the inside forward. There is quite a lot of room for error in heading any ball, so, in case the ball is headed across the goal mouth, the outside right tries when the movement starts to get between the full back and the goalkeeper.

The first time we tried this, the move worked perfectly until I came to shoot. I missed the ball completely and landed on my back! But our second attempt proved successful.

Some of the moves I have described are admittedly complex, so don't expect them to come off first time. But if you keep on practising and win complete harmony with your colleagues, then I am sure that as a winger you will not only 'make' goals for others, but also score quite a few yourself.

Chapter Thirteen

The People's Hero

Evidence of Billy Liddell's enduring place in the history of British football is provided by the number and variety of people who testify to his enriching impact on their lives. He truly was a public hero with an all-embracing appeal that echoed one Sunday newspaper's claim that 'all human life is there'.

His is a powerful legacy encompassing the gamut of society, from a man who filled one of the highest offices of state to the supporters who stood on the Kop, and from Liddell's footballing contemporaries to the country's top comedians and an award-winning broadcaster. To them all he was an icon and an inspiration.

For a youngster in South Wales a lifetime's allegiance to Liverpool FC was spawned through the deeds of Liddell – despite the fact that he never saw him play! The long-distance admirer was Michael Howard, who rose to become an MP and a QC, home secretary, shadow chancellor of the exchequer and now Leader of the Opposition.

'When I was growing up in Llanelli I was inspired by Billy's exploits and that's where my support for Liverpool all began,' Howard revealed. 'It was my admiration for Billy that started it all.

'I have remained faithful to the club ever since and watch them whenever I can, either in person or on television, though that is nothing like as frequently as I would wish.

'Regrettably, I never did see Billy in action but I was an avid reader of match reports of games in which he played, although for obvious reasons I used to have a real problem when Scotland met

Wales! I was bowled over by his talent and his skills and his generosity as a team player. He was a real sporting hero.

'Billy was always known as a true gentleman, quite apart from his wizardry on the field. His example could well be followed with advantage by many of today's players and I am delighted this biography of him has been written.'

Here is a selection of personal recollections of Billy Liddell, the man and player:

Tommy Docherty, Liddell's Scotland team-mate, former Preston and Arsenal wing half and manager of Scotland, Chelsea and Manchester United (among other clubs):

When you played against Billy he was like a torpedo coming towards you. He had strength, skill, bravery and a big heart. He was a winner. He had everything that epitomised a Liverpool and Scotland player.

They rightly called Liverpool 'Liddellpool'. For what he did for them they should still call it that. Kenny Dalglish is the best Scottish player I've ever seen but Billy is right up there with him.

I played with Billy for Scotland at Hampden and at Wembley. There were times when we were the only two Anglos in the team. The Scottish press didn't like players with English clubs. They looked upon them as traitors.

But that didn't bother Billy and me. We were born and bred in Scotland and considered it a great privilege to play for our country. That's the way we looked on it. In fact, we'd have paid to play for Scotland. I don't think players should be paid for the honour of representing their country.

Billy was equally at home at outside left or outside right and I played against him for Preston when he was at centre forward. I tackled him once or twice and it was like trying to stop a runaway tank. You were likely to bounce off him.

He was as hard as they come yet he would never commit a deliberate foul in his life. He was very fair. When it comes to great wingers I would say that Billy was the

Scottish Tom Finney and when you take into account my
feelings about Tom, my team-mate at Preston, there is no
higher praise than that.

I'm very proud to be able to say that I played with and
against Billy Liddell. To be in the same team as him was an
honour. He was a great role model and off the field he did so
much for the community.

I remember Billy telling me when we were away with
Scotland once that he was studying to become an accountant.
It meant he trained only twice a week but he probably trained
harder on those two mornings than most of today's players
do in a week.

You've got to be careful today in case the players get tired.
You've got to put them to bed early. Some of them get
injured on their day off. I can think of one big centre foward
who'd get injured on *A Question Of Sport*!

Then they talk about pressure! I'll tell you what pressure
is. It's having a mortgage and not having the money to pay
for it. Billy Liddell never talked about pressure. I don't think
he even thought about it. If he was playing today he'd be a
sensation.

Ken Dodd, celebrated comedian and friend of the Liddell family:

Billy Liddell was my hero and was reminiscent to me of his
namesake, the great athlete Eric Liddell. Their names were
pronounced differently but they shared one quality: they
were both men of great principle.

Kids come to me nowadays and say they want to be
footballers. I tell them two things. First, make sure that they
learn another skill to fall back on and, second, if they do
overcome all the hurdles to make it and become players they
should strive to be like Billy Liddell, not only as a footballer
but as a man.

I remember I was appearing in the panto *Cinderella*
with the Beverley Sisters at the Liverpool Empire in 1957.

I discovered that Billy had booked tickets for himself, his wife and some friends to come to see the show one Saturday night.

I was really excited. In fact, I was discumknockerated to know that the great man would be in the audience! As it happened he got injured that afternoon in a match against Doncaster at Anfield. He was knocked unconscious and had to have his head stitched.

So that was that, I thought. There was no way Billy would come to see the show after that. How wrong I was. When the curtain went up there, sitting in the front stalls, was Billy, sporting a huge black eye, with his lovely wife Phyllis. I was absolutely thrilled to bits that he'd still come along.

At the time I was a vice president of Liverpool Supporters Club and after the show Billy, Phyllis and their party came to see me in the dressing room. Billy told me that the player he'd collided with needed six stitches and he'd only had three. I told Billy, for a laugh, that he must have a very thick skull!

I got to know Billy and Phyllis, and their twin sons Malcolm and David, very well. Liverpool and Everton have been blessed with a lot of great players in their history but none greater than Billy Liddell. To me he was a king.

Billy Bingham, 56–times capped former Northern Ireland, Sunderland, Luton and Everton winger and manager of Northern Ireland, Greece and Everton (among other posts):

The first thing to say about Billy Liddell is that in physique he was a bit bigger than usual for a winger. I thought he was built more like a rugby wing forward. He was very strong, so consequently he could take a tackle and ride them, too.

He was a very determined player and very penetrative. He had an impressive goal record for a winger and I tried to follow his example of scoring goals as well as making them. But he had a very different style from me.

He was very direct, hard and strong running. Yet for all his physical attributes he was quite passive on the field. He wasn't an angry player and it would have been very difficult for any opponent to rile him.

When he cut in he had a terrific shot, he could head a ball well and, overall, he was a very powerful player of his time, as good as any winger in the game. The only player I'd put on a par with him was Tom Finney who, like Billy, could also play right wing, left wing or centre forward.

I played against Billy in his last appearance for Scotland in Belfast in 1955. If I was a manager given a pick of any player, regardless of age or time, Billy would be in my team.

Wally Fielding, former Everton inside forward who made 410 appearances, scoring 54 goals, for the Goodison club between 1945 and 1958:

Billy was one of the best, one of the all-time greats, and such a wonderful chap to know and be with. It used to make my day when people told me that Billy rated me highly as a player.

He had a wonderful left foot, a match winner in his own right. He was nonstop and he was a hard worker. He wasn't one of those wingers who just stayed out wide. He'd be there wherever he was needed.

When we met Liverpool in the FA Cup at Goodison in 1955, Billy had to switch to wing half because of injuries to one of the other players. It meant he was marking me. I never got a kick and we lost 4–0. I had a terrible game. He never left me. He blotted me out of the match.

He was a good all-round player. You could put him in any position and he'd perform well. Billy Liddell *was* Liverpool. He was such a good-living man and never swore.

I remember in another Mersey derby match one of Billy's team-mates fouled me. It was a bad one. He kicked me in the back. Billy saw what happened, went over to this chap and played hell with him. He said: 'What did you do that for? We don't want any more of that. Cut it out.'

That was the sort of fellow Billy was. I met him a few times at various functions and he was as great a chap off the field as he was great player on it. A lovely man.

I've only recently discovered that Billy and I have another link. During the war when I was stationed in Bari, Italy, I played for a services side against the British Army football team, comprising the cream of football talent including Joe Mercer and Tommy Lawton with Matt Busby in charge.

After the match Matt came up to me and asked: 'How would you like to join us, son?' I told him that I needed permission from my CO. Matt obtained that within a few hours and I joined the Army squad and played for them on the rest of their tour.

That's how I made my name and I signed for Everton in 1945. So like Billy Liddell, I've got Matt Busby to thank for my career on Merseyside.

Sir Tom Finney, brilliant former England and Preston winger and centre forward, with 30 goals in 76 internationals and 250 goals in 569 first-class appearances:

Bill was a legend and a great servant to Liverpool. He was a bit like me in that he played both on the wing and at centre forward.

I remember him saying that he had decided to follow a career in accountancy as a fall-back from football and then, in later life, he was assistant bursar at Liverpool University Students Union. Not many players have filled a responsible post like that.

I had a plumbing company but I trained with the rest of the Preston squad every morning. We finished at lunchtime and then I went back to the business in the afternoons.

But Bill had only two morning training sessions each week and to be the player he was is a great achievement. I was very surprised when I discovered that he trained only twice a week. To play for so long and so consistently well for Liverpool and Scotland as a part-timer, which he effectively was, speaks volumes for him. It was incredible, really.

Given how crucial Bill was to Liverpool, I'm sure the club were hugely relieved that he turned down the invitation to go to Bogota. The offers coming from Colombia were mind-boggling for players in England who were then on a maximum wage. And although it all sadly collapsed, and led to players coming home branded as rebels, it must have been very tempting at the outset.

Bill was up there with the best players and a great goalscorer, too. We each played in the other's testimonial match. But Bill was more than just a great player. He was a gentleman, a genuinely nice person and a great ambassador for the game.

Bill's conduct on the field was exemplary and he was highly regarded and respected by his fellow professionals. Bill was bigger than me and, like me, took a lot of stick from defenders. But neither of us was ever booked by a referee.

Whenever you played Liverpool, Bill was always a thorn in your side which you might expect from a player who was chosen, along with Stan Matthews, for both Great Britain teams.

Bill and Stan were fine wingers but very different types of player. Bill was so direct and as a big chap was very good in the air and he could shoot with both feet. He'd certainly be in my all-time best team.

John Peel, disc jockey and radio presenter, 2002 Sony Gold Award winner for four decades of broadcasting, and Liverpool fan since boyhood leading to his children being named William Robert Anfield, Alexandra Mary Anfield, Thomas James Dalglish and Florence Victoria Shankly:

One of my most treasured possessions is an advertising fly sheet for the long-defunct newspaper *Reynolds News*. I treasure it because it contains the signature of the one and only Billy Liddell.

I was born on the Wirral and went to prep school in North

Wales, which was a boys' boarding establishment. The boys there who had any interest in football were mainly Manchester United supporters so I guess that as a reaction to that I decided to follow Liverpool.

To follow football at that school at that time, in the late 1940s and 1950s, was considered rather proletarian, but during the holidays I would travel to Anfield on my own to watch Liverpool, which is when I first saw the great man Liddell.

I think I went once with my mother but my parents were not football fans. I followed my own path as a football supporter. It was when I was going to a match in the 1950s that I came across a guy near the stadium distributing the *Reynolds News* fliers.

At that moment I spotted Billy Liddell getting off the bus! So I grabbed one of the fly sheets and asked Billy to sign it. It was a great thrill then and even today it's one of my few remaining treasured possessions.

On another occasion on my way to a game I emerged from the Mersey Tunnel on my bike and was struck by a real buzz about the city. Then somebody shouted: 'Billy's back!'

Billy had been out of the team for quite a few matches and this was his comeback game. I must admit that I cried when he ran out of the players' tunnel onto the field before kick-off. And all around me there were burly dockers and stevedores in tears, too. It was quite a sight and the memory of it has never left me.

I have a feeling it was a match against Middlesbrough, who had two men marking Billy all afternoon. They repeatedly tried to bring him down. In the end Billy got a bit fed up with trying to swerve to avoid them and decided he'd just run straight through them!

That gave me a rather wonderful *Boys Own* moment of this great, heroic figure striding past opponents as if they weren't there! He had such great upper body strength.

Years later, around the late 1960s or very early 70s by which time I was married and in broadcasting, my wife Sheila and I were living in a rather grim flat in St Stephens

Lane, Bayswater. I was asked to interview Billy for a BBC2 programme called *One Man's Week*.

Billy travelled to London by train to be my guest. But when I came face to face with the great man I was so tongue-tied I could hardly say a word beyond 'How are you?'. Having all those boyhood memories of him really got to me and I struggled to ask questions!

I got through it somehow and after we'd done the programme I asked him if he'd like to come to my place for a cup of tea. Amazingly, he said yes. I thought: 'My God! Billy Liddell's going to be in my flat drinking a mug of tea.'

Even Sheila, a Yorkshire girl who'd been a Leeds fan, was impressed because she could see from my reaction that I was going through some general trauma at having Billy Liddell in our flat! I'd like to be able to say that I kept the mug he drank from but, sadly, I didn't.

My worship of Billy, though, extended to a tour of Scotland I made in the 1970s when I made a point of visiting Lochgelly, near to Billy's home and where he played for the local team before joining Liverpool.

I don't like the way football is today when someone like Bill Shankly probably wouldn't be able to get a job, because of coaching qualifications and red tape, and England is going the way of Scotland, which has a two-club domination by Rangers and Celtic.

Billy belonged to a very different era yet, when I reflect on all the players I've seen, he and Kenny Dalglish are up there at the top.

Ian Callaghan, member of England's 1966 World Cup-winning squad and Liverpool's 856–game record holder, who made his debut in place of his boyhood hero Liddell:

When I was a youngster Billy was my hero. I was just so absolutely impressed by him . . . by his speed and how hard he hit the ball. Dear me! He looked so big and he had a pair of legs on him like I don't know what!

He was the top player at Liverpool. They were in the Second Division when I was a boy supporting them and everyone loved the bones of Billy. He was the top man.

For me to then join the club as a fifteen-year-old amateur training two nights a week, to meet Billy and then take over from him on my first-team debut, just after my eighteenth birthday, was a huge thing for me.

We'd played a couple of games together in the reserves but to take his place in the first team was something I'd never bargained for. And if anyone had said then, back in April 1960, that I'd go on to break Billy's club record of 492 League appearances I'd have laughed at them!

I was about twelve when I first saw him play. I used to walk with my mates from the Dingle area of the city. It took more than an hour there and an hour back although I didn't see him or Liverpool as much as I'd have liked to.

That was because I used to play for the school team on Saturday mornings and the boys club side in the afternoon. But when I got the opportunity to go to Anfield, it was always a thrill to see Billy in full flow.

For such a star Billy was an unbelievably quiet man. Even in later years when he very kindly served on my testimonial committee and we were also members of the Littlewoods 'Spot The Ball' panel, of which Billy was chairman, he was always quiet and very softly spoken.

When Billy had to step down from the panel through ill health I was asked to succeed him. So I had the honour of following in the great man's steps on and off the field.

Billy was an introvert and, as such, it must have been very difficult for him to fulfil his duties as a magistrate, for example, and to speak publicly at functions. But he just got on with it and he also did a lot of charity work that people never knew about.

Football in Billy's era was very different from today and the debate will continue about the merits of the game now and in the past. But players of Billy's calibre would flourish in any era.

I've been fortunate to see and play alongside some marvellous players but Billy has to be right up there with the greatest, especially as he could play brilliantly on either wing, or at centre forward, and score goals.

He was simply unforgettable. Everton had Dixie Dean. Liverpool had Billy Liddell. Both are legends.

Brian Phillips, lifelong Liverpool supporter, Liddell admirer and one of his former tennis opponents:

As an impressionable youngster during and after the war Billy was my great hero and my admiration of him only grew as the years went by. I have a multitude of memories of him as a player and I was privileged to get to know him and face him across a tennis court.

It's difficult to know where to start when I begin to recollect some of my most treasured moments of Billy in a Liverpool jersey. There are so many. There was, of course, the famous FA Cup occasion against Manchester City in 1956. With the final seconds ticking away, Billy let fly from just inside the penalty area with a shot that left Bert Trautmann helpless but the referee, Mervyn Griffiths, had blown for time as the ball was in flight!

The 1950 FA Cup Final also stands out for the treatment the strong-tackling the Arsenal half backs, particularly Alex Forbes, meted out to Billy. But there was no retaliation or complaint from Billy, even though he must have been black and blue at the end of the game.

As a Liverpool fan I was proud that Billy played for the two postwar Great Britain teams against the Rest of Europe, in 1947 and 1955, and I travelled to Belfast to watch him in the second one.

I was also at Anfield in November 1957 to see him set what was then a new League record of appearances for Liverpool and more than ten years before that was another game that remains foremost in my memory.

It was an FA Cup tie against Birmingham and centre forward Albert Stubbins scored one of Anfield's greatest ever goals when he ran in and dived horizontally, just above the snow-covered pitch, to meet Billy's low cross and head past England goalkeeper Gil Merrick.

After Billy's retirement from football I had some stirring encounters with him on the tennis courts. As with his football, Billy was a competitive yet sporting player when he turned out for the Mossley Hill and, later, East Wavertree clubs.

He was a very obliging man and he kindly found the time to travel with me to North Wales to kick off a charity match. After the game there was a buffet in the presence of the local mayor who thanked everyone for coming and I knew that Billy was expected to say a few words in reply.

But, to be frank, with Billy being so quiet and softly spoken the palms of my hands were sweating worrying that he might be lost for words. I needn't have had any anxieties at all. He just stood up and said exactly what needed to be said. So that was another facet of Billy that I discovered.

He was a great player, a lovely man and a role model before they had role models.

Tommy Lawrence, Liverpool and Scotland goalkeeper who was on the Anfield playing staff with Liddell:

My dad, who played football with Bill Shankly at junior level in Scotland, knew Billy Liddell before he came south to join Liverpool not long before the war. And I was literally in the picture with Billy after I joined Liverpool as an amateur in 1956, turning professional the following year.

In those days when a player signed for Liverpool you went through a club ritual – having your photograph taken with Billy Liddell. You were then given a copy of the picture. My mother kept mine.

Billy was a tremendous figure at Liverpool. As the youngest goalkeeper on the club's books I was the one

chosen to go in when Billy did shooting practice. That was
the era of the big, heavy caseballs yet even so Billy could put
amazing swerve and bend on his shots.

I was never near them! Never had a sniff. You just
couldn't stop them. He kicked with such power that if he'd
hit one of the lightweight balls they play with today you'd
never have seen it again! He packed the hardest shot I've
ever known, he was one of the greatest players I've ever seen
and he was a real gentleman.

I never had the privilege of playing in the first team with
him – I made my debut after Billy had retired – but we played
together in the reserves and he was always kind to the
younger players.

In fact, I often wondered how he could sit on the bench as
a magistrate. He was so nice it's a wonder he didn't let
everyone off!

Many people ask whether Billy or Kenny Dalglish is the
greatest Liverpool player of all. But it's an unfair question.
Kenny was magnificent but he had other great players with
him. Usually, though, if Billy didn't play, Liverpool didn't win.

**Jimmy Tarbuck, top comedian and Liverpool fan who hero-
worshipped Liddell from boyhood:**

It was the great Billy Liddell who began my love affair with
Liverpool Football Club. My dad was an Evertonian and a
close pal of Dixie Dean. One day, when I was a kid, he took
me to a Mersey derby match with his Evertonian pals and
decked me out in a blue and white scarf.

Suddenly, Liddell cracked a shot into the Everton net to
score for Liverpool. I jumped up and cheered and one of my
dad's pals exclaimed: 'The little b—'s a Red!' I certainly
was from then on!

I used to get the 46 bus to Anfield and I'd see Billy getting
out of his little car. But I never had the nerve to approach him
and ask him for an autograph. Billy was *the* hero figure for
me and in Liverpool's Hall of Fame they should just have an

exclusive Liddell section and perhaps something even more permanent. I firmly believe that, considering what he did for this club.

Because of the passage of time, which means that many of today's fans don't really know who Billy was or what he did, I feel it is even more important that there is a lasting tribute to him at the club either at Anfield or if and when they move to a new stadium.

To those who never had the privilege of seeing Billy play, let me say that he carried the team. He carried the club. In those days it really was Liddellpool. The aura of the man meant so much to everyone: it lifted his team and worried the opposition. Yet, quite remarkably, he was a part-timer training only twice a week! That speaks volumes for his dedication.

Even when he might not have been as quick as he once was, you just had to give him the ball to hit with either foot, or with his head, and there was danger. There was the chance of a goal. And he could play anywhere.

He was brave and tough but the epitome of sportsmanship and also shared with Stanley Matthews the great distinction of being the only players to appear in both of the only two Great Britain teams that have played.

Ironically, my fondest memory of him was bathed in disappointment. I was standing in the Kop the day he hit that last-gasp shot against Manchester City in the FA Cup. It flew in for what we all thought was the equaliser.

The players went off the pitch but we thought they were just going to have a drink to get ready for extra time. They had to announce over the Tannoy that the referee had whistled for full time seconds before Billy's shot went in and that the game was over. Judging by the famous picture next day I don't think the ref had blown before Billy kicked it and I still think that.

Another great memory is of Tom Finney coming out of retirement to play in Billy's testimonial match at Anfield and running dear Ronnie Moran ragged. The atmosphere that night showed the amazing respect and affection the Kop had for Billy.

But the biggest, almost frightening thrill, was meeting
Billy for the first time. He was playing in the reserves and my
pal Bobby Campbell, also a Liverpool player, came over to
introduce me and said: 'This is Billy.' I couldn't speak. I was
just in awe. I just looked at him.

I was struck by what a beautifully proportioned guy he was
physically. Not an ounce of spare flesh. Just muscle. Many
years later, when I had my Dream Team on *This Is Your Life*,
Billy came on last and I was absolutely overcome that he had
made the effort to make the trip and appear on the show.

Billy would have to be in the top three Liverpool players
I've ever seen and I've seen some great ones. You think,
obviously, of Dalglish, Souness, Hansen and Clemence. Of
Yeats and St John. Of Keegan. You can go on and on.

But Dalglish and Liddell would be my top two. And I rate
Liddell that highly not through some faded memory of a little
boy who worshipped him. Billy simply has to be up there,
not least because of what he meant to the club. Liverpool
were not the most fashionable football team in those days but
we had Liddell . . . a one-club player of myth and legend.

Yet he was a very modest man, a gentleman on and off the
field and a wonderful ambassador for Liverpool Football
Club. Could he play in modern football? Could Dixie Dean,
Tom Finney and Stan Matthews play today?

Not much! Let me tell you – if you're great in any era you
can play in any era. The greats adapt and there is no question
that Billy Liddell would be a sensation today. It might sound
funny but I absolutely loved him.

**Dave Horridge, former *Liverpool Echo* sub-editor and *Daily
Mirror* sportswriter:**

As a boy I lived in a street off City Road, on the doorstep of
Goodison Park, and I was an Evertonian. But my father, who
was a Liverpool fan, took me to Anfield to see Billy
Liddell's League debut in the 7–4 win over Chelsea in
September 1946.

Then, as a twelve-year-old, I won a competition and the prize was an autographed photograph of Billy Liddell in a heading duel with the great Wolves and England centre half Billy Wright. Little did I know then that I would go on to become friends with both men and, sadly, attend both their funerals.

Another Liverpool match my father took me to was against Sheffield Wednesday in March 1951, when Jackie Sewell made his debut as the most expensive player in the history of English football at that time. He had cost Wednesday £34,500 from Notts County.

The pitch was heavily waterlogged and the game would not have been played today. It was so bad that it was the first football match I ever saw where nobody would head the ball because it had absorbed so much water it was like a medicine ball!

They had to scoop the ball even to kick it. Yet Billy stepped up just before half-time and hit a free kick of such power that it flew into the net at the Anfield Road end with the defenders ducking to get out of the way of it!

Billy's follow-through was such that his shooting leg was chest high, perpendicular to the ground. Sewell scored that day but Billy scored another, from a penalty, in the second half and Liverpool won 2–1.

His team-mate, Albert Stubbins, told me a story of Billy playing against Huddersfield. Liverpool got a free kick, Billy took it with his left foot and it smashed against the stanchion inside the net and came out again with the goalkeeper, Bob Hesford, who had played against Preston in the 1938 Cup Final, unaware of what had happened.

In the event the referee ordered a retake because of an infringement. This time Billy hit it with his right foot and again the ball smashed against the stanchion and came out. And again Hesford never saw it. This time, though, the goal stood.

Another example of his shooting power was in a game against Burnley at Anfield. He hit one that visiting

goalkeeper Jim Strong, unusually wearing a white jersey
when most keepers wore green, caught into his stomach as
he stood on the six-yard line at the Kop end. It was so hard
that it knocked Strong back a few feet. If he'd been standing
on his line it would have carried him into the net.

Opposing full backs, including the great Johnny
Carey,would try to stop Billy by positioning themselves tight
to the touchline to try to force him inside. But Billy would
curl the ball with the outside of his right foot, step over the
line and go round the defender, giving him a hefty shoulder
charge as he went past him which was quite permissible and
part of the game in those days.

When I was a sub-editor on the *Liverpool Echo* I used
to handle Billy's weekly column and he would
always write them himself – in longhand on a big piece of
writing paper.

They were so well composed articles and, invariably, they
appeared in the paper as he'd written them. I just had to tick-
sub them – as we say in the trade – and mark them up for
type-size and headlines.

The situation was exactly the same for Everton captain
Peter Farrell who also wrote a weekly article, and both
columns used to appear in the *Echo*'s Saturday football
edition. Because of that I got to know both Billy and Peter
quite well.

I was only a young journalist at the time and I was called
up for National Service. I joined the Army and was posted to
Egypt. One day I received a letter from Billy, who had got
my military address from the *Echo*.

He just signed the letter 'Bill' and the rest of the lads in the
tent didn't believe it was from Billy Liddell. I wrote back to
Billy and told him and when he sent another letter he made a
point of making sure there was no mistake!

I still have the letter, dated 11 August 1953, eight days
before the start of the 1953–4 season. Billy wrote it in longhand on letter-headed notepaper from his home, which was
then in Windsor Road, Huyton. This is what he wrote:

Dear Dave (or should it be Corporal?),

It was good to hear from you again and to know that you are now enjoying life in the Army. Don't talk about professional footballers having all the luck. How about yourself? You must have had a good cruise out to Egypt and now you are in the land of sunshine and you don't have to play in the heat like we used to do.

No worries (for you) for the next year or so while we are in the throes of a bitter League struggle and wondering, like thousands of others, whether this is to be Liverpool's year.

I see Everton are now importing players to try and get them out of the Second Division. A Canadian (believed to be Gordon Stewart) is playing in the reserves in their trial game and Nobby Fielding is not in either team.

We have our trial game tomorrow night and then Wednesday week we start off at home against Portsmouth followed by Manchester United and Newcastle United while Everton have three away engagements. What's the betting we finish higher in the League and go farther in the Cup?

I think I have to write again in the *Echo* but I have not seen the sports editor for a fortnight and as usual he is waiting for permission from the general manager.

I was sorry I could not help your father the other week but the family and I were just off to Devon where we had a marvellous time with some very good weather. Of course, since we started training it has been very warm and we have had rain only once.

The only startling news is that Lawrie Reilly won't sign for Hibs. He wants a benefit like Gordon Smith got. Mr Welsh [Don Welsh, the Liverpool manager] was in the queue at the weekend but I expect the £35,000 fee will scare him off. Anyhow, I don't think Lawrie will come to England. He knows he can get more in Scotland.

Well Dave, I have a few business letters to write now.
I have opened a sweets and tobacco shop in Oakfield
Road. So I will draw to a close hoping this finds you in
the best of health and always enjoying yourself.

Best wishes, Yours Sincerely, Bill.

Just in case they don't believe you I will append my
autograph below

Best Wishes

Bill Liddell

Liverpool F.C. and Scotland

Billy's apology in the letter for not being able to help my
father refers to the fact that he was unable to attend the West
Derby Darts League awards night that year. But a year later
he was able to go and I've got a superb photograph of Billy
and my father at that function.

The forecast Billy makes for Liverpool to finish higher
than Everton that season came good if you claim that
finishing 22nd – and last – in the old First Division is higher
than second in the old Second Division. Because that's what
happened! Liverpool went down and Everton came up.

But Billy, a quiet, placid man, was always the Liverpool
star and in all my years watching the game as fan and
journalist I don't think I have ever seen anyone who could hit
the ball as hard with either foot.

I once asked Ian St John to name his all-time Liverpool
team and even though he had never seen Liddell play he
included him in the side. He did so on the strength of Billy's
reputation.

My mother, who was not a football fan, used to say that
Merseyside's three most famous footballers were Dixie
Dean, Dave Hickson and Billy Liddell and my own view is
that Billy would be an even more celebrated player now than
he was in his own era.

There is a strong emphasis on athleticism in the modern
game and Billy, being so strong, fast and powerful, would be
tailor-made for it.

John Thornhill, chairman of Merseyside Magistrates Association:

Billy became a magistrate in 1958 and by the time he reached the compulsory retirement age of seventy in 1992 he was the Father of the local Bench. He was a man of great dignity and honour who dispensed justice in a very even-handed way.

He was a very gentle man and gentle as a magistrate but if he felt a custodial sentence was appropriate he would hand it down. He did not shirk his responsibilities. He was never frightened to do his job.

But he was always compassionate and in court he always listened and looked to see both sides of the story. He had a great sense of community and was interested in trying to ensure that those people who had transgressed could be rehabilitated, if at all possible, back into society.

Different Justices bring different qualities to their work on the Bench. They are drawn from varying backgrounds, which is the richness of the system, and it is why we always sit as magistrates in a group of three.

It is to achieve that important balance so that if there are extremes they can be evenly tempered. Billy was the sort of person who could evenly temper a group. He would often provide, if necessary, that nice balance between his two other magistrate colleagues. He would stop extremes taking control.

I first met Billy at Scottish country dancing. I thought to myself: 'That's where he practises those dribbling skills!' Actually, he was quite a good Scottish country dancer, tall and elegant.

Billy was a member of Liverpool St Andrews Society and I'm a member of the Liverpool Scots and the Liverpool Burns Club so we met each other quite regularly on the circuit.

He also regaled us with some wonderful anecdotes. He was a mine of stories and was good to listen to. He was always very willing to talk about his football life and his early days and also his family because he was a keen family man.

He was a religious man but his creed of living was a straightforward simple one – that everyone should be treated fairly and justly. He brought that quality to his work on the Bench.

Billy was a naturally quietly spoken man and in court, while he might have raised his voice slightly, it was more a case that he had a presence. In a sense people would listen intently to hear what he said. He certainly never shouted and he didn't raise his voice unduly.

Some people have a presence, others don't. Billy had a presence. Not because he was bombastic or loud but because he was gentle and honourable. He had people's respect, as a famous footballer but also for his manner in court.

To us, as magistrates, he was not a star player. He never basked in that. He was just Billy Liddell our colleague. And if there is one phrase to sum him up I would echo the one that his former Liverpool team-mate Albert Stubbins used to describe Billy – an honourable man.

Arthur Ellis, world-renowned referee:

I refereed Billy many times in my 23 years in League football. One incident among many was typical of the man. It happened in an important game between Liverpool and Wolves at Anfield, in which I was officiating.

Bob Paisley pushed a ball through to Billy in the Wolves penalty area. He was in the act of shooting for goal when he was charged off the ball and finished up on the ground.

The Kop crowd immediately howled for a penalty, which might well have looked justified. But I decided not and the game continued. As Billy ran past me he said: 'That was a really good shoulder-charge, ref!'

I can pay him no greater tribute than to say that if there were 22 Billy Liddells on a football field there wouldn't be any need for a referee.

Al Capleton, long-time Liverpool supporter voicing the views of many:

I remember Bill Liddell in 1947, a young powerful Scottish international who played on the left wing for Liverpool. He possessed phenomenal speed, great determination, skill and a real powerhouse of a shot. His football was tough and hard to the limit of the rules of the game.

I remember (when it was legal) Bill shoulder-charged the giant England goalkeeper Frank Swift, as he was holding the ball, and knocked him into the back of the net to score for Scotland.

He never complained when he was fouled. He just picked himself up and got on with the game. He was so tough he seemed to be made of Scottish granite and in those early years he seemed to have instructions to stay on the left.

As he raced down the line towards the Kop, 50,000-plus spectators would roar encouragement. As his cross came over into the goalmouth the crowd on the Kop would wave back and forth like a field of corn on a breezy day as perhaps Stubbins or Balmer or fiery Bobby Paisley would head or shoot the ball into the net.

It is ridiculous the way they are giving titles to footballers and this wonderful modest hero was ignored. To us old-timers Bill Liddell will always be the king. When you pick the all-time greats, start with Liddell – the greatest of the great.

Tommy Smith, former Liverpool captain who made 639 appearances for the club, scoring 48 goals, between 1963 and 1978:

One day in 1960 I thought I was in heaven. It was the day I lined up in the same Liverpool reserve team as the incomparable Billy Liddell. The match was a Central League fixture against Aston Villa. Billy was outside left and I was inside left.

What a feeling to be in the same side as the great man! Billy has always been my idol, my great hero. If we were playing in the street or on the rec [recreation ground] I was always Billy Liddell.

I'll never forget the winter's day in 1956 when I got out of school and stood on the Kop to watch the FA Cup replay against Manchester City. Right at the end of the game Billy charged down the pitch and smacked a shot past Bert Trautmann in the City goal for what we all thought was the equaliser.

Unfortunately, it didn't count because the referee said he blew for full time seconds before Billy shot. I never dreamed that day that about four years later I'd be playing alongside him in Liverpool reserves.

He was at the end of his career and I was just starting mine and I think I played about five reserve games with him. It was a great experience. Even then he was still a good player and, of course, an Anfield icon.

Many of the younger players, like myself, had the benefit of learning from him and his influence at Anfield was immense. Billy was my epitome of a footballer, a great player and head and shoulders above the rest of the team. He was very direct, had blistering pace, a rocket shot and his acceleration was tremendous. He was just magnificent.

And we mustn't forget that Billy, in common with other fine players like Stan Matthews, John Charles, Nat Lofthouse and Len Shackleton, played in an era when the ball was like a brick and the pitches were heavy and often like quagmires. But they still performed brilliantly.

Billy was one of the most modest, quiet, unassuming players ever to grace the game. He was a true professional and off the field he was a lovely man and a true gentleman.

The word 'great' is often over-used these days. But Billy Liddell was a true great. I've seen grown men get all emotional just recalling his feats. I can understand why.

Dave Abrahams, long-time Everton supporter:

Ian St John, Roger Hunt, Kevin Keegan, Kenny Dalglish, Ian Rush, Robbie Fowler and Michael Owen have all been idolised by Liverpool fans over the last forty years. But none of them has been held in the same sort of reverence as Billy Liddell.

In my opinion Alan Hansen uses the word 'awesome' too often and too easily. Yet Billy Liddell, with his power, strength and speed – allied to blistering shots with either foot and bullet-like headers – was really and truly absolutely awesome.

Billy was a gentleman on and off the field, a true sportsman and a player who was a wonderful role model for every aspiring footballer of his day. Although I didn't see him, we Evertonians will always have our Dixie Dean. And the Liverpudlians will always have their Billy Liddell.

I can pay him no bigger tribute than that.

Steve Faye, comedian, lifelong Liverpool supporter and friend of Liddell:

When I was a kid in the Huyton area of Liverpool we were playing a kick-about football match on the local playing fields when one of the lads hoofed the ball into the road.

A guy who happened to be walking past picked up the ball and booted it back to us. It was Billy Liddell! The lad who owned the ball kept it for years on a shelf in his kitchen as a treasured memento.

The ball was all ripped and had the bladder hanging out. But it had been touched by the foot of a Liverpool legend and he just wouldn't part with it.

In fact, the lad stopped our kick-about and told us he was taking the ball home 'because Liddell kicked it'. Billy's achievements for Liverpool FC were incredible. I'll never forget the sight of him in action.

He was the greatest and it's hard to explain just how much

he meant to the fans, who hero-worshipped him. He was a fantastic player and hit the ball with so much power it turned oblong!

When Billy became a magistrate this guy came out of court with a big smile on his face and explained: 'Billy was on the Bench and he fined me £2. But I was so pleased to come face to face with him that I'd have given him four quid if he'd asked! And if he'd sentenced me to six months I'd have done twelve!'

That was what people thought of Billy Liddell. I feel privileged to have seen him play and to have known him.

Chapter Fourteen

Epilogue

It was during the grim and poignant aftermath of the Hillsborough Disaster in 1989 that Phyllis Liddell observed the first signs of the illness that was to blight her husband Billy for the last dozen years of his life.

'We were at Anfield paying our respects to the victims of Hillsborough when I got the first indication that something was wrong,' Phyllis recalled. 'I realised that Billy didn't seem able to comprehend or accept what had happened which, of course, was totally out of character for him.

'In due course it was diagnosed that he was suffering from Parkinson's Disease. But it was very well controlled, as it can be to a certain extent, and for several more years Billy continued to sit on the Littlewoods "Spot The Ball" panel of which he was chairman, having succeeded Joe Mercer.

'Ian Callaghan and Brian Labone were also on the panel and Billy, despite his worsening illness, did the job well. I kept in touch with Littlewoods and they wanted him to carry on, even sending a chauffeur-driven car to collect him. Eventually, though, in December 1993, I had to call a halt. It was difficult for everybody.'

Billy and Phyllis continued to watch Liverpool matches from their seats in Anfield's Main Stand and in July 1996 the couple celebrated their fiftieth wedding anniversary, with *Brookside* star and comedian Vince Earl providing some impromptu entertainment for the Liddell family and friends.

But Billy's deteriorating condition meant his eventual move into a nursing home in Liverpool's Mossley Hill district, the victim of a disease which has afflicted many footballers, in particular those who played the game in the era of the heavy, water-absorbent, lace-up caseballs and at a time when far more physical challenges were allowed than in today's strictly regulated regime.

Media articles, notably by my journalist colleague Jim Holden in the *Daily Express* and former FA Chief Executive Graham Kelly in the *Independent*, urging greater action and investigation by the football authorities into neurological degenerative diseases such as Parkinson's and Alzheimer's, were given powerful emphasis by a coroner's landmark verdict.

Andrew Haigh, the South Staffordshire coroner, ruled in November 2002 that the premature death of former West Bromwich Albion and England striker Jeff Astle, at the age of 59, was due to 'industrial disease'. In Astle's case it was brain disease caused by constantly heading the old-style footballs which, when wet, became 20 per cent heavier. Astle, who had likened it to 'heading a bag of bricks', sadly swelled a list of former players to have been similarly afflicted.

The more famous of them include Sir Alf Ramsey, Danny Blanchflower, Stan Cullis, Stan Mortensen, Joe Mercer as well as Liddell and his long-term friend and former Anfield team-mate Bob Paisley, the most successful English club manager of them all, who died in 1996 after long suffering the effects of Alzheimer's.

Liddell's favourite player John Charles, the Wales giant idolised at Leeds and Juventus, is another Alzheimer's sufferer and countless other former professionals who are not household names are carrying the legacy of playing Britain's national game.

In 1998 former Celtic player Billy McPhail lost his legal battle to claim benefits for dementia which he said was caused by heading the old-style footballs. But the coroner's ruling has at last recognised the link and could signal overdue action by the game's authorities as well as legal action by claimants. As Graham Kelly declared: 'The coroner has given succour to those who feel it is no coincidence that so many former footballers have fallen to the disease. There must surely be sufficient resources available to the game to ensure that adequate measures are taken to alleviate the suffering.'

The Football Association in England, Europe's ruling body UEFA and world governing association FIFA have all said they are studying the verdict, which has been welcomed by brain disease expert Professor Andrew Lees, Professor of Neurology at London's National Hospital for Neurology and Neurosurgery.

'I thought it was a very brave verdict by the coroner,' said Professor Lees. 'I say that because, as yet, there is no absolutely incontrovertible evidence for the conclusion he came to. But while the medical studies continue his verdict sets down a marker.

'Circumstantial evidence exists that the pathological processes which underlie Parkinson's and Alzheimer's may be triggered by head injury and further research is required.

'The candidate gene which puts people at greater risk of developing Alzheimer's is, in its shortened name form, Apo E4. There is some very preliminary evidence to link this with a greater predisposition to the punch-drunk syndrome in professional boxers.

'We must also remember that in football there can be traumas from incidents other than heading a ball. Players can clash heads and be involved in collisions with opponents on the field. These can all have a cumulative effect.

'Moreover, in Billy Liddell's era, in addition to the fact that they played with a much heavier ball, the game was more physical because the laws and the prevailing disciplinary climate allowed more contact and challenges. This could trigger neurological problems, especially if the player concerned was predisposed to such a condition.

'The most extensive current medical research on football players is being carried out in Scandinavia but, certainly, there is a strong possibility of a link between football injuries and degenerative neurological diseases such as Alzheimer's and Parkinson's.'

Neurologists at the Walton Centre on Merseyside have been carrying out research on 500 former players to establish if there is a link between heading footballs and the onset of dementia.

Research published in Holland in 1998 made the alarming claim that almost half of professional footballers suffered some form of brain injury from repeatedly heading a ball.

The Professional Footballers Association, the players' union, are monitoring 24 young players who will be given tests and scans every five years.

Ray Kennedy, a League and FA Cup double-winning striker with Arsenal before being converted by Bob Paisley into a left midfielder feared throughout Europe in Liverpool's unprecedented trophy-seizing sweep in the 1970s and 1980s, has long been battling Parkinson's. His plight has prompted the Liverpool FC Former Players Association to make charitable donatations to the Merseyside office of the Parkinson's Disease Society at the Glaxo Neurological Centre in Norton Street, Liverpool.

The Alzheimer's Society also has an office at this venue. 'Anyone wishing to obtain information from either society should call the centre on 0151 298 2999,' said a spokesman. 'There is also a national freephone helpline for Parkinson's sufferers which is 0808 800 0303.'

'Parkinson's is a terrible disease,' affirmed Phyllis Liddell, who for so long carried the strain of Billy's brave battle. 'Eventually it takes over and with Billy the last four years were very rough.'

Billy died on 3 July 2001, aged 79, in the middle of a massively sad week for the Liverpool club and their supporters. A few days earlier had seen the passing of Joe Fagan, a member of Liverpool's back-room staff during Liddell's final playing years and, later, the first ever English club manager to win a treble. Club director and former youth development officer Tom Saunders died shortly after, the third Anfield stalwart to pass away in eight days.

Within minutes of Billy Liddell's death being announced on the 8 p.m. BBC Radio Merseyside news bulletin the station was swamped with tributes, many from people trying to choke back tears as they went on air.

One caller, Brian, said: 'I'm an Evertonian but when it comes to gentlemen I don't think Billy had any peers. And as a player he was awesome. He had the hardest shot I've ever seen. It would be a great game if the football fraternity was full of Billy Liddells.'

Another, Paul in Bootle, declared: 'There was an aura about Billy Liddell. Whenever the ball went to him there was a roar from the crowd as if a miracle was going to happen.

'Whenever we played away from home the fans had only one question: "Is Liddell playing?" They weren't interested in anyone else. No wonder they called it Liddellpool.'

Tony rang in from West Derby to say: 'Me and my mates used to call him Sir William Liddell. He should have got a knighthood. He was one wonderful man. I hooked off school when I was about eight just to watch him play one Wednesday afternoon.

'Dalglish was a craftier player but Billy was *the* man and I've got a crush barrier from the old Kop terracing in my back garden to remind me of the days I saw Billy in action in a red jersey.'

Another caller, Alf from Heswall, remembered: 'Before games at Anfield they used to walk round the ground with a big sheet for the crowd to throw coins in for charity, usually in aid of the St John ambulance. Every time, some of the coins would miss and land on the pitch.

'In one particular match – it would be in the late 1940s or early 50s – Billy Liddell spotted a penny on the pitch and tossed it back into the Kop. I caught it and still have it today. I wouldn't part with it. I cherish it as a memory of a fantastic man and fantastic footballer.'

Columnist Len Capeling observed pertinently in the *Liverpool Daily Post*: 'The tributes to Billy Liddell touched on his many kindnesses. His many good deeds. His courtesy, his charm. He was truly a man who walked with kings but never lost the common touch.'

Ivan Ponting, that accomplished compiler of football obituaries for the *Independent* newspaper, wrote: 'Anfield, the famous home of Liverpool FC, has been graced by a plethora of footballing heroes since the Second World War.

'Roger Hunt and Ian St John, Kevin Keegan and Kenny Dalglish, Ian Rush and John Barnes; it is difficult to imagine a more exalted collection. Yet not one of these luminaries, each

worshipped rabidly in his prime by the fanatics who stood on the
Kop, was more revered on Merseyside than Billy Liddell.

'From 1945 until the onset of the Bill Shankly-inspired soccer
revolution at Anfield in the early 1960s popular perception had it
that the durable, self-effacing yet explosively exciting winger-
cum-centre forward *was* Liverpool.'

The impact of his death reverberated around the world and
outside Liverpool, nowhere was it felt more deeply than in New
York. The Liverpool FC Supporters Club there ran a special
appreciation of Billy Liddell in their impressive magazine which
proclaimed:

It is simply not possible to overstate how important Billy
Liddell was for Liverpool FC. As a footballer he thrilled
Anfield for fifteen years but as a man he was a symbol of all
that was good, fine and right in the sport.

From the left wing he would run at speed at defenders and
then cut inside to goal – a Stevie Heighway and an Emile
Heskey rolled into one except far better. He was muscular
and skilful, had sprinter's speed, a rocket shot, was good in
the air and gave his all in every game.

We roared to the League title on his broad shoulders.
Sadly our club then went into the doldrums. Even a man as
great as Liddell couldn't make up for the bad players and
management which surrounded him. He was in the sad
position of being a star in a team which went progressively
downhill.

But no transfer requests from this chivalrous, loyal man.
The support of the fans remained, loyal to Billy Liddell. This
was the birth of the spirit of Liverpool FC that Bill Shankly
and Bob Paisley were to build into the greatest club the world
has ever seen . . . the spirit of Billy Liddell.

Billy's funeral service was held on 9 July 2001 at Court Hey
Methodist Church in Huyton, where he and Phyllis had worshipped for many years. It was conducted by the Rev. Malcolm

Carter and relayed from the packed church to an overspill congregation in a nearby hall.

Liverpool chairman David Moores, who idolised Liddell, and stars from the club's past – including Roger Hunt, Ian Callaghan, Alan A'Court, Ron Yeats and Gerry Byrne – as well as family, friends, and members of the public who just wanted to say farewell to their idol, heard the Rev. Carter say:

'This is not a gloomy service. It's a time of thanksgiving and celebration – and praise to God for Billy Liddell's life. There is plenty to celebrate.

'His quiet but committed involvement in vast areas of life, in addition to being a professional footballer, tell you a great deal about the man. Youngsters throughout the area were thrilled that their hero would come so freely into their club meetings.

'As for his exploits on the football pitch, these have been expounded by experts galore – and rightly so. He was a perfect role model for any young footballer, giving 110 per cent in every game, win or lose. His colleagues all speak glowingly of him. Nobody spoke ill of him.

'This is the hallmark of the man: loyalty, commitment and courage, strength and, not least, humility. Such a great player but quite unaware of it. Some well-known players today, like David Beckham, get a migraine before a home game because they don't know whether to travel to the ground in their Porsche, Mercedes or Jaguar!

'Billy went to work on a Saturday morning when the Reds were playing at home. He worked from 9 a.m. until 1 p.m., then travelled on a tram to the match, chatting with supporters about the forthcoming game.

'No wonder he endeared himself to Joe Public. He was one of them. If anybody wanted his autography they used to knock on his front door and Billy would always willingly oblige.

'But he would be in his place at Court Hey on Sunday morning to worship his God, whether he had scored a hat trick or Liverpool had lost. Such was his commitment – and that's why a minibus of our Court Hey folk have travelled back this morning, interrupting their holiday in the Lake District to be here.

'By no means least, Billy was a family man. As his son David told me: "To us he was a good father, not a famous footballer." High praise indeed. So this is a worthy moment to salute a truly great sportsman and family man, a humble Christian who preached the gospel by the quiet but effective example of his life, on and off the pitch.

'When I was a theological student forty years ago I wrote to Billy and asked him if he would come to our Manchester college and open our missionary garden party. My fellow students were amazed that he agreed to come so readily. He also brought a Scotland international jersey for me to auction.'

After the service, Rev. Carter told a personal story of how one of Liddell's most famous yet fruitless moments in football came to be part of his learning curve of life.

'When I entered theological college in 1957 I kept a newspaper cutting of Billy's almost brilliant FA Cup "goal" against Manchester City pinned to my study wall for the four years I was there,' he said.

'It browned with age. I kept it for years to remind me that just as the referee blew for full time seconds before Billy's shot hit the net, so there would be cruel disappointments ahead in my, or anyone's, job. It was an ideal disappointment to learn from and I never forgot it.'

Phyllis was so touched by the public response to Billy's passing that she publicly expressed her appreciation in the *Liverpool Echo*. 'I would like to say a very special "thank you" to all the Merseyside football fans who sent me letters and flowers after my husband's death,' she wrote.

'It was really moving and we appreciated it as a family. We always knew that Bill was loved and respected by supporters throughout the city but the cards and comments that poured in gave us a real sense of pride.

'We will never forget Bill. Clearly, many of the fans who saw my husband play and met him will retain wonderful memories of their own. This means a lot to us and I would like to say a very big "thank you" to everyone who took the trouble to write to me.'

This public adulation of Billy Liddell was powerfully evident when Radio Merseyside conducted a poll to select the 'Team of the Century' in which the BBC station asked listeners to pick their best players of the twentieth century drawn from the ranks of all Merseyside's major clubs.

The votes flooded in for Liddell, from supporters of varied allegiance, and he duly took his place on the left wing in this side, lining up in 4–4–2 formation: Ray Clemence; Alex Parker, Alan Hansen, Tommy (T G) Jones, Ray Wilson; Alan Ball, Peter Reid, Graeme Souness, Billy Liddell; Dixie Dean, Kenny Dalglish.

Since his death there have been campaigns in the media and calls from the public, supported by former stars such as Tommy Smith and Ian Callaghan, for Liverpool FC to erect a permanent Liddell memorial.

'I was the first to sign a petition calling on the club to salute Liddell,' said Smith. Callaghan, who holds the club's 856-match appearance record, agreed. 'I certainly endorse the calls for a memorial to Billy and I'm sure it will happen,' he said.

Liddell has been inducted into Liverpool FC's new 'Hall Of Fame' but the prospect of anything further has gone on ice because of the club's proposed move to a new stadium in nearby Stanley Park.

'We are, of course, more than aware of the contribution Billy made but we don't have an official position yet because we are in the process of finalising plans for the new stadium,' said Liverpool chief executive Rick Parry.

'One of my ideas was to create a "Walk of Fame", perhaps leading from the Kop to the new stadium. This would enable us to pay tribute not only to Billy but also to other Liverpool legends.'

It would be fitting and overdue, also, if his birthplace of Townhill near Dunfermline erected a permanent memorial to their most famous son, who twice represented Great Britain, starred for Scotland and was idolised by Liverpool's Kop. His brother George revealed: 'They've got photographs of Billy in the village school at Townhill but nothing else to remember him by. Obviously, it would be very welcome if there was.'

Liddell was much more than a football icon. He was, in the words of one of his Liverpool wing successors, Brian Hall, 'a complete person'. Hall, now the club's public relations manager, reflected: 'Every aspect of Billy's life seemed to be in its right place – and there aren't many people you can say that about.

'He really knew himself, he knew what he wanted and he tried desperately to fulfil it. But not in a madcap way. He had his family, his football, his other sport, his career outside the game and his faith. Complete. That's the word to describe Billy.'

Among Billy's cherished possessions was a miniature pair of leather football boots, specially made by a Liverpool supporter and sent to him on his retirement from the game.

There was also an anonymous poem, discovered by Phyllis.'I found it among Billy's papers. I don't know who wrote it but Billy had kept it and it clearly meant something to him. It also sums him up.' This was the poem:

> Be there ever a player so loyal
> In the soccer world today
> Like the big-hearted Scotsman
> Leading Liverpool Wembley Way
> Your name will live forever
> Let no man this deny
> In the sportsman's book of heroes
> Down Anfield plain och aye
> Dour, determined, faithful servant
> Every inch a gentleman
> Loved by all his fans
> Let's drink health to a MAN

The only known surviving Liverpool jersey worn by Liddell went on display at the Liverpool FC Museum in February 2002, after almost half a century hanging in a wardrobe. The famous No. 11 shirt was loaned to the museum by former Liverpool reserve Jimmy Rolfe, an outside right who asked to keep the jersey when he left Anfield to join Chester in 1953.

Jimmy explained: 'It was the custom then that after at least two years' wear the first-team players' shirts would be handed down to the reserves – then they were used as training tops until they wore out. That's why they're so rare.

'When I left Liverpool I asked the trainer Albert Shelley if I could keep Billy's shirt as a memento of my time at the club and he said it was alright. Even though I played alongside Billy only once, in a pre-season match, I learned a lot from him.

'He was a great man and a wonderful footballer. He was a character but he was a quiet and modest man. At the time he was probably more famous than Michael Owen is now and he carried the Liverpool team most weeks.'

Museum curator Stephen Done was pleasantly surprised at the good condition of the red cotton Halbro-manufactured shirt. 'It's a real coup getting Billy's shirt here because he was an astonishing footballer and a true gentleman,' he declared.

'There were no replica kits then and the culture of keeping things didn't exist in those days. It's rare for a League shirt to survive because usually they were worn until they were threadbare.'

It was the great American golfer Bobby Jones who observed: 'In golf, as in life, it's no use just playing by the rules. If you don't play by the etiquette it's not worth a damn.'

No player adhered to the etiquette of football more rigidly than Liddell, never booked and a shining symbol of the true spirit of competition. And perhaps no opponent quite captured the essence of the great Scot better than Danny Blanchflower, as erudite in his writing as he was gifted as a wing half for Aston Villa, Tottenham and Northern Ireland.

'I always think of Billy when I hear or recall that terrifying Anfield roar,' said Blanchflower. 'Billy seemed to inspire that roar and it seemed to inspire him. Come to think of it, his play was something akin to it . . . a wonderful, stirring, awesome force, liable to erupt at any moment and strike fear into opponents.'

The legend of William Beveridge Liddell, King of the Kop, icon of the people, will endure as long as Liverpool Football Club exists, as long as men and boys kick a football and their dreams of glory take wing.

Chapter Fifteen

The Statistics

Liddell's wartime League and Cup record for Liverpool:

Season	Appearances	Goals
1939–40:	16	9
1940–41:	37	12
1941–42:	35	22
1942–43:	15	5
1943–44:	6	4
1944–45:	15	13

Liddell's transitional season league record for Liverpool:

1945–46:	28	17

Liddell's Football League and FA Cup record for Liverpool:

	Division One		FA Cup		Total	
	Apps	Goals	Apps	Goals	Apps	Goals
1945–46:			2	1	2	1
1946–47:	34	7	6	1	40	8
1947–48:	37	10	2	1	39	11
1948–49:	38	8	4	1	42	9
1949–50:	41	17*	7	2	48	19
1950–51:	35	15*	1	0	36	15
1951–52:	40	19*	3	0	43	19

1952–53:	39	13*	1	0	40	13
1953–54:	36	7	1	0	37	7
Division Two						
1954–55:	40	30*	4	1	44	31
1955–56:	39	27*	5	5	44	32
1956–57:	41	21*	1	0	42	21
1957–58:	35	22*	5	1	40	23
1958–59:	19	14	0	0	19	14
1959–60:	17	5	0	0	17	5
1960–61:	1	0	0	0	1	0
Totals:	**492**	**215**	**42**	**13**	**534**	**228**

(*Denotes leading League scorer for club that season)

Liddell's appearances and goals in friendly and tour games:
(Liverpool score first in each case, Liddell goals in parenthesis)

16 December 1939: 'Grand Match' v Preston North End (h) 0–1 (first-team debut at age of 17 years 11 months)

30 December 1939: Preston North End (h) 3–1

25 March 1940: Bolton Wanderers (h) 0–1

5 May 1940: Oldham Athletic (a) 4–2 (1 goal)

6 June 1942: Army Red Rose XI (h) 2–3

21 August 1943: Everton (Lord Mayor's War Fund) (h) 5–2 (1 goal)

28 July 1945: RAF XI (in Germany) 7–0 (2 goals)

29 July 1945: 21st Army XI (in Germany) 3–3

14 February 1948: Newcastle United (a) 3–0 (1 goal)

16 May to 20 June 1948: Canada and North America tour: A I Met All Stars (New York) 5–1; Baltimore All Stars 9–2; Philadelphia 5–2; NE All Stars (Fall River) 6–0; American S L All Stars (New York) 9–2; St Louis All Stars 4–2; Montreal 4–2; American S L All Stars (Ebbets Field, Brooklyn) 5–2; Ulster United (Toronto) 5–1; Djurgarden of Sweden (Ebbets Field, Brooklyn) 5–2; Kearney Scots Celtics (Kearney, New Jersey) 8–0. (Liddell tour total: 11 games, 13 goals)

26 February 1949: Newcastle United (a) 1–1

5 December 1949: AIK Stockholm (h) 4–2 (1 goal, a penalty)

28 May 1950: Anderlecht (a) 1–1 (1 goal)

30 April 1951: Brighton (a) 1–1 (1 goal)

9 May 1951: Saarbrucken (h) (Festival of Britain match) 1–1

May 1951: Sweden tour: AIK Stockholm 7–0; Malmö 4–1; Norrköping 1–0; Gothenburg Select 5–3; Malmö 1–2. (Liddell tour total: 5 games, 5 goals).

4 August 1951: Edinburgh Select (Easter Road) 2–1 (2 goals)

May 1952: West Germany, Austria and Spain tour: Essen Select 2–2; Austria Select 0–2; Ausberg 4–1; Madrid Select 1–3. (Liddell tour total: 4 games, 2 goals)

31 January 1953: Leeds United (a) 0–1

14 May to 14 June 1953: Canada and North America tour: Northern Ireland (New York) 4–0; American Soccer League (Triborough Stadium, Randalls Island, New York) 4–1; New England All Stars (Fall River, Massachusets) 4–0; Nuremburg (Triborough Stadium, Randalls Island, New York) 4–3; Montreal All Stars 10–0; Toledo All Stars 10–3; Chicago All Stars 4–2; St Louis 5–1; Northern Ireland (Varsity Stadium, Toronto) 3–1; Young Boys Berne (Yankee Stadium, New York) 1–1. (Liddell tour total: 13 goals)

20 February 1954: St Mirren (h) 4–2 (2 goals)

30 November 1954: Watford (a) 2–3 (1 goal)

19 September 1955: Eddie Spicer Benefit: Liverton v Lancashire XI (h) 2–2

May 1956: France tour: Angers 0–0, Contors 8–1; Rouen 6–2; St Etienne 1–1; Toulouse 1–3. (Liddell tour total: 4 goals)

10 September 1956: Hibernian (a) 2–1 (1 goal)

26 January 1957: Bolton Wanderers (a) 3–5

3 May 1957: Brighton (a) 2–0 (1 goal)

30 October 1957: Everton (h) (inaugural floodlight game) 3–2 (2 goals)

9 November 1957: Hibernian (h) 3–3 (1 goal)

May 1958: Spain tour: Real Sociedad 1–0; Osasuna 3–1; Elche 0–1; San Hospitalet 1–2; Perpignan 4–0. (Liddell tour total: 3 goals)

2 August 1958: Edinburgh Select (Tynecastle Park) 2–2 (2 goals)

21 September 1960: International XI (Billy Liddell Testimonial) 4–2 (Liddell: 1 goal for International XI)

Liddell also appeared as a wartime guest player for Chelsea (five appearances, two goals) and Cambridge Town in 1942–43; played one match for Hearts in a 3–2 win over the RAF in August 1943; played four games for Dunfermline Athletic in 1944 and made two appearances and scored two goals for Irish League club Linfield, both games against Ards, in February 1945.

For Liverpool, he made ten Lancashire Senior Cup appearances, scoring seven goals, and was twice a competition winner. He made nine Liverpool Senior Cup appearances, scoring one goal, and was twice a competition winner.

In 1957 he guested for Ellesmere Port Town against a Football League Select side in a testimonial match for the club's long-serving left back Ken Roberts, which drew an attendance of 3,600. Lidell scored the home side's only goal in a 7–1 defeat by the League team, which included Joe Mercer and David Hickson.

Liddell's Liverpool hat tricks:

Wartime football:

1939–40: v Manchester City (a) (Football League Wartime Western Division) 6 January 1940

1941–42: v Chester (h) (Football League Northern Section) 15 November 1941

v Rochdale (h) (League War Cup) 28 March 1942

Football League:

1951–52: v Tottenham Hotspur (a) (First Division) 1 December 1951

1954–55: v Fulham (h) (Second Division), including two penalties, 18 September 1954

v Ipswich Town (h) (Second Division), Liddell scored 4 goals, including one penalty, 25 December 1954

1955–56: v Nottingham Forest (h) (Second Division) 17 December 1955

1957–58: v Blackburn Rovers (a) (Second Division) 22 February 1958

Liddell's penalty record for Liverpool:

Liddell took 44 penalties in first-class football for Liverpool and
scored from 36. Four of his spot kicks were saved, two hit a
post and two went wide, one of them in the opening game of the
1949–50 season at home to Sunderland and the other in the
opening game of the 1952–53 season away at Preston. He also
scored for the club from four penalties in wartime football. His
scoring penalties are as follows:

Wartime football:

1939–40: v Manchester City (a) (Football League Wartime
           Western Division) 25 May 1940

1940–41: v New Brighton (h) (Football League Wartime North
           Regional League) 14 December 1940

         v Southport (h) (League Cup North) 15 February
           1941

1941–42: v Blackpool (a) (Football League Northern Section) 25
           May 1942

First-class football

1948–49: v Middlesbrough (h) (First Division) 23 October
           1948

         v Sunderland (a) (First Division) 1 January 1949

1949–50: v Manchester City (h) (First Division) 5 November
           1949

         v Charlton Athletic (a) (First Division) 12 November
           1949

         v Charlton Athletic (h) (First Division) 1 April 1950

1950–51: v Newcastle United (h) (First Division) 4 November
           1950

         v Wolverhampton Wanderers (h) (First Division) 16
           December 1950

         v Sheffield Wednesday (h) (First Division) 17 March
           1951

1951–52: v West Bromwich Albion (h) (First Division) 27
           October 1951

         v Tottenham Hotspur (a) (First Division) 1 December
           1951

1952–53: v Tottenham Hotspur (h) (First Division) 10 September
1952

v Wolverhampton Wanderers (h) (First Division) 1
November 1952

v Derby County (a) (First Division) 22 November
1952

v Burnley (h) (First Division) 26 December 1952

1953–54: v Sheffield United (a) (First Division) 13 March 1954

v Sunderland (h) (First Division) 3 April 1954

1954–55: v Fulham (h) (Second Division), 2 penalties scored, 18
September 1954

v Luton Town (a) (Second Division) 13 November
1954

v Nottingham Forest (h) (Second Division) 20
November 1954

v Middlesbrough (h) (Second Division) 4 December
1954

v Ipswich Town (h) (Second Division) 25 December
1954

v Blackburn Rovers (h) (Second Division) 22 January
1955

v Lincoln City (h) (Second Division) 19 March 1955

v Birmingham City (h) (Second Division) 30 April
1955

1955–56: v Leeds United (a) (Second Division) 19 November
1955

v Stoke City (h) (Second Division) 26 December 1955

v Leicester City (h) (Second Division) 21 January 1956

1956–57: v Huddersfield Town (h) (Second Division) 18 August
1956

v Bury (h) (Second Division) 22 December 1956

v Bristol Rovers (h) (Second Division) 19 April 1957

v West Ham United (h) (Second Division) 27 April
1957

1957–58: v Grimsby Town (h) (Second Division) 26 December
1957

v Stoke City (h) (Second Division) 7 April 1958

1958–59: v Grimsby Town (h) (Second Division) 23 August
1958
v Charlton Athletic (h) (Second Division) 13
September 1958

Liddell took two penalties for Scotland, against France in Paris
(27 May 1950) and against Hungary in Budapest (29 May 1955),
and missed both.

'Factoids' on Liddell's Liverpool career:

- Liddell's first appearance in a Liverpool first team was in a
  wartime friendly against Preston North End at Anfield, 16
  December 1939. Lost 0–1. Attendance: 3,000.
- Liddell scored his first goal for Liverpool's first team two
  minutes into his competitive debut, wearing No. 11, against
  Crewe Alexandra at Anfield in a Wartime Western Division
  game, 1 January 1940. Won 7–3. Attendance: 2,000.
- Liddell scored on his Liverpool debut in official, top-class
  football – an FA Cup third-round, first-leg match at Chester, 5
  5 January 1946. Won 2–0. Attendance: 12,000.
- Liddell's last Liverpool goal in a League or FA Cup game came
  in the Second Division match against Stoke City at Anfield, 5
  March 1960. Won 5–1. Attendance: 35,101.
- Liddell's last senior appearance for Liverpool was in the No. 9
  shirt in the Football League Second Division match against
  Southampton at Anfield, 31 August 1960. Lost 0–1.
  Attendance: 37,604. He was aged 38 years 234 days, the second
  oldest postwar player to appear for Liverpool. (The oldest was
  his fellow Scot, Kenny Dalglish at 39 years 58 days.)
- Liddell's last Liverpool appearance was in the reserve team in
  the Central League match against Blackburn Rovers at Anfield,
  29 April 1961, in which he also scored his last goal for the club.
  Won 5–0. Attendance: 2,173.
- Liddell's career spanned four Liverpool managers: George
  Kay, Don Welsh, Phil Taylor and Bill Shankly.
- Liddell is one of only ten players in Liverpool history to appear

for the club in three different decades, playing in the 1940s, 1950s and 1960s. The others are: Jack Parkinson (1890s–1910s); Elisha Scott (1910s–1930s); Tommy Lucas (1910s–1930s); Jack Balmer (1930s–1950s); Willie Fagan (1930s–1950s); Ray Clemence (1960s–1980s); Kenny Dalglish (1970s–1990s); Alan Hansen (1970s–1990s); Steve Staunton (1980s–2000s).

- Liddell is one of only three Liverpool players to score for the club in three different decades. The others are Jack Balmer and Willie Fagan.
- Liddell's favourite League opponents on the basis of the number of goals he scored against them are, with goal totals in parentheses:

    Fulham; Middlesbrough (13); Blackburn (12); Sunderland (10); Stoke City (9); Sheffield United (8); Huddersfield Town (7); Chelsea; Charlton Athletic; Derby County; Grimsby Town; Nottingham Forest; Tottenham Hotspur (6); Birmingham City; Barnsley; Bury; Bristol City; Ipswich Town; Leicester City; Lincoln City; Rotherham United; West Ham United (5); Arsenal; Preston North End; Sheffield Wednesday; Portsmouth (4); Aston Villa; Burnley; Bolton Wanderers; Hull City; Leeds United; Manchester City; Notts County; Newcastle United; Port Vale; West Bromwich Albion (3); Bristol Rovers; Doncaster Rovers; Manchester United; Swansea Town; Wolverhampton Wanderers (2); Brighton and Hove Albion; Cardiff City; Everton; Luton Town; Leyton Orient; Scunthorpe United (1). Grand total: 215 League goals against 47 opponents.

- Liddell's total of 492 League appearances for Liverpool, between September 1946 and August 1960, has been bettered by only one player in the club's history. Ian Callaghan made 640 League appearances between April 1960 and February 1978.
- Despite playing most of his games as a winger, Liddell is the fourth highest scorer in Liverpool history, both in League matches alone and overall. His total of 228 goals (215 League, 13 FA Cup) is bettered only by recognised strikers Ian Rush, Roger Hunt and Gordon Hodgson.

- In an era before substitutes were permitted, injury situations in matches meant that Liddell played in every department of the Liverpool team except in goal. He was selected in five different numbered jerseys ranging across the forward line: 7, 8, 9, 10, 11.
- Liddell won a League championship medal in 1946–47, his first season of League football, a campaign in which he made 34 appearances, scoring seven goals. He won an FA Cup runners-up medal in the 1950 Final against Arsenal.
- Liddell made most League appearances for Liverpool both in the 1940s (135 games) and 1950s (348 games). He was also the club's top League scorer in the 1950s with 178 goals.
- Liddell was a Liverpool ever-present in 40 FA Cup games between January 1947 and March 1958, scoring twelve goals in that sequence.
- Liddell played twice for Great Britain and won 28 full Scotland caps, scoring six goals, between 1946 and 1955. He also made eight appearances, scoring five goals, in wartime, Victory and fundraising internationals between 1942 and 1946.

Liddell's appearances in official internationals:

19 OCTOBER 1946
Racecourse Ground, Wrexham (30,000)
Wales 3 (Bryn Jones, Ford, Stephen o.g.)
Scotland 1 (Waddell)
Wales: Sidlow (Liverpool); Lambert (Liverpool), Hughes (Birmingham City); Witcomb (West Bromwich Albion), TG Jones (Everton), Burgess (Tottenham Hotspur); E Jones (Swansea Town), Powell (Leeds United), Ford (Swansea Town), B Jones (Arsenal), Edwards (Birmingham City).
Scotland: Miller (Celtic); Stephen (Bradford), D Shaw (Hibernian); Brown (Partick Thistle), Brennan (Newcastle United), Husband (Partick Thistle); Waddell (Rangers), Dougall (Birmingham City), Thornton (Rangers), Blair (Blackpool), Liddell (Liverpool).
Referee: W H Evans (Liverpool, England)

27 NOVEMBER 1946

Hampden Park, Glasgow (98,776)

Scotland 0

Northern Ireland 0

Scotland: Brown (Rangers); Young (Rangers), D Shaw (Hibernian); Campbell (Morton), Brennan (Newcastle United), Long (Clyde); Smith (Hibernian), Hamilton (Aberdeen), Thornton (Rangers), Duncanson (Rangers), Liddell (Liverpool).

Northern Ireland: Hinton (Fulham); Gorman (Brentford), Feeney (Linfield); Martin (Glentoran), Vernon (Belfast Celtic), Farrell (Everton); Cochrane (Leeds United), Carey (Manchester United), Walsh (West Bromwich Albion), Stevenson (Everton), Eglington (Everton).

Referee: G Reader (Southampton, England)

(The Northern Ireland team included some Republic of Ireland players)

4 OCTOBER 1947

Windsor Park, Belfast (52,000)

Northern Ireland 2 (Smyth 2)

Scotland 0

Northern Ireland: Hinton (Fulham); Martin (Leeds United), Aherne (Belfast Celtic); W Walsh (Manchester City), Vernon (West Bromwich Albion), Farrell (Everton); Cochrane (Leeds United), Smyth (Wolverhampton Wanderers), D Walsh (West Bromwich Albion), Stevenson (Everton), Eglington (Everton).

Scotland: Miller (Celtic): Young (Rangers), J Shaw (Rangers); Macaulay (Arsenal), Woodburn (Rangers), Forbes (Sheffield United); Delaney (Manchester United), Watson (Motherwell), Thornton (Rangers), Steel (Derby County), Liddell (Liverpool).

Referee: T Smith (Atherstone, England)

(The Northern Ireland team included some Republic of Ireland players)

12 NOVEMBER 1947

Hampden Park, Glasgow (88,000)

Scotland 1 (McLaren)

Wales 2 (Ford, Lowrie)

Scotland: Miller (Celtic); Govan (Hibernian), Stephen (Bradford); Macaulay (Arsenal), Woodburn (Rangers), Forbes (Sheffield United); Smith (Hibernian), McLaren (Preston North End), Delaney (Manchester United), Steel (Derby County), Liddell (Liverpool).

Wales: Sidlow (Liverpool); Sherwood (Cardiff City), Barnes (Arsenal); L Powell (Queens Park Rangers), T G Jones (Everton), Burgess (Tottenham Hotspur); S Thomas (Fulham), A Powell (Leeds United), Ford (Aston Villa), Lowrie (Coventry City), Edwards (Birmingham City).

Referee: A E Lewis (Halifax, England)

10 APRIL 1948

Hampden Park, Glasgow (135, 376)

Scotland 0

England 2 (Finney, Mortensen)

Scotland: Black (Southampton); Govan (Hibernian), D. Shaw (Hibernian); Campbell (Morton), Young (Rangers), Macaulay (Arsenal); Delaney (Manchester United), Combe (Hibernian), Thornton (Rangers), Steel (Derby County), Liddell (Liverpool).

England: Swift (Manchester City); Scott (Arsenal), Hardwick (Middlesbrough); Wright (Wolverhampton Wanderers), Franklin (Stoke City), Cockburn (Manchester United); Matthews (Blackpool), Mortensen (Blackpool), Lawton (Notts County), Pearson (Manchester United), Finney (Preston North End).

Referee: D Maxwell (Belfast, Northern Ireland)

9 NOVEMBER 1949

Hampden Park, Glasgow (73,782)

Scotland 2 (McPhail, Linwood)

Wales 0

Scotland: Cowan (Morton); Young (Rangers), Cox (Rangers); Evans (Celtic), Woodburn (Rangers), Aitken (East Fife); Liddell (Liverpool), McPhail (Celtic), Linwood (Clyde), Steel (Derby County), Reilly (Hibernian).

Wales: K. Jones (Aston Villa); Barnes (Arsenal), Sherwood (Cardiff City); I Powell (Aston Villa), TG Jones (Everton),

Burgess (Tottenham Hotspur); M Griffiths (Leicester City), Paul (Swansea Town), Ford (Aston Villa), Clarke (Manchester City), Edwards (Cardiff City).
Referee: S E Law (West Bromwich, England)

15 APRIL 1950
Hampden Park, Glasgow (133,300)
Scotland 0
England 1 (Bentley)
Scotland: Cowan (Morton); Young (Rangers), Cox (Rangers); McColl (Rangers), Woodburn (Rangers), Forbes (Arsenal); Waddell (Rangers), Moir (Bolton Wanderers), Bauld (Hearts), Steel (Derby County), Liddell (Liverpool).
England: Williams (Wolverhampton Wanderers); Ramsey (Tottenham Hotspur), Aston (Manchester United); Wright (Wolverhampton Wanderers), Franklin (Stoke City), Dickinson (Portsmouth); Finney (Preston North End), Mannion (Middlesbrough), Mortensen (Blackpool), Bentley (Chelsea), Langton (Bolton Wanderers).
Referee: R J Leafe (Nottingham, England)

21 MAY 1950
Nacional Stadium, Lisbon (68,000)
Portugal 2 (Travacos, Albano)
Scotland 2 (Brown, Bauld)
Portugal: Ernesto; Barrosa, Angelo Carvalho; Canario, Felix, Serafim; Pacheco Nobre, Vasques, Ben David, Travacos, Albano.
Scotland: Cowan (Morton); Young (Rangers), Cox (Rangers); Evans (Celtic), Woodburn (Rangers), Forbes (Arsenal); Campbell (Falkirk), Brown (East Fife), Bauld (Hearts), Steel (Derby County), Liddell (Liverpool).
Referee: Anzano (Spain)

27 MAY 1950
Colombes Stadium, Paris (35,568)
France 0
Scotland 1 (Brown)

France: Ibrir; Huguet, Lamy; Marche, Gregoire, Cuissard; Strappe, Grumellon, Baillot, Baratte, Dard.

Scotland: Cowan (Morton); Young (Rangers), Cox (Rangers); McColl (Rangers), Woodburn (Rangers), Forbes (Arsenal); Campbell (Falkirk), Brown (East Fife), Reilly (Hibernian), Steel (Derby County), Liddell (Liverpool).

Referee: Argue (Spain)

21 OCTOBER 1950

Ninian Park, Cardiff (60,000)

Wales 1 (A Powell)

Scotland 3 (Reilly 2, Liddell)

Wales: Parry (Swansea Town); Barnes (Arsenal), Sherwood (Cardiff City); I Powell (Aston Villa), Paul (Manchester City), Burgess (Tottenham Hotspur); Williams (Leeds United), Allen (Coventry City), Ford (Aston Villa), A Powell (Birmingham City), Clarke (Manchester City).

Scotland: Cowan (Morton); Young (Rangers), McNaught (Raith Rovers); McColl (Rangers), Woodburn (Rangers), Forbes (Arsenal); Collins (Celtic), McPhail (Celtic), Reilly (Hibernian), Steel (Dundee), Liddell (Liverpool).

Referee: A E Ellis (Halifax, England)

1 NOVEMBER 1950

Hampden Park, Glasgow (75,000)

Scotland 6 (Steel 4, McPhail 2)

Northern Ireland 1 (McGarry)

Scotland: Cowan (Morton); Young (Rangers), McNaught (Raith Rovers); McColl (Rangers), Woodburn (Rangers), Forbes (Arsenal); Collins (Celtic), Mason (Third Lanark), McPhail (Celtic), Steel (Dundee), Liddell (Liverpool).

Northern Ireland: Kelly (Southampton); Galloghy (Huddersfield Town), McMichael (Newcastle United); Blanchflower (Barnsley), Vernon (West Bromwich Albion), Cush (Glenavon); Campbell (Fulham), McGarry (Cliftonville), McMorran (Barnsley), Doherty (Doncaster Rovers), McKenna (Huddersfield Town).

Referee: B M Griffiths (Newport, Wales)

13 DECEMBER 1950

Hampden Park, Glasgow (68,000)

Scotland 0

Austria 1 (Melchior)

Scotland: Cowan (Morton); Young (Rangers), McNaught (Raith Rovers); Evans (Celtic), Woodburn (Rangers), Forbes (Arsenal); Collins (Celtic), Turnbull (Hibernian), McPhail (Celtic), Steel (Dundee), Liddell (Liverpool).

Austria: Zemann; Rickl, Happel; Hanappi, Ocwirk, Gernhardt; Melchior, Decker, Wagner, Stojaspal, Aurednik.

Referee: W Ling (Stapleford, England)

14 APRIL 1951

Wembley Stadium (98,000)

England 2 (Hassall, Finney)

Scotland 3 (Johnstone, Reilly, Liddell)

England: Williams (Wolverhampton Wanderers); Ramsey (Tottenham Hotspur), Eckersley (Blackburn Rovers); Johnston (Blackpool), Froggatt (Portsmouth), Wright (Wolverhampton Wanderers); Matthews (Blackpool), Mannion* (Middlesbrough), Mortensen (Blackpool), Hassall (Huddersfield Town), Finney (Preston North End).

*(Mannion, injured in 11th minute, took no further part in game.)

Scotland: Cowan (Morton); Young (Rangers), Cox (Rangers); Evans (Celtic), Woodburn (Rangers), Redpath (Motherwell); Waddell (Rangers), Johnstone (Hibernian), Reilly (Hibernian), Steel (Dundee), Liddell (Liverpool).

Referee: G Mitchell (Scotland)

6 OCTOBER 1951

Windsor Park, Belfast (56,946)

Northern Ireland 0

Scotland 3 (Johnstone 2, Orr)

Northern Ireland: Uprichard (Swindon Town); Graham (Doncaster Rovers), McMichael (Newcastle United); Dickson (Chelsea), Vernon (West Bromwich Albion), Ferris (Birmingham City); Bingham (Sunderland), McIlroy (Burnley),

McMorran (Barnsley), Peacock (Celtic), Tully (Celtic).

Scotland: Cowan (Morton); Young (Rangers), Cox (Rangers); Evans (Celtic), Woodburn (Rangers), Redpath (Motherwell); Waddell (Rangers), Johnstone (Hibernian), Reilly (Hibernian), Orr (Morton), Liddell (Liverpool).

Referee: W H Evans (Liverpool, England)

14 NOVEMBER 1951

Hampden Park, Glasgow (71,272)

Scotland 0

Wales 1 (Allchurch)

Scotland: Cowan (Morton); Young (Rangers), Cox (Rangers); Docherty (Preston North End), Woodburn (Rangers), Forbes (Arsenal); Waddell (Rangers), Orr (Morton), Reilly (Hibernian), Steel (Dundee), Liddell (Liverpool).

Wales: Shortt (Plymouth Argyle); Barnes (Arsenal), Sherwood (Cardiff City); Paul (Manchester City), Daniel (Arsenal), Burgess (Tottenham Hotspur); Foulkes (Newcastle United), Morris (Burnley), Ford (Sunderland), I Allchurch (Swansea Town), Clarke (Manchester City).

Referee: P Morris (Belfast, Northern Ireland)

5 APRIL 1952

Hampden Park, Glasgow (134, 504)

Scotland 1 (Reilly)

England 2 (Pearson 2)

Scotland: Brown (Rangers); Young (Rangers), McNaught (Raith Rovers); Scoular (Portsmouth), Woodburn (Rangers), Redpath (Motherwell); Smith (Hibernian), Johnstone (Hibernian), Reilly (Hibernian), McMillan (Airdrieonians), Liddell (Liverpool).

England: Merrick (Birmingham City); Ramsey (Tottenham Hotspur), Garrett (Blackpool); Wright (Wolverhampton Wanderers), Froggatt (Portsmouth), Dickinson (Portsmouth); Finney (Preston North End), Broadis (Manchester City), Lofthouse (Bolton Wanderers), Pearson (Manchester United), Rowley (Manchester United).

Referee: P Morris (Belfast, Northern Ireland)

30 APRIL 1952

Hampden Park, Glasgow (107,765)

Scotland 6 (Reilly 3, McMillan 2, O'Connell o.g.)

United States of America 0

Scotland: Cowan (Morton); Young (Rangers), Cox (Rangers);
   Scoular (Portsmouth), Woodburn (Rangers), Kelly (Black-
   pool); Smith (Hibernian), McMillan (Airdrieonians), Reilly
   (Hibernian), Brown (Blackpool), Liddell (Liverpool).

USA: Borghi; O'Connell, Keough; Sheppell, Colombo, Bahr;
   Monsen, E.Souza, Roberts, J Souza, McLaughlin.

Referee: D Gerrard (Aberdeen, Scotland)

25 MAY 1952

Copenhagen (39,000)

Denmark 1 (Rasmussen)

Scotland 2 (Thornton, Reilly)

Denmark: K. Jorgensen; P Petersen, S. Nielssen; E Terkelsen, C
   Brogger, S Blicher; C Holm, P Rasmussen, J Tortensen, K
   Lundberg, H Seebach.

Scotland: Cowan (Morton); Young (Rangers), Cox (Rangers);
   Scoular (Portsmouth), Paton (Motherwell), Forbes (Arsenal);
   Reilly (Hibernian), McMillan (Airdrieonians), Thornton
   (Rangers), Brown (Blackpool), Liddell (Liverpool).

Referee: Ahlner (Sweden)

30 MAY 1952

Stockholm (32,000)

Sweden 3 (Sandberg, Losgrem, Bengtsson)

Scotland 1 (Liddell)

Sweden: Svensson; Samuelsson, Nilsson; Hauson, Gustafsson,
   Lindh; Bengtsson, Losgrem, Eriksson, Brodd, Sandberg.

Scotland: Cowan (Morton); Young (Rangers), Cox (Rangers);
   Scoular (Portsmouth), Paton (Motherwell), Forbes (Arsenal);
   Reilly (Hibernian), Humphries (Motherwell), Thornton
   (Rangers), Brown (Blackpool), Liddell (Liverpool).

Referee: Van Der Meer (Netherlands)

18 OCTOBER 1952
Ninian Park, Cardiff (60,000)
Wales 1 (Ford)
Scotland 2 (Brown, Liddell)
Wales: Shortt (Plymouth Argyle); Lever (Leicester City), Sherwood (Cardiff City); Paul (Manchester City), Daniel (Arsenal), Burgess (Tottenham Hotspur); Foulkes (Newcastle United), Davies (Newcastle United), Ford (Sunderland), I Allchurch (Swansea Town), Clarke (Manchester City).
Scotland: Farm (Blackpool); Young (Rangers), Cox (Rangers); Scoular (Portsmouth), Brennan (Newcastle United), Aitken (Sunderland); Wright (Sunderland), Brown (Blackpool), Reilly (Hibernian), Steel (Dundee), Liddell (Liverpool).
Referee: A Bond (London, England)

5 NOVEMBER 1952
Hampden Park, Glasgow (65,057)
Scotland 1 (Reilly)
Northern Ireland 1 (D'Arcy)
Scotland: Farm (Blackpool); Young (Rangers), Cox (Rangers); Scoular (Portsmouth), Brennan (Newcastle United), Aitken (Sunderland); Wright (Sunderland), Logie (Arsenal), Reilly (Hibernian), Steel (Dundee), Liddell (Liverpool).
Northern Ireland: Uprichard (Swindon Town); Graham (Doncaster Rovers), McMichael (Newcastle United); Blanchflower (Aston Villa), Dickson (Chelsea), McCourt (Manchester City); Bingham (Sunderland), D'Arcy (Brentford), McMorran (Barnsley), McIlroy (Burnley), Tully (Celtic).
Referee: R E Smith (Newport, Wales)

18 APRIL 1953
Wembley Stadium (97,000)
England 2 (Broadis 2)
Scotland 2 (Reilly 2)
England: Merrick (Birmingham City); Ramsey (Tottenham Hotspur), Smith (Arsenal); Wright (Wolverhampton

Wanderers), Barrass (Bolton Wanderers), Dickinson (Portsmouth); Finney (Preston North End), Broadis (Manchester City), Lofthouse (Bolton Wanderers), R Froggatt (Sheffield Wednesday), J. Froggatt (Portsmouth).

Scotland: Farm (Blackpool); Young (Rangers), Cox (Rangers); Docherty (Preston North End), Brennan (Newcastle United), Cowie (Dundee); Wright (Sunderland), Johnstone (Hibernian), Reilly (Hibernian), Steel (Dundee), Liddell (Liverpool).

Referee: T J Mitchell (Northern Ireland)

4 NOVEMBER 1953

Hampden Park, Glasgow (71,378)

Scotland 3 (Brown, Johnstone, Reilly)

Wales 3 (Charles 2, I Allchurch)

Scotland: Farm (Blackpool); Young (Rangers), Cox (Rangers); Evans (Celtic), Telfer (St Mirren), Cowie (Dundee); McKenzie (Partick Thistle), Johnstone (Hibernian), Reilly (Hibernian), Brown (Blackpool), Liddell (Liverpool).

Wales: Howells (Cardiff City); Barnes (Arsenal), Sherwood (Cardiff City); Paul (Manchester City), Daniel (Sunderland), Burgess (Tottenham Hotspur); Foulkes (Newcastle United), Davies (Newcastle United), Charles (Leeds United), I Allchurch (Swansea Town), Clarke (Manchester City).

Referee: TJ Mitchell (Northern Ireland)

4 MAY 1955

Hampden Park, Glasgow (20,858)

Scotland 3 (Reilly, Gemmell, Liddell)

Portugal 0

Scotland: Younger (Hibernian); Parker (Falkirk), Haddock (Clyde); Evans (Celtic), Young (Rangers), Cumming (Hearts); Smith (Hibernian), Robertson (Clyde), Reilly (Hibernian), Gemmell (St Mirren), Liddell (Liverpool).

Portugal: Gomez; Caldeira, Carvalho; Caidao, Passos, Gracia; Aguas, Matateu, Coluna, Travassos, Marteno.

Referee: D J Gardeazabal (Spain)

15 MAY 1955

JNA Stadium, Belgrade (20,000)

Yugoslavia 2 (Veselinovic, Vukas)

Scotland 2 (Reilly, Smith)

Yugoslavia: Beara; Delin, Zakovic; Cajkowski, Svraka, Boskov;
Veselinovic, Milutinovic, Vukas, Bobek, Zabak.

Scotland: Younger (Hibernian); Parker (Falkirk), Haddock
(Clyde); Evans (Celtic), Young (Rangers), Cumming (Hearts);
Smith (Hibernian), Collins (Celtic), Reilly (Hibernian),
Gemmell (St Mirren), Liddell (Liverpool).

Referee: Orlandini (Italy)

19 MAY 1955

Praterstadion, Vienna (54,000)

Austria 1 (Docherty o.g.)

Scotland 4 (Robertson, Smith, Liddell, Reilly)

Austria: Schmied; Halla, Barschandt; Hanappi, Roeckl, Ocwirk;
Hofbauer, Wagner, Brousek, Probst, Schleger.

Scotland: Younger (Hibernian); Parker (Falkirk), Kerr (Patrick
Thistle); Docherty (Preston North End), Evans (Celtic), Cowie
(Dundee); Smith (Hibernian), Collins (Celtic), Reilly
(Hibernian), Robertson (Clyde), Liddell (Liverpool).

Referee: G Bernardi (Italy)

29 MAY 1955

Nep Stadium, Budapest (102,000)

Hungary 3 (Hidegkuti, Kocsis, Fenyvesi)

Scotland 1 (Smith)

Hungary: Danka; Buzinsky, Varhidi; Lantos, Bozsik, Szojka;
Sandor, Hidegkuti, Kocsis, Puskas, Fenyvesi. (Danka and
Sandor were replaced by Farago and Palotas in the second
half.)

Scotland: Younger (Hibernian); Kerr (Partick Thistle), Haddock
(Clyde); Docherty (Preston North End), Evans (Celtic), Cowie
(Dundee); Smith (Hibernian), Collins (Celtic), Reilly
(Hibernian), Robertson (Clyde), Liddell (Liverpool).

Referee: Seilpelt (Austria)

8 OCTOBER 1955
Windsor Park, Belfast (50,000)
Northern Ireland 2 (J Blanchflower, Bingham)
Scotland 1 (Reilly)

Northern Ireland: Uprichard (Portsmouth); Graham (Doncaster Rovers), Cunningham (Leicester City); D Blanchflower (Tottenham Hotspur), McCavana (Coleraine), Peacock (Celtic); Bingham (Sunderland), J Blanchflower (Manchester United), Coyle (Coleraine), McIlroy (Burnley), McParland (Aston Villa).

Scotland: Younger (Hibernian); Parker (Falkirk), McDonald (Sunderland); Evans (Celtic), Young (Rangers), Glen (Aberdeen); Smith (Hibernian), Collins (Celtic), Reilly (Hibernian), Johnstone (Manchester City), Liddell (Liverpool).

Referee: J Kelly (Chorley, England)

Liddell's appearances for Great Britain:

10 MAY 1947
Hampden Park, Glasgow (135,000)
Great Britain 6 (Mannion 2 (1 pen), Lawton 2, Steel, Parola o.g.)
Rest of Europe 1 (Nordahl)

Great Britain: Frank Swift (England and Manchester City); George Hardwick (England and Middlesbrough, captain), Bill Hughes (Wales and Birmingham City); Archie Macaulay (Scotland and Brentford), Jackie Vernon (Northern Ireland and West Bromwich Albion), Ron Burgess (Wales and Tottenham Hotspur); Stanley Matthews (England and Blackpool), Wilf Mannion (England and Middlesbrough), Tommy Lawton (England and Chelsea), Billy Steel (Scotland and Morton), Billy Liddell (Scotland and Liverpool).

Rest of Europe: Da Rui (France); Petersen (Denmark), Steffen (Switzerland); Carey (Republic of Ireland, captain), Parola (Italy), Ludl (Czechoslovakia); Lambrechts (Belgium), Gren (Sweden), Nordahl (Sweden), Wilkes (Holland), Praest (Denmark).

Referee: G Reader (England)

13 AUGUST 1955

Windsor Park, Belfast, Irish FA 75th anniversary match (58,000)

Great Britain 1 (Johnstone)

Rest of Europe 4 (Vukas 3, Vincent)

Great Britain: Jack Kelsey (Wales and Arsenal); Peter Sillett
(England and Chelsea), Joe McDonald (Scotland and Sunder-
land); Danny Blanchflower (Northern Ireland and Tottenham
Hotspur, captain), John Charles (Wales and Leeds United),
Bertie Peacock (Northern Ireland and Celtic); Stanley
Matthews (England and Blackpool), Bobby Johnstone
(Scotland and Manchester City), Roy Bentley (England and
Chelsea), Jimmy McIlroy (Northern Ireland and Burnley),
Billy Liddell (Scotland and Liverpool).

Rest of Europe: Buffon (Italy); Gustafsson (Sweden), Van Brandt
(Belgium); Ocwirk (Austria, captain), Jonquet (France),
Boskov (Yugoslavia); Sorensen (Denmark), Vukas (Yugo-
slavia), Kopa (France), Travassos (Portugal), Vincent (France).

Referee: J Bronkhorst (Holland)

**Liddell's appearances in Scotland's unofficial wartime
internationals 1939–45 and Victory internationals 1945–46:**

18 APRIL 1942

Hampden Park, Glasgow (75,000)

Scotland 5 (Dodds 3, Liddell, Shankly)

England 4 (Lawton 3, Hagan)

Scotland: Dawson (Rangers); Carabine (Third Lanark), Beattie
(Preston North End); Shankly (Preston North End), Smith
(Preston North End), Busby (Liverpool); Waddell (Rangers),
Herd (Manchester City), Dodds (Blackpool), Bremner
(Arsenal), Liddell (Liverpool).

England: Marks (Arsenal); Bacuzzi (Fulham), Hapgood
(Arsenal); Willingham (Huddersfield Town), Mason
(Coventry City), Mercer (Everton); Matthews (Stoke City),
Edelston (Reading), Lawton (Everton), Hagan (Sheffield
United), Kirchen (Arsenal).

10 OCTOBER 1942

Wembley Stadium (75,000)

England 0

Scotland 0

England: Marks (Arsenal); Bacuzzi (Fulham), Hapgood (Arsenal); Britton (Everton), Cullis (Wolverhampton Wanderers), Mercer (Everton); Matthews (Stoke City), Edelston (Reading), Lawton (Everton), Hagan (Sheffield United), D. Compton (Arsenal).

Scotland: Dawson (Rangers); Carabine (Third Lanark), Beattie (Preston North End); Shankly (Preston North End), Corbett (Celtic), Busby (Liverpool); Waddell (Rangers), Walker (Hearts), Dodds (Blackpool), Bremner (Arsenal), Liddell (Liverpool).

17 APRIL 1943

Hampden Park, Glasgow (105,000)

Scotland 0

England 4 (Carter 2, Westcott, D Compton)

Scotland: Dawson (Rangers); Carabine (Third Lanark), Shaw (Rangers); Shankly (Preston North End), Young (Rangers), Kean (Hibernian); Waddell (Rangers), Buchan (Blackpool), Wallace (Clyde), Venters (Rangers), Liddell (Liverpool).

England: Swift (Manchester City); Hardwick (Middlesbrough), L Compton (Arsenal); Britton (Everton), Cullis (Wolverhampton Wanderers), Mercer (Everton); Matthews (Stoke City), Carter (Sunderland), Westcott (Wolverhampton Wanderers), Hagan (Sheffield United), D Compton (Arsenal).

3 FEBRUARY 1945

Villa Park, Birmingham (66,000)

England 3 (Mortensen 2, Brown)

Scotland 2 (Delaney, Dodds)

England: Swift (Manchester City); Scott (Arsenal), Hardwick (Middlesbrough); Soo (Stoke City), Franklin (Stoke City), Mercer (Everton); Matthews (Stoke City), Brown (Charlton Athletic), Lawton (Everton), Mortensen (Blackpool), Smith (Brentford).

Scotland: Brown (Queens Park); Harley (Liverpool), Stephen (Bradford); Busby (Liverpool), Thyne (Darlington), Macaulay (West Ham United); Delaney (Celtic), Fagan (Liverpool), Dodds (Blackpool), Black (Hearts), Liddell (Liverpool).

10 NOVEMBER 1945
Hampden Park, Glasgow (80,000)
Scotland 2 (Waddell, Dodds)
Wales 0
Scotland: Brown (Queens Park); McPhee (Falkirk), Shaw (Rangers); Campbell (Morton), Paton (Motherwell), Paterson (Celtic); Waddell (Rangers), Smith (Hibernian), Dodds (Blackpool), Deakin (St Mirren), Liddell (Liverpool).
Wales: Sidlow (Wolverhampton Wanderers); Dearson (Birmingham City), Hughes (Birmingham City); Witcomb (West Bromwich Albion), Davies (Nottingham Forest), Burgess (Tottenham Hotspur); J. Jones (Swansea Town), Squires (Swansea Town), Lowrie (Coventry City), Cumner (Arsenal), Edwards (Birmingham City).

2 FEBRUARY 1946
Windsor Park, Belfast (53,000)
Northern Ireland 2 (Walsh 2)
Scotland 3 (Liddell 2, Hamilton)
Northern Ireland: Breen (Linfield); McMillan (Belfast Celtic), Feeney (Linfield); Todd (Blackpool), Vernon (Belfast Celtic), Ahearne (Belfast Celtic); Dr K O'Flanagan (Arsenal), Stevenson (Everton), Walsh (Linfield), Carey (Manchester United), Bonnar (Belfast Celtic).
Scotland: Brown (Queens Park); McGowan (Partick Thistle), Shaw (Rangers); Campbell (Morton), Paton (Motherwell), Paterson (Celtic); Waddell (Rangers), Hamilton (Aberdeen), Dodds (Blackpool), Chisholm (Queens Park), Liddell (Liverpool).

13 APRIL 1946

Hampden Park, Glasgow (139,468)

Scotland 1 (Delaney)

England 0

Scotland: Brown (Queens Park); D Shaw (Hibernian), J Shaw (Rangers); Campbell (Morton), Brennan (Airdrie), Husband (Partick Thistle); Waddell (Rangers), Dougall (Birmingham City), Delaney (Manchester United), Hamilton (Aberdeen), Liddell (Liverpool).

England: Swift (Manchester City); Scott (Arsenal), Hardwick (Middlesbrough); Wright (Wolverhampton Wanderers), Franklin (Stoke City), Mercer (Everton); Elliott (West Bromwich Albion), Shackleton (Bradford Park Avenue), Lawton (Chelsea), Hagan (Sheffield United), D Compton (Arsenal).

15 MAY 1946

Hampden Park, Glasgow (113,000)

Scotland 3 (Liddell 2, Delaney)

Switzerland 1 (Aeby)

Scotland: Brown (Rangers); D Shaw (Hibernian), J Shaw (Rangers); Campbell (Morton), Brennan (Airdrie), Husband (Partick Thistle); Waddell (Rangers), Thornton (Rangers), Delaney (Manchester United), Walker (Hearts), Liddell (Liverpool).

Switzerland: Ballabio; Gyger, Steffen; Rickenback, Andreoli, Bouquet; Amado, Fink, Friedlaender, Maillard, Aeby.

Liddell's appearance in Bolton Disaster Fund Appeal match:

24 AUGUST 1946

Maine Road, Manchester (70,000)

England 2 (Welsh 2)

Scotland 2 (Thornton 2)

England: Swift (Manchester City); Walton (Manchester United), Hardwick (Middlesbrough); Wright (Wolverhampton Wanderers), Leuty (Derby County), Mitchell (Birmingham

City); Matthews (Stoke City), Welsh (Charlton Athletic),
Lewis (Arsenal), Fielding (Everton), Mitten (Manchester
United).

Scotland: Miller (Celtic); D Shaw (Hibernian), J Shaw (Rangers);
Campbell (Morton), Brennan (Airdie), Husband (Partick
Thistle); Waddell (Rangers), Dougall (Birmingham City),
Thornton (Rangers), Hamilton (Aberdeen), Liddell
(Liverpool). (Match raised £11,000 for the Appeal Fund.)

Liddell's appearances in wartime representative games:

19 APRIL 1941

Anfield (12, 000)

Football League 9 (Lawton 3, Dorsett 2, Hanson 2, Stephenson,
Liddell)

All British XI 7 (Nieuwenhuys, Cullis, Busby, Fagan 2,
Stevenson, Stephenson o.g.)

Football League: Hobson (Chester); Lambert (Liverpool),
Gorman (Sunderland); Willingham (Huddersfield Town),
Pryde (Blackburn Rovers), Galley (Wolverhampton
Wanderers); Worrall (Portsmouth), Dorsett (Wolverhampton
Wanderers), Lawton (Everton), Stephenson (Leeds), Hanson
(Chelsea). Substitute: Liddell at half time for Hobson, with
Galley going in goal.

All British XI: Poland (Liverpool); Cook (Everton), Jones
(Blackpool); Dearson (Birmingham City), Cullis (Wolver-
hampton Wanderers), Busby (Liverpool); Nieuwenhuys
(Liverpool), Mutch (Preston), Fagan (Liverpool), Stevenson
(Everton), McShane (Blackburn Rovers).

2 MAY 1942

Molineux (5,443)

Football League 5 (Dodds 3, Fagan, Dearson)

Western Command 3 (Robinson 2, Balmer)

Football League: Scott (Wolverhampton Wanderers); Brigham
(Stoke City), Smith (Chelsea); Shankly (Preston North End),
Morgan (Walsall), Haydock (Aston Villa); Matthews (Stoke

City), Fagan (Liverpool), Dodds (Blackpool), Dearson (Birmingham City), Liddell (Liverpool).

Western Command: Hamilton (Queens Park); Reid (Kilmarnock), Cumberbridge (Stoke City); Chilton (Manchester United), Pryde (Blackburn Rovers), Angus (Exeter City); Hamilton (Newcastle United), Balmer (Liverpool), Robinson (Wolverhampton Wanderers), Dix (Tottenham Hotspur), Armes (Middlesbrough).

21 NOVEMBER 1942

Victoria Ground, Stoke-on-Trent (20,000)

FA XI 4 (Mercer, Broome, Goulden, Liddell)

RAF 3 (Dodds 2, Soo)

FA XI: Fairbrother (Preston North End); Bacuzzi (Fulham), Cook (Everton); Hall (Sunderland), Cullis (Wolverhampton Wanderers), Mercer (Everton); Finney (Preston North End), Broome (Aston Villa), Westcott (Wolverhampton Wanderers), Goulden (West Ham United), Liddell (Liverpool).

RAF: Marks (Arsenal); Hardwick (Middlesbrough), Hapgood (Arsenal); Shankly (Preston North End), Joy (Arsenal), Paterson (Celtic); Matthews (Stoke City), Carter (Sunderland), Dodds (Blackpool), Steel (Stoke City), Kirchen (Arsenal). (Frank Soo of Stoke City went on as a substitute.)

5 DECEMBER 1942

St James's Park, Newcastle (35,000)

RAF 4 (Carter 3, Drake)

Scotland 0

RAF: Marks (Arsenal); Hardwick (Middlesbrough), Hapgood (Arsenal); Soo (Stoke City), Joy (Arsenal), Paterson (Celtic); Matthews (Stoke City), Carter (Sunderland), Drake (Arsenal), Doherty (Manchester City), Kirchen (Arsenal).

Scotland: Dawson (Rangers); Carabine (Third Lanark), Beattie (Preston North End); Shankly (Preston North End), Corbett (Celtic), Busby (Liverpool); Waddell (Rangers), Walker (Hearts), Dodds (Blackpool), Herd (Manchester City), Liddell (Liverpool).

30 JANUARY 1943

Upton Park, London (6,200)

RAF 2 (Soo, Carter)

National Police 0

RAF: Marks (Arsenal); Scott (Arsenal), Hardwick (Middlesbrough); Shankly (Preston North End), Joy (Arsenal), Paterson (Celtic); Grainger (Southport), Carter (Sunderland), Drake (Arsenal), Soo (Stoke City), Liddell (Liverpool).

National Police: Tootill (Crystal Palace); Bicknell (West Ham United), F Dawes (Crystal Palace); Forsyth (Millwall), Smith (Preston North End), Weaver (Chelsea); Fisher (Millwall), A Dawes (Crystal Palace), Richardson (West Bromwich Albion), Brocklebank (Burnley), Spence (Chelsea).

27 MARCH 1943

Griffin Park, Brentford, London

Dutch Forces 1

RAF 15 (including Liddell 5, Whittingham 4)

RAF: Williams (Walsall); Hardwick(Middlesbrough), Hapgood (Arsenal); Soo (Stoke City), Franklin (Stoke City), Burgess (Tottenham Hotspur); Briscoe (Hearts), Carter (Sunderland), Whittingham (Bradford City), Doherty (Manchester City), Liddell (Liverpool).

25 NOVEMBER 1944

Hillsborough, Sheffield (40,172)

RAF 1 (Mortensen)

Scotland 7 (Black 2, Liddell 2, Busby, Fagan, Dodds)

RAF: Williams (Walsall); Scott (Arsenal), Hughes (Birmingham City); Soo (Stoke City), Joy (Arsenal), Burgess (Tottenham Hotspur); Matthews (Stoke City), Carter (Sunderland), Drake (Arsenal), Mortensen (Blackpool), Smith (Brentford).

Scotland: Brown (Queens Park); Harley (Liverpool), Stephen (Bradford); Busby (Liverpool), Thyne (Darlington), Macaulay (West Ham United); Delaney (Celtic), Fagan (Liverpool), Dodds (Blackpool), Black (Hearts), Liddell (Liverpool).

6 JANUARY 1945

Brussels

Belgium 2

Scottish Services 3 (Black 2, Fagan)

Scottish Services: Brown (Queens Park); Nennie (Kilmarnock), Harley (Liverpool); Macaulay (West Ham United), Thyne (Darlington), Paterson (Celtic); Oakes (Hearts), Fagan (Liverpool), Dodds (Blackpool), Black (Hearts), Liddell (Liverpool).

7 JANUARY 1945

Bruges (12,000)

Flanders 6

Scottish Services 4 (Black 3, Dodds)

Scottish Services: Brown (Queens Park); Nennie (Kilmarnock), Cox (Third Lanark); Macaulay (West Ham United), Thyne (Darlington), Paterson (Celtic); Liddell (Liverpool), Fagan (Liverpool), Dodds (Blackpool), Black (Hearts), Pearson (Newcastle).

Liddell's guest club appearance in wartime representative match:

7 AUGUST 1943

Tynecastle Park, Edinburgh (35,000)

Hearts 3 (Black, Walker, Mortensen)

RAF 2 (Carter, Docherty)

Hearts (guest players' clubs in parenthesis): Dawson (Rangers); Shaw (Hibernian), Carabine (Third Lanark); Massie (Aston Villa), Baxter (Middlesbrough), Miller; Black, Walker, Dodds (Blackpool), Mortensen (Blackpool), Liddell (Liverpool).

Bibliography

Ashton, Ken. *The Liverpool FC Book*, Stanley Paul, 1967.

Ball, Dave and Rea, Ged. *Liverpool FC: The Ultimate Book of Stats and Facts*. The Bluecoat Press, 2001.

Barrett, Norman. *World Soccer From A–Z*. Pan Books, 1973.

Busby, Matt. *My Story*. Souvenir Press, 1957.

Goble, Ray. *Manchester City FC: A Complete Record*. Breedon Books, 1987.

Keith, John and Thomas, Peter. *Daily Express A–Z of Mersey Soccer*. Beaverbrook Newspapers, 1973.

Keith, John. *Bob Paisley: Manager of the Millennium*. Robson Books, 1999.

Keith, John. *The Essential Shankly*. Robson Books, 2001.

Liddell, Billy. *My Soccer Story*. Stanley Paul, 1960.

Payne, Mike. *England: The Complete Post War Record*. Breedon Books, 1993.

Pead, Brian. *Liverpool FC: A Complete Record*. Breedon Books, 1990.

Prole, David. *Come On The Reds*. Robert Hale, 1967.

Rollin, Jack. *Soccer At War 1939–45*. Willow Books, 1985.

Rous, Sir Stanley. *Football Worlds*. Faber and Faber, 1978

Taylor, Rogan and Jamlich, Klara. *Puskas on Puskas: The Life and Times of a Footballing Legend*. Robson Books, 1997.

The FA Book For Boys 1952–53, The Naldrett Press, 1952.

Ward, Andrew. *Scotland The Team*. Breedon Books, 1987.

Young, Percy M. *Football On Merseyside*, Stanley Paul, 1963.